# STUBBORN
# RESISTANCE

# STUBBORN RESISTANCE

*New Brunswick Maliseet and Mi'kmaq
in Defence of their Lands*

## BRIAN CUTHBERTSON

NIMBUS
PUBLISHING
nimbus.ca

Nimbus Publishing Limited
3731 Mackintosh St, Halifax, NS B3K 5A5
(902) 455-4286   nimbus.ca

Printed and bound in Canada

NB1200

Cover photo: Lieutenant Robert Petley, 1837, *Mi'kmaw hunter with fish, spear, musket, and paddle*, coloured lithograph. Library Archives Canada, C-023349
Design: Peggy & Co. Design, Halifax

Library and Archives Canada Cataloguing in Publication

Cuthbertson, Brian, 1936-, author
Stubborn resistance : New Brunswick Maliseet and Mi'kmaq in defence of their lands / Brian Cuthbertson.

Includes bibliographical references and index.
Issued in print and electronic formats.
ISBN 978-1-77108-346-1 (paperback).—ISBN 978-1-77108-347-8 (html)

1. Malecite Indians—Land tenure—New Brunswick—History—19th century. 2. Micmac Indians—Land tenure—New Brunswick—History—19th century. 3. Malecite Indians—New Brunswick—Government relations—History—19th century. 4. Micmac Indians—New Brunswick—Government relations—History—19th century. 5. Land tenure—Government policy—New Brunswick—History—19th century. 6. New Brunswick—Race relations—History—19th century. I. Title.

E99.M195C88 2015   971.5'10049734   C2015-904337-9
                                     C2015-904338-7

Canada Council   Conseil des arts
for the Arts     du Canada

Nimbus Publishing acknowledges the financial support for its publishing activities from the Government of Canada through the Canada Book Fund (CBF) and the Canada Council for the Arts, and from the Province of Nova Scotia. We are pleased to work in partnership with the Province of Nova Scotia to develop and promote our creative industries for the benefit of all Nova Scotians.

# CONTENTS

# FOREWORD

As a Maliseet woman, a teacher, a lawyer, a chief, and a mother, I cannot overstate the importance of learning about our past. The Mi'kmaq and Wolastoqiyik have struggled to maintain their traditional lands since the first arrival of European immigrants. Even those who participated in this so-called "settlement" of the New World have recognized this struggle, or resistance, to our homeland encroachment. Today this resistance continues and is evident through the many specific land claims, comprehensive claims, grassroots and leadership protests, as well as in the Canadian court system. Brian's book is a shining example of how we can begin to understand the daily details of this struggle in those days when New Brunswick was becoming a province.

I first had the pleasure of working with Brian when I worked for the federal government in the Specific Claims Branch of Aboriginal and Northern Affairs Canada. Brian's analytic skills and attention to detail made him the perfect historian for joint research projects between the Government of Canada and First Nations. Currently, Brian is also working with the Madawaska Maliseet First Nation as an expert witness in their specific claim, which is now at the Specific Claims Tribunal.

Much has been written about historical federal Indian legislation, but little about how colonial and provincial legislation discriminated against First Nations in this country. Brian's detailed accounts about New Brunswick's discriminatory 1844 act and its purpose to eliminate our homelands demonstrate not only the thinking of the time, but also how non-Aboriginal leaders saw how this was wrong and unfair to First Nations in the province. In a time when settlement of the colony was vital to many politicians, there were some who understood that this land was never sold, nor ceded, nor obtained by conquest, and that the "Indians were the rightful possessors and Lords of the soil."

*Stubborn Resistance* is important because it illustrates that First Nations people in New Brunswick have not only recently begun to speak out, but have been doing so since before the creation of the province. Brian's dedication and hard work in hunting down primary documents and piecing them together is extremely helpful for those looking to better understand the foundations of the frustrations faced by today's Mi'kmaq and Wolastoqiyik.

Chief Patricia Bernard
Madawaska Maliseet First Nation
July 2015

# PREFACE

My purpose in writing this book is to tell the story of New Brunswick's Maliseet and Mi'kmaw resistance to the loss of lands that had been set aside in good faith as reserves for them. The story begins with the twenty thousand acres Chief John Julian of the North West Miramichi River Tribe received for his loyalty to George III during the American Revolution. It ends in 1974 with the Department of Indian Affairs decision to remove squatters from the Red Bank Reserve on the Little South West Miramichi River instead of insisting on a surrender of the reserve lands for sale to the squatters. The story has contemporary relevance because of the dramatically changing relationship between First Nations and Canada as reflected in the ongoing negotiations over such issues as environmental concerns, education, and governance. Although the paternalistic role of Indian Affairs that so dominated in the past has dramatically changed, I hope the story, as I tell it, reminds our generation that much of present attitudes have historical roots that cannot be ignored.

In the case of New Brunswick, the past is still very much with us because of the 1844 Act to Regulate the Management and Disposal of the Indian Reserves. The act gave the government of the day the legislative authority to auction reserve lands, regardless of opposition by the Maliseet and Mi'kmaq, who had been occupying these lands for generations. The method chosen was to sell by public auction lots of reserve lands occupied by squatters and other reserve lands, which could then be opened to settlement by non-Aboriginals. The money raised by sales was to create an Indian Fund for their permanent betterment.

As I describe it, the act failed on both accounts: as a means of improving the livelihood of the Maliseet and the Mi'kmaq and of dealing with the squatters who, with few exceptions, refused to purchase the lots they illegally occupied. As a result, the substantial funds predicted by the government for the Indian Fund never materialized, the Maliseet and Mi'kmaq still on the reserves received no financial benefit from the sales made, and they also lost the lands occupied by squatters.

Even at the time the 1844 act was passed, there were doubts whether the government could sell reserve lands. It is an open question today, in the context of more recent court decisions favourable to Aboriginal peoples, whether the 1844 act could be challenged. Between 1849 and 1867, under the authority of the 1844 act, the government put 20,456 acres up for auction that were lost to eleven New Brunswick reserves of the time. Most of these reserves still exist. If a court challenge proved successful, the compensation could be in the tens of millions of dollars.

The genesis of this book derives from a series of reports that I researched and prepared for the New Brunswick First Nations of Red Bank (now Metepenagiag), Buctouche, and Tobique. Copies of these reports, with their indexed documentation in bound volumes, have been deposited with the Provincial Archives of New Brunswick in Fredericton.

The objective was to submit these reports for Red Bank, Buctouche, and Tobique under the specific claims policy of the Department of Indian Affairs (now Department of Aboriginal Affairs and Northern Development Canada). Generally, the term *specific claims* refers to claims made by a First Nation against the federal government, which relates to the administration of land and other First Nation assets and to the fulfillment of Indian treaties, though the treaties themselves are not open to renegotiation. None of my research involved *comprehensive claims*, which deal with the unfinished business of treaty-making in Canada. Nearly all of my research was related to non-Aboriginals squatting on lands set aside as reserves for the Mi'kmaq and Maliseet by the New Brunswick government beginning in 1789 with Eel Ground Reserve. By the 1840s the total amounted to 60,000 acres. By the end of the nineteenth century, most of this acreage had been lost to squatters.

The process for preparing these documents involved the Joint Research Working Groups, consisting of officials from the Specific Claims Directorate of Indian Affairs and the Chief and band council of the relevant First Nation. Approval of a report by a Joint Working Group, to which I reported, meant there was agreement on the historical facts as presented and the claim could proceed to the next stage. The next step entailed First Nations' legal advisors preparing a set of allegations relating to the claim, which would be submitted to the federal Department of Justice for a decision on whether it could be accepted as a valid claim. If accepted, then appraisers would be employed to determine values, usually for loss of use. In the reports I prepared, there were extensive databases citing acreages, values of improvements, and contemporary prices (which all can be found in the documentation donated to the Provincial Archives of New Brunswick). These databases were to prove valuable to the appraisers in arriving at their conclusions on loss of use. The final stage in the specific claims process is the negotiation for the amount of compensation, in which I have never been involved. In writing this manuscript I have relied largely on primary sources concerning the use of licences of occupation and other means to establish reserves in New Brunswick after its separation from Nova Scotia in 1784. For the story of the 1844 act (see Chapter 3: Passage of the Act to Regulate the Management and Disposal of the Indian Reserves), I relied on sources not used before, especially reports of the New Brunswick House of Assembly debates, which appeared in newspapers of the day. These proved to be invaluable for following the assembly debates on the act and controversies surrounding its passage within the executive council. Other primary sources I have used were in the Provincial Archives of New Brunswick, in particular RS965 Indian Documentation Inventory. The Harriet Irving Library Archives has a valuable collection of New Brunswick Indian records in MG H54. I also made good use of the William Francis Ganong papers in the New Brunswick Museum in Saint John.

Of the secondary sources used, the *Dictionary of Canadian Biography* proved most helpful. L. F. S. Upton, in his seminal *Micmacs and Colonists: Indian-White Relations in the Maritimes, 1713–1867*, published in 1979, still remains an important source up to Confederation. However, Upton gave only passing reference to the 1844 act. Neither Upton, nor any other source of which I am aware examines in any detail post-Confederation surrenders of reserve lands in New Brunswick with the exception of W. D. Hamilton, whose *The Julian Family* (1984) and his article "Indian Lands in New Brunswick: The Case of the Little South West Reserve" in *Acadiensis*, vol. 13, No. 2 (1984), describe events surrounding the surrender of Red Bank lands in 1895.

I was able to obtain two sets of previously unpublished images. Most important are the five watercolours of 1764, the earliest known portrayals of Maliseet, done by the Reverend Richard Byron and published only in a 1991 Sotheby's catalogue (the asking price for each was between £5,000 and £8,000). Their whereabouts remain unknown. The other set of images are by Captain Henry Dunn O'Halloran in 1841 while visiting Mi'kmaw villages in northern New Brunswick with Moses Perley. These parchment drawings in the collection of the Provincial Archives of New Brunswick are believed to be among some of the earliest of the Mi'kmaq in New Brunswick.

On the use of such terms as Indian, Aboriginal, Indigenous, Native, non-Native, I have only used Indian(s) when it appears in directly quoted text, as is the general practice by Canadian publishers and the scholarly community. Because this book is about Maliseet and Mi'kmaq, wherever context allows, I have used those terms as opposed to Aboriginal(s) or Indigenous. Native and non-Native has occasionally seemed appropriate, as also the use of tribe. On the separate uses of Mi'kmaq and Mi'kmaw, I can do no better than to quote from *The Language of this Land, Mi'kma'ki* by Trudy Sable and Bernie Francis (Cape Breton Press, 2012, p. 16): "The word Mi'kmaq is plural and is also used when referring to the whole nation. For instance: 'The Mi'kmaq of Eastern Canada.' Mi'kmaw is the singular and adjectival form of Mi'kmaq. Examples: 'I am a Mi'kmaw' or 'A Mi'kmaw man told me a story'...It is also used to refer to the language itself."

The reports I completed for the Joint Working Groups involving Indian Affairs, Red Bank, Tobique, and Buctouche First Nations were done for them exclusively. I am most obliged to the band councils of these First Nations for their hospitality; we often met on their reserves or they arranged for other locations. I still remember well a meeting at Red Bank where the ladies provided a meal of a large Miramichi salmon. The considerable leftover fish was packed for me to take back to Halifax. I drove like hell and my wife and I had a wonderfully fresh salmon meal that evening.

Patricia Bernard and Sara Sixsmith of Indian Affairs not only gave direction to the research, but also ensured I received endless reels of microfilm of relevant government documentation, which I could use at home. Band council members made a major contribution to discussions relating to the reports for their reserves. Each First Nation had a solicitor whose advice ensured I kept in mind that I was preparing reports with a legal purpose, not academic treatises. Ronald Gaffney served as legal counsel for both Red Bank and Buctouche First Nations and Harold Doherty served for Tobique. They prepared the allegations for all the specific claims submitted for validation.

The task of turning the reports into book form proved daunting. I initially decided to create an e-book so I could reduce printing costs and incorporate more visual material than would be the case with a printed book. I was turned down by a number of publishers, mostly, I believe, because they were not prepared to publish in the e-book form. Finally, I submitted the manuscript to Nimbus Publishing. Patrick Murphy read the full manuscript, and two weeks later we had a signed contract to publish printed and e-book versions. I am much indebted to Dr. Henry Roper, formerly of the University of King's College, Halifax, for reading the manuscript and commenting as a good editor should. Paula Sarson of PLS Editing Services did yeoman service in turning my manuscript into a publishable book. In 1980 Nimbus published my first book on Nova Scotian history, entitled *The Old Attorney General: A Biography of Richard John Uniacke*. With the publication of *Stubborn Resistance* I have, so to speak, returned to the fold and in Patrick Murphy found a most congenial editor.

Brian Cuthbertson

# CHAPTER 1

# PEACE TREATIES AND SETTING ASIDE LANDS FOR THE MI'KMAQ AND MALISEET

At the time of Halifax's founding in 1749, of the approximately 3,000 Mi'kmaq and Maliseet, the Mi'kmaq were the most numerous with 1,500 to 2,000 spread throughout the present Nova Scotia and eastern New Brunswick as far as the Gaspé; the Maliseet of the Saint John River numbered fewer than 2,000.[1] Acadia had been ceded to the English by the Treaty of Utrecht in 1713, but the French influence still predominated. The construction of the fortress town of Louisbourg in 1720 had further strengthened the French presence. Halifax was founded to offset Louisbourg.

Although the English sought by treaty process to have good relations with the Mi'kmaq, the Aboriginals saw Halifax as the beginning of settlement and hence a threat to the continued occupation of their lands. As a consequence, they declared war and began to seize fishing and other vessels. Two priests, L'Abbé Pierre Maillard and L'Abbé Jean-Louis Le Loutre, played a major role in urging the Mi'kmaq to make war on the English. When a Mi'kmaw raiding party killed four unarmed men and carried away another as they worked at a sawmill near Halifax Harbour, Governor Edward Cornwallis and his council angrily reacted by issuing the infamous proclamation of October 1–2, 1749, ordering British subjects to "annoy, destroy, take or destroy, the savage commonly called Micmacks wherever they are found" and offering a reward for every Mi'kmaw taken alive or killed "to be paid upon producing such savage taken or his scalp (as is the custom of America)."[2] Sometimes referred to as the

Anglo-Mi'kmaq War, the fighting continued unabated with both the French and English paying for scalps.

Both sides attempted to make peace overtures, though unsuccessfully. In particular the Mi'kmaq made two attempts. Through a British officer at Fort Lawrence on the Chignecto Isthmus, Le Loutre sent a message that the Mi'kmaq wished to make a proposal "towards establishing a General and lasting peace." In a detailed letter he stated news had arrived that British soldiers had penetrated Mi'kmaw hunting grounds on the Shubenacadie River. According to Le Loutre the Mi'kmaq at Chignecto had called a council to determine a course of action. He said they proposed a large portion of Nova Scotia should be recognized by the British as Mi'kmaw territory. It would run from the Chignecto Isthmus to Minas, then to Cobequid and Shubenacadie, across to Musquodoboit, then along the eastern shore and finally through the strait separating mainland Nova Scotia and Cape Breton Island, along the north shore and back to Baie Verte. Le Loutre contended this was a reasonable demand for a people who lived by hunting and fishing. His motives, however, were questionable. He had been trying to attract Acadians to move to the Chignecto Isthmus and surrounding area, thereby increasing the numbers supporting the French claim under the 1713 Treaty of Utrecht. The English would be confined to a small area bordering on the Atlantic. In Halifax the council had good reason to be suspicious of Le Loutre whose letter it considered "too insolent and absurd to be answered through the Author." They sent a general letter to all Mi'kmaq stating if they were serious about making peace, they should come to Halifax "where they will be treated with reasonable conditions."[3]

The Mi'kmaq at Chignecto and further up the Northumberland Strait decided to send Paul Laurent, who could speak English, with a message to the governor and his council.[4] His message was that a peace treaty depended on a land grant. He could not negotiate, but asked for a reply in writing, which would specify the "Quantity of Land, that they would allow them." The council replied that the peace overtures were "very general and the demands you make in our opinion, are extremely exorbitant." But they added they were quite willing to set aside a tract of land for "your hunting, fishing etc. as shall be abundantly sufficient for you and what we make no doubt, yourselves will like and approve."[5] They asked for their chiefs to come to Halifax to work out the details, while noting that in the past promises made by them had not been kept. Yet the English made clear they were still ready to negotiate setting aside lands for them, but it had to be within the framework of a general treaty requiring the sanction of all the chiefs together. There was no further attempt by either the Mi'kmaq or the British to negotiate an end to hostilities.

Although war between Britain and France had not been officially declared, the British captured Fort Beauséjour in June 1755. The Expulsion of the Acadians followed. The consequence for the Maliseet and Mi'kmaq was immediate and devastating because of their dependence on the Acadians to provide much of their food and on the French military for the shot and powder they needed for hunting; in expelling the Acadians, the British had destroyed their logistical support.[6] The capture of Fortress Louisbourg in 1758 essentially ended the Anglo-French struggle for Acadia. The French defeat meant both Maliseet and Mi'kmaq had no recourse but to seek to make peace with the English because of their dependence on European goods.

The Maliseet were the first to make peace. In February 1760, two delegates, Mitchell Neptune and Ballomy Glode, arrived in Halifax where they met with members of the governor and council. John G. Reid, who has written extensively on Aboriginal history, is of the opinion that although the Maliseet and the Mi'kmaq were facing serious difficulties, the English, too, were desperate for peace.[7] They sought the stability and further settlement that peace would allow. There was to be no formal surrender of land. Rather, officials sought only the renewal of the past treaties of 1726 and 1749 by incorporating them into a new Treaty of Peace and Friendship. Of major concern for the Maliseet delegates was the re-establishment of trade relations so there could again be trade in furs for European goods upon which they had become so dependent. The negotiations were conducted in French, and the treaty, dated February 23, 1760, was written in that language.[8] After the terms of the treaty were read to the delegates, they agreed to make peace.

Later in February the first of the Mi'kmaw delegates from the villages of Richibucto, La Hève, and Shubenacadie arrived to sign a treaty of peace and friendship. After the same treaty terms concluded with Glode and Neptune were read to them, they agreed to make peace as well. Later six other villages—Pictou and Malagomich, Cape Breton, Chignecto, Shediac, Miramichi, and Poke-mouche—ratified the treaty. As with the Maliseet, the critical issue was trade relations. The Nova Scotia government proceeded to establish government-run truck houses with set prices, where both Maliseet and Mi'kmaq could exchange their furs for such items as powder and shot, axes, provisions, blankets, and clothing. The extent of this trading can be grasped from the records of the firm Simonds, Hazen and White at the mouth of the Saint John River. During ten years of uninterrupted trade with the Maliseet until the American Revolution, the firm would export forty thousand beaver skins, as well as skins of such animals as muskrat, marten, otter, fox, moose, and deer.

*Jonathan Belcher, 1756,* oil on canvas. John
Singleton Copley (American, 1738–1815).

Gift of the Canadian International Paper Co. The Beaverbrook
Art Gallery, Fredericton, New Brunswick.

However, the major ceremony for treaty signing took place on June 25, 1761, when representatives of the Miramichi, Shediac, Pokemouche, and Cape Breton villages assembled at Lieutenant-Governor Jonathan Belcher's farm in Windsor on the Avon River, which drained into Minas Basin and the Bay of Fundy, and was the most convenient site for these Mi'kmaq village representatives. Belcher conducted the proceedings because of the death of Governor Charles Lawrence. Lawrence had earlier invited L'Abbé Pierre Maillard (Le Loutre had been taken prisoner by the English in 1755 and was being held in England) to come to Halifax and assist in reconciling the Mi'kmaq to English rule. At the ceremony Maillard served as an interpreter. Officials recorded every part of the ceremony for inclusion in a dispatch to the secretary of state. Belcher's speech emphaized that, henceforth, the Mi'kmaq would be bound by the laws of Nova Scotia: "The Laws will be like a great Hedge about your Rights and properties." Moreover, "your cause of War and Peace may be the same as ours under one mighty Chief and King, under the same Laws for the same Rights and Liberties."[9]

In reply to Belcher, the chief of the Cape Breton band, with Maillard translating from Mi'kmaw, said they had come to yield themselves up without requiring any terms because they must have "wretchedly perished" unless relieved by humanity. He was willing "to swear on behalf of all his people that I sincerely comply with all and each of the Articles that you have proposed to be kept inviolably on both sides…As long as the Sun and Moon shall endure, as long as the Earth on which I dwell shall exist in the same State you this day see it, so long will I be your friend and Ally, submitting myself to the Laws of your Government, faithful and obedient to the Crown."[10] Stephen Patterson considers this reply the largest single recorded statement "by any Indian in the region."[11]

Although the French had been finally defeated with the capture of Quebec and Montreal, the British government considered it wise to send a royal order to colonial governments, dated November 23, 1761, instructing them "to support and protect the Indians in their just Rights and Possessions" and warning of the "fatal Effects which would attend a Discontent among the Indians in the present Situation of Affairs."[12] Governors were prohibited from making any grants of land "which at any time had been reserved or claimed by them."

At the time of the order, Chief Justice Jonathan Belcher was acting lieutenant-governor. Although the royal order required him to issue a public proclamation of its contents, he did not do so. Later, he would justify his inaction on the grounds that it might have generated certain hostility from the Indians, who would have been incited by the disaffected Acadians and others to have made extravagant and unwarrantable demands. Instead, he had a search made of records to determine whether any official demands or claims for land had ever been made by "Nova Scotia Indians." The only substantiated Indian claim that could be found was for hunting and fishing rights to a piece of shoreline based upon a common right to sea coast. The specific area ran from Musquodoboit on the Eastern Shore to Canso and then along the Northumberland Strait shoreline to the Bay of Chaleur. Belcher did not provide a source for his conclusion, though it was most likely a reference to the attempts in 1754 and 1755 by the Chignecto Mi'kmaq to seek a partition of Nova Scotia in return for ending hostilities.

Belcher misinterpreted the royal instruction concerning all lands "which at any time had been reserved or claimed by them." He proceeded to issue a proclamation on May 4, 1762, setting "aside lands for Indians, incorporating the coastal area from the Strait of Canso to the Bay of Chaleur with lands set aside for Indians for the special purpose of hunting, fowling and fishing."[13] When the Board of Trade received the proclamation, their Lordships expressed concern over his "impudent" action, which would encourage the Aboriginals to put in any claim whatever to lands in the Province of Acadia to the exclusion of His Majesty's other subjects.[14] The board further explained that the proclamation of May 4, 1762, was not warranted by His Majesty's Order in Council of December 9, 1761. This document referred "only to such Claims of the Indians as had heretofore at long usage admitted and allowed on the part of Government and confirmed to them by solemn Compacts."[15] In issuing his proclamation Belcher seems to have had no support at the council table; rather, there was a campaign to secure his dismissal, which would result in the appointment of Montagu Wilmot as governor.

Upon Wilmot's arrival in Halifax during September 1763, his instructions on becoming governor reiterated the board's concerns that "the very extraordinary Claims made by the Indians of Nova Scotia were so injurious to the settler's commercial interests." The board informed Wilmot officially that Belcher's proclamation of May 4, 1762, had been disallowed.[16] At a council meeting attended by both Wilmot and Belcher on December 26, 1763, the council ruled the proclamation void.[17] In 1764, eleven months after Belcher's proclamation was made public, Wilmot was ordered to inform the Mi'kmaq that any claims they might have as a result of Belcher's proclamation had been "disallowed" since the document was "inconsistent with His Majesty's Rights" and "injurious to the Commercial Interests of His Subjects."[18] Other than this instruction, Wilmot was told merely to cultivate a good friendship with the Nova Scotia tribes, to induce them to become good British subjects, and to grant a sum of money to any British subject who married a Native. His instructions from the Board of Trade included a copy of the Royal Proclamation of October 7, 1763. The proclamation had as its prime objective "to maintain peace with the Indians" through the creation of an immense territory to the west of the American seaboard colonies. Among its provisions was that no lands could be "privately purchased from Indians that had not been ceded to, or purchased by the Crown from Indians." Wilmot informed the Board of Trade that the proclamation was immediately published in Halifax and would be proclaimed in the distant and remote parts of the colony.[19]

The general view of historians has been that Wilmot and his successors considered the proclamation did not apply to Nova Scotia. In the words of Leslie Upton, "it was as though it had never been made."[20] However, there is considerable evidence that Wilmot and his council did observe the proclamation, particularly regarding grants to military men. In the council minutes there are many entries granting lands to reduced officers and soldiers as provided for in terms of Part III of the proclamation. On the death of Wilmot on May 23, 1766, Benjamin Green, a member of the council, became administrator (acting governor) of Nova Scotia. In writing to the Board of Trade, Green noted the council had been making grants that were not strictly conformable to His Majesty's instructions.[21] Green and his fellow councillors must have been fully aware of the proclamation. A month after Green's dispatch, the council resolved on September 10, 1766, that "for the future all reduced officers claiming lands under the King's Proclamation shall be required to make Oath that they have obtained not that Bounty in any of the Provinces, before they shall obtain the Grant."[22]

The Royal Instructions addressed to the recently appointed governor Francis Legge on August 3, 1773, forbade him to issue any warrant of survey or to pass any patents for lands or to grant any licence for the purchase for lands in the province, or to grant any licence for the purchase by private persons "of any lands from the Indians without especial directions from us for that purpose."[23]

An instruction, dated February 3, 1774, for a new system of patenting lands was sent to a number of the American colonies, including Nova Scotia. It had the following exception: "only in case of such commissioned officers and soldiers as are entitled to grants of land in virtue of our royal proclamation of 7th of October, 1763." Moreover, the Nova Scotia minutes of council for September 23, 1766, noted on the representation that "many irregularities were committed by several persons in the Indian commerce"; it was resolved that "notice be given of the King's Proclamation requiring all Traders with Indians to take out Licences."[24] Brian Slattery concludes: "In the case of Nova Scotia, then, there cannot be much doubt that it was a 'colony' to which the Proclamation of 1763 applied."[25]

Any issue surrounding the proclamation of 1763 ceased to be a matter of concern because in 1773 speculation in Nova Scotian lands caused the British government to prohibit any granting of lands. This prohibition would remain in effect until 1782, when instructions to Governor John Parr allowed grants, with strict limits on acreages, to be made to Loyalists. Instructions to governors on granting lands did not prohibit the granting of lands by licences of occupation. Such licences mainly differed from outright grants in that they allowed occupation "during pleasure" and could be issued without having to pass under the seal of the colony, as was required for grants. Licences of occupation became the preferred means of setting aside lands for the Maliseet and Mi'kmaq.

The first case of using licences for occupation occurred in 1782, when the Nova Scotia government set aside five hundred acres for the Mi'kmaq on the Nova Scotian South Shore in the expectation that they would take up farming. A major precedent for using licences of occupation for setting aside lands for the Mi'kmaq came a year later and before the creation of New Brunswick as a separate colony. During the American War of Independence, after the French became allied with the Americans, the French admiral Comte d'Estaing issued a proclamation calling for a general uprising in all of France's former colonies. It caused the South West Mi'kmaq on the Miramichi River to threaten to kill every English settler on the river. However, Chief John Julian and his tribe came from the Northwest Miramichi River to intervene on behalf of the settlers. The fortuitous arrival of a British warship resulted in subduing the uprising. On the captain's recommendation, the Nova Scotia government appointed John Julian "Chief of the Miramichi Indians for his Loyalty to His Majesty, and Friendship to His Subjects."[26] In addition, the government by licence of occupation also set aside twenty thousand acres on the Northwest Branch of the Miramichi River for John Julian and his tribe.[27]

Lieutenant-Governor Thomas Carleton

Provincial Archives of New Brunswick Assorted Photo
Acquisitions #4 P37-309

After New Brunswick was established as a separate colony in the summer of 1784, the executive council of the new government created a lands committee. It consisted of a number of council members and the surveyor general. Petitions for grants of lands would come before the lands committee, which would recommend whether the requested lands should be granted to the petitioners. Lieutenant-Governor Thomas Carleton's instructions for the granting of lands to the incoming tide of Loyalists provided one hundred acres for each head of family and fifty acres for other family members. However suitable this formula was for Loyalist settlements, it was obviously not applicable for setting aside lands for the Maliseet and Mi'kmaq. Although the government initially adopted licences of occupation, it was inconsistent in its use and was never able to establish criteria for determining the size of reserves before issuing these licences.

When in 1785 the New Brunswick government discovered that the Nova Scotia council had, in 1765, issued a grant of 100,000 acres to John Cort and William Davidson on the Miramichi, it immediately began escheat proceedings. In the process, the New Brunswick government learned of the licence of occupation for the 20,000 acres given to John Julian and that it overlapped the Davidson and Cort grant. The government ordered Benjamin Marston, recently appointed sheriff for Northumberland County, to report on the state of Mi'kmaw settlements within the Cort-Davidson grant. It is likely that Julian had his copy of the licence of occupation from which another copy was made and sent to Fredericton as proof of his claim.[28] When the Davidson and Cort grant was escheated in 1786, no action was taken to confirm John Julian's claim of 20,000 acres. Instead, the government issued a licence of occupation to John Julian in 1789 for 3,033 acres of what would become Eel Ground Reserve.[29] As a result of later surveys in 1804 and 1805, the government also issued licences to Andrew Julian (son of John) and to Francis Julian to occupy tracts of what would become Red Bank, Big Hole, and Indian Point Reserves.[30]

The government encountered the most difficulties with establishing reserves for the small numbers of Mi'kmaq who inhabited villages on the coastal rivers draining into Northumberland Strait. These varied in extent. Those in the southeast like Shediac, Cocagne, and Aboushagan were comparatively small rivers and were inhabited by only a few Mi'kmaq. Further up the coast were villages on the Buctouche and Richibucto rivers whose drainage basins were around 207,200 hectares. Between the Miramichi River and Chaleur Bay there were villages at the entrances of the Tabusintac, Burnt Church, and Pokemouche rivers. In 1788 the government decided that it needed to determine the limits of these Mi'kmaw villages all along the Northumberland Strait shore.

Provincial Secretary Jonathan Odell, ca. 1770
John Clarence Webster Canadiana Collection, W1294,
New Brunswick Museum, Saint John, NB

Captain George Sproule, who had been appointed surveyor general in 1784, probably convinced the government of the need to act. He had served in the Gulf of St. Lawrence with James Cook and Samuel Holland and was probably more knowledgeable than any other New Brunswick official about the geography of the Northumberland shore.[31] Sproule's instructions to Deputy Surveyor Stephen Millidge were to go to Northumberland County and ascertain the limits of the Mi'kmaw villages and to lay out as much land as contiguous to them "to afford them a sufficient limit." Should their claims be extravagant he was only to report them, but at the same time he was "to sooth them & endeavour to keep them in temper."[32]

Sproule recommended that Millidge proceed from Shediac to Chaleur Bay, but no record is extant of what he reported on Shediac, nor of any consideration given for a licence of occupation to be authorized. The next village of importance was Buctouche, where he would have found that five Acadian families had taken up lands around the inner harbour, who would be the beginning of a sizable Acadian migration to Buctouche. Millidge made no mention that these families were squatters. He met with the "Sachem (Supreme Chief) of the Chebuctouche" and travelled up the river at least to the rapids or falls, which he recorded on a plan that has disappeared.[33] He seems not to have undertaken a survey of the tract of land requested by the Sachems because he probably considered it too large an area. The Sachems then petitioned the government in the spring of 1789 through Gervas Say, Justice of the Peace, for a tract of land to be set aside for them. In his reply to the Sachems through Gervas Say, Provincial Secretary Jonathan Odell noted that Millidge had been sent into their country with instructions to survey a village for their exclusive use in which no other inhabitants should interfere. If the Buctouche Mi'kmaq were to form a settlement, they would have all due encouragement, but if they continued to insist, as apparently they had to Millidge, on having a large tract of land, they would not receive it.

There matters remained until 1798, when Chief John Noel (also known as Noel John) went to Fredericton for an interview with Lieutenant-Governor Thomas Carleton.[34] Carleton instructed George Sproule to send Deputy Surveyor James Watson with John Noel, who would take him by canoe to Buctouche. Watson would survey a tract of land for Chief John Noel and the others of the band that would extend up the Buctouche River for eight miles, then extend into the countryside on both sides of the river.[35] The band was to provide both axemen and chainmen. The result was that approximately 40,940 acres were set aside for a Buctouche population of probably not more than two hundred individuals. Odell wrote Joseph Gueguen, who operated a trading establishment at nearby Cocagne, he was prepared to certify that Watson had surveyed a tract of this description. However, no licence of occupation would ever be issued for this acreage.[36]

The Richibucto Band members were concerned not only about having lands set aside for them, but also with settlers attempting to encroach within the district of their village. Chief Matthew Andrew complained that a man from Miramichi had been fishing for salmon in their river without permission. What is particularly interesting about this petition is Chief Andrew's opening statement that the Richibucto Tribe had remained peaceable subjects of King George ever since the "year sixty" without interfering with any of the King's subjects in their settlements or trade. In making the point that they had upheld their promises in the 1760 treaty, they now expected the government, in the name of the Crown, to use the law to defend their rights. The government did act on Andrew's petition by issuing an order strictly forbidding anyone from occupying lands within the Richibucto village, which would be in due time ascertained by an actual survey.[37] Squatting, however, continued.

When the Richibucto Band had not received notice of the lands they wished set aside for them, they petitioned in 1800 through Joseph Gueguen.[38] In reply,

Jonathan Odell wrote Gueguen that he had done all that could be done at present, which was to give the Richibucto Band a certificate that he enclosed. Like the one sent earlier to the Buctouche Band, the certificate stated the Richibucto Band had made application for an allotment of lands on the upper part of the Richibucto River extending down the stream about ten miles, including such breadth on each side as might in actual survey be found allowable in the judgment of the governor and his council.

It seems no further action was taken due to increasing concern in the government about setting aside such large acreages as were being contemplated for the Buctouche and Richibucto bands. Nonetheless, the Richibucto Band persisted. Again in 1801 they asked Gueguen to intervene while stating their hope and desire for "the same indulgence" received by members of the Buctouche Band through the survey carried out by James Watson. In supporting their request, Gueguen emphasized that the Richibucto Mi'kmaq, with fifty-four males, were more numerous than those at Buctouche. Finally, in 1802, George Sproule provided a description of the lands to be reserved for the Richibucto Band, stating that these lands extended ten miles up the Richibucto River and four miles on each side, containing on the whole 51,200 acres.[39] Moses Perley, who in 1841 had access to the records of the executive council and surveyor general's office, claimed that the government issued a licence of occupation on September 9, 1805, for setting aside lands in Sproule's description.[40] This is highly improbable and no licence has ever been found. However, the government did set aside nearly 100,000 acres for the combined population on the two reserves, which likely did not exceed five hundred individuals. No explanation has been found for the government setting aside such large tracts for the Buctouche and Richibucto reserves.

Hardly had the government given sanction for setting aside these lands, than petitions began arriving from settlers attracted to both river basins with the inevitable squatting. The pressures to reduce the size of the reserves increased. For the government, matters were greatly complicated by the death of Surveyor General George Sproule in 1817. One of the first tasks of his successor, Anthony Lockwood, was dealing with petitions from both band members and whites at Richibucto. Chief Paul Tenans petitioned for a survey of the Richibucto Reserve to protect it against trespassers, to which the government gave its approval.[41] The white population expressed frustration in a petition that claimed settlers from England were going on to the United States because they could not obtain land. The petitioners felt the loss of these possible settlers when "they see the land cloaked under the names of these poor infatuated Indians who derive no benefits."[42]

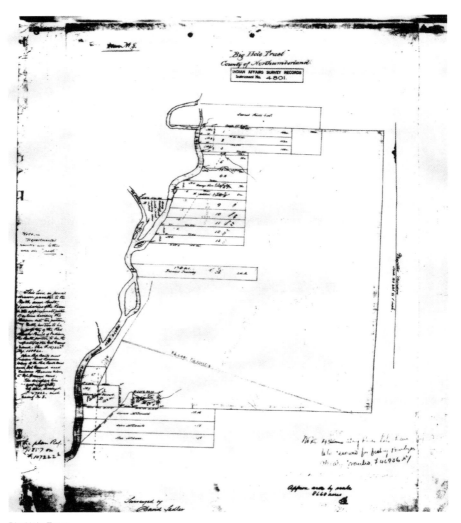

Big Hole Tract
Courtesy Natural Resources Canada

In 1820 the executive council ordered issue of a licence of occupation for the Richibucto Reserve, but no such licence has ever been located. Lockwood reported that same year to the executive council on lands for the Richibucto Band.[43] In 1823 he presented to the council a plan of the Richibucto River that showed the reserve lands and another of the Buctouche River. It is probable that the decision was made at this time or the following year to reduce the 40,960

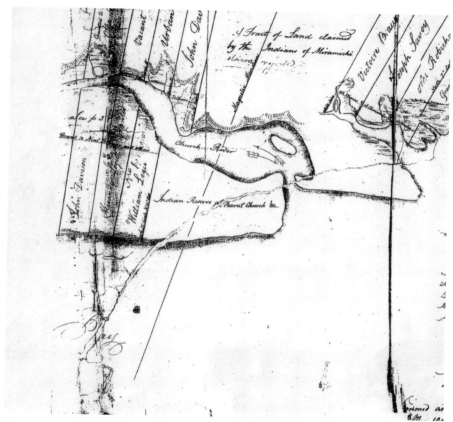

Survey by Dugald Campbell of Indian lands at Burnt Church, 1804.
Courtesy Natural Resources Canada

acres of the Buctouche Reserve to 4,665 acres and to reduce the 51,320 acres of Richibucto to 5,720 acres.[44] After Thomas Baillie became surveyor general in 1824, a licence of occupation was issued for the use of the Richibucto Band on the north side of the Richibucto River, extending to include two miles to the rear of the river. Reserve lands on the south side had been lost to squatters who would later receive grants. Facing the same pressures at Buctouche, the government chose to throw open for settlement all the reserve land on the south side of the Buctouche River. It proceeded to issue grants for 6,307 acres. The two reserves in their reduced form were virtual twins.

The Maliseet of the Saint John River, though fewer in number than the Mi'kmaq, were of greater interest to the government. Once the war with

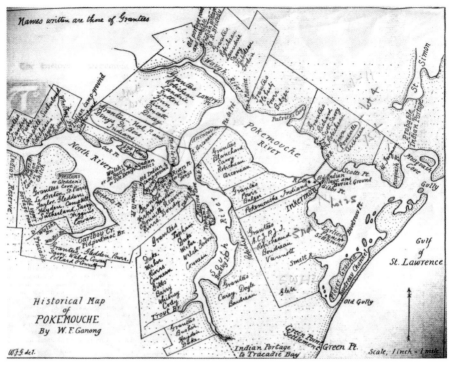

Historical map of Pokemouche by W. F. Ganong
Courtesy Natural Resources Canada

revolutionary France began in 1793, the government became concerned about any signs of disaffection. The fear was that they would come under the influence of the neighbouring Massachusetts Tribe and side with the French. François Ciquard, a French Royalist priest serving the Abenaki mission at Penobscot, contacted Lieutenant-Governor Carleton about transferring to New Brunswick. Carleton was able to obtain for him an annual allowance of £50. In turn, Carleton made clear to him his expectations that "he would work in sincerity of his zeal to contribute what may be in his power towards civilizing the Savages of this province and attaching them to our Government."[45]

In the upper Saint John River, tracts of land had been set aside for Loyalist regiments, but lands in the area of Tobique River were still un-granted wilderness. Further up the river there was a considerable settlement of Acadians who had moved there from the lower part of the Saint John River after the Loyalists' arrival. There was also a Maliseet village further up the river. The government decided that Tobique would become the area for settlement of the Maliseet nation. In the second half of the 1790s, a few Maliseet, probably from Madawaska, seem to have removed to the mouth of the Tobique, almost certainly attracted by the salmon fishery. Ciquard began the construction of a chapel and probably a house for himself. In 1801 Noille Bernard and nineteen other Maliseet petitioned that they were destitute. They wished to settle on land commencing at Roche a Tobic and extending further up the Saint John River to the mouth of Tobique River.[46] The executive council on September 4, 1801, ordered that the land described in the petition be reserved for the Maliseet.[47] Neither a reference to a subsequent licence of occupation nor a full description of the lands to be set off, would have been required for issuing a licence of occupation, have ever been found.

The problems created by the lack of any description of lands were noted by George Shore when he was acting surveyor general for a brief time in 1818, after the death of George Sproule. He reported that in August of 1818 Chief Joseph Toma of the Tobique Band had complained to him about trespassers cutting pine timber and erecting buildings and clearing the land. Because no limits or bounds had been established as to how far their land extended back from the Tobique River, Toma wanted the government to set out a portion for their purposes. He concluded, however, by stating that the "Tribe always considered it as their right, to possess the Land from the Mouth to the Sources of [the] Tobique River," which was about six miles.[48] In what appears to have been a rough calculation, the office of the surveyor general arrived at a figure of 16,000 acres for the reserve.[49]

The government encountered the most difficulties with establishing reserves for the small number of Mi'kmaq who inhabited villages on the coastal rivers draining into Northumberland Strait. These varied in extent. Those in the southeast like Shediac, Cocagne, and Aboushagan were comparatively small rivers and were inhabited by only a few Mi'kmaq. Further up the coast were villages on the Buctouche and Richibucto rivers whose drainage basins were around 207,200 hectares and had larger populations. Between the Miramichi River and Chaleur Bay, there were villages at the entrances of the Tabusintac, Burnt Church, and Pokemouche rivers.

Stephen Millidge's instructions in 1788 required him to proceed as far as Chaleur Bay. After dealing with the Richibucto Band, he went directly to Burnt Church, bypassing the Miramichi villages, presumably because they were already being dealt with by the government. At Burnt Church he seems to have marked off a tract—probably by no more than shooting compass bearings and blazing trees—near the mouth of the river, where the English under James Wolfe had destroyed the church after the capture of Louisbourg in 1758, hence the name of the village. At Tabusintac he would have found no more than a dozen Mi'kmaw families with their campsites located at the mouth of the river and a nearby burial ground. There was a close association between the Burnt Church and Tabusintac Mi'kmaq: they were virtually one tribe or band. English settlement dated from 1798, when four families settled on the river adjacent to the Mi'kmaw campsites.

Although the Mi'kmaq did not object initially to the English taking up lands, relations quickly deteriorated because settlements were encroaching on the eeling ground, which the Mi'kmaq claimed was licensed to them. They petitioned through James Thom, Justice of the Peace, for a permanent licence of occupation of a tract of land on both sides of the river to secure their eeling ground. Thom supported the petition, stating that they were the most industrious tribe in Northumberland County. Some of them brought the petition to Fredericton, where they met with George Sproule. He recommended the executive council issue a licence of occupation, to which the council agreed, but for reasons he apparently explained to the tribe, no licence would ever be issued.

However, Moses Perley, writing in 1846, believed there was a minute of council of February 18, 1802, which stated that a licence was granted to the Mi'kmaq of the Tabusintac district to occupy 240 acres at Burnt Church Point, 1,400 acres on the north side of Burnt Church River, and 9,035 acres on the Tabusintac River. On the same date Jonathan Odell issued an order referring to these acreages and using the similar description to those he had issued for Buctouche and Richibucto. Undoubtedly, George Sproule would have prepared the descriptions. It is likely that Perley was referring to Odell's order because no minute of council has been found authorizing a licence of occupation. His acreage figures came from an 1839 Schedule of Reserves prepared by the surveyor general's office and were presumably based on Odell's order.[50]

If Deputy Surveyor Stephen Millidge had followed the instructions given to him by Surveyor General George Sproule in 1788, he would have continued up the coast from the Miramichi River to Burnt Church, Tabusintac, and further on to Pokemouche, but there is no record of him having done so. There seems to have been only very few Mi'kmaq there. There would be no settlers attracted to the area until the late 1790s, when some Acadian fishermen settled on the south side of the river. They were soon followed by numerous Irish immigrants. This sudden influx probably stemmed from the petition of 1803 by the de Boss family for a grant to lands "that from time immemorial their ancestors" had occupied and known as Pointe de la Croix. In support of this petition William Ferguson, Justice of the Peace at Tracadie, certified that the de Boss family had "priority of possession," which was now reduced to only two families. Although the petition did not state the acreage requested, when it came before the land committee of the executive council on May 15, 1804, the wording was that Denny de Boss and three sons had been settled and had cultivated a tract of land on the north side of the Pokemouche River, about six miles from its mouth, and were asking for lots of 200 acres each. Moses Perley, however, states that at that meeting a tract of 2,600 acres on the river was ordered to be surveyed for the Pokemouche Mi'kmaq. No survey seems to have been made.

A memorial in 1810 from Chief John Baptiste Pomeville and sixteen other members of the tribe residing at Pokemouche was arguably the most authentic Native voice to address government in this period of drastic change for the Mi'kmaq. It began, "the memorialists were a remnant of the mickmac nation of Aboriginals whose ancestors have inhabited said River time immemorial—hunting and fishing the primitive pursuit of our forefathers is from the increase of setters nearly Extinct." They had observed the full allotments of land given their brethren who inhabited the Tabusintac, Miramichi, and Richibucto rivers. Also they had seen how their brothers were profiting from the only natural resource common to all, the timber trade, which they wished to promote on their river. They requested land on the Pokemouche River to cover the eel fishery, to erect cabins, and to "drink at same springs, and smoke the calumet of peace with our Brothers and be ever faithful to King George, our Great Chief beyond the great lake onwards to the rising sun."[51] Representatives of the Pokemouche village were present at the ceremonial proceedings for the treaty signing that had been held at Lieutenant-Governor Jonathan Belcher's farm in 1761. Those proceedings likely were passed down orally from generation to generation.

William Ferguson certified that lands the Mi'kmaq asked for were three miles above any other granted lands. Because hunting had failed, he recommended the memorial for consideration. The committee of council for lands ordered that John Baptiste Pomeville and the other Mi'kmaq might have 4,000 acres lying on both sides of the river and extending up the river two miles.[52] At the surveyor general's office a mix-up seems to have occurred between the acreages of Denny de Boss and his sons for the 2,600 acres on the river and for John Pomeville and the sixteen others for 4,000 acres on the south side of the river. A survey was probably carried out in 1811, though it has never been located, with the result that 2,600 acres were set aside on the south side of the river and the order for 4,000 acres was never acted upon. The most likely explanation is that Deputy Surveyor William Ferguson carried out the 1811 survey and on orders of George Sproule reduced the reserve's extent on the south side of the Pokemouche River on the grounds that 2,600 acres should be ample for the Mi'kmaq population of around fifty.

By 1810–11 the government had set aside around 60,000 acres for the combined Maliseet and Mi'kmaq population. In doing so it was never able to institute a firm policy for establishing reserves. At first, it followed the Nova Scotia precedent of licences of occupation when setting aside lands at Miramichi. When it came to lands for the Buctouche and Richibucto Mi'kmaq the government was prepared to set aside 100,000 acres initially for a combined population of no more than five hundred for which there seems to have been no known rationale. Instead of issuing licences of occupation, the government adopted a policy of the provincial secretary providing a certificate with a brief description of the lands prepared by the surveyor general. When it became apparent that squatters on both reserves were openly seizing reserve lands, the government simply reduced the reserves to one-tenth their original extent. What seems to have become policy was based on whether or not land petitioned for by Maliseet on the Saint John River and Mi'kmaq on the Northumberland Strait shore hindered settlement. This was definitely the policy followed at Tabusintac and Pokemouche.

A major factor in abandoning the use of licences of occupation was the necessity of a survey to provide a description for the lands to be set aside. Surveys were expensive to undertake. Yet without surveys, as in the particular case of Tobique for example, it was impossible to deal with the continued and extensive squatting on reserve lands. Other than issuing orders in the *Royal Gazette* strictly forbidding anyone from occupying reserve lands, the government took no action.

## NOTES

1. Stephen E. Patterson, "Indian-White Relations in Nova Scotia, 1749–61: A Study of Political Interaction," *Acadiensis* 13, no. 1 (Autumn 1993): 25.

2. Minutes, His Majesty's Council (hereafter Council Minutes), October 1–2, 1749, CO 217/9, pp. 117–8, United Kingdom National Archives (hereafter UKNA).

3. Council Minutes, July 29, September 9, 1754, vol. 187, RG1, Nova Scotia Archives (hereafter NSA); William Cotterell to Captain Hamilton, June 3, 1754, in Thomas Akins, ed., *Selections from the Pubic Documents of Nova Scotia* (Halifax, 1869), p. 210.

4. Micheline D. Johnson, "Paul Laurent," *Dictionary of Canadian Biography* (hereafter *DCB*), vol. 3, pp. 358–9.

5. Council Minutes, February 12 and 13, 1755, RG1 vol. 187, PANS.

6. Patterson, "Indian-White Relations in Nova Scotia, 1749–61," p. 51.

7. John Reid to author by email, March 17, 2012.

8. Patterson, "Indian-White Relations in Nova Scotia, 1749–61," p. 55, fn. 69. For the various treaties signed in 1760 and 1761 see William C. Wicken, *Mi'kmaq Treaties on Trial: History, Land, and Donald Marshall Junior* (Toronto: University of Toronto Press, 2002), pp. 198–209.

9. Patterson, "Indian-White Relations in Nova Scotia, 1749–61," pp. 56–57. The treaties were, however, largely silent on land issues. Both Wicken and Patterson note this fact.

10. Order of the King in Council, November 23, 1761, E. B. O'Callaghan, *Documents relative to the Colonial History of the State of New York*: 477.

11. Patterson, "Indian-White Relations in Nova Scotia, 1749–61," p. 57.

12. Order of the King in Council, November 23, 1761, E. B. O'Callagan, *Documents relative to the Colonial History of the State of New York*: 477.

13. Proclamation of May 4, 1762, RG1, vol. 31, PANS.

14. Extracts of Minutes of Proceedings of the Lord Commissioners of Trade and Plantations, December 3, 1762, RG1, vol. 31, no. 10, PANS.

15. Ibid.

16. Lords of Trade to Wilmot, March 20, 1764, CO 218/6/387-88, UKNA.

17. Wilmot to Lords of Trade, January 28, 1764, CO 217/21, ff. 7-8, UKNA

18. Lords of Trade to Wilmot, March 29, 1764, CO 218/6/387-88, UKNA

19. Wilmot to Lords of Trade, January 28, CO 217/21, 7–8ff., UKNA. For the Royal Proclamation see John Borrows, "Wampum at Niagara: The Royal Proclamation, Canadian Legal History, and Self-Government," in *Aboriginal and Treaty Rights in Canada*, ed. Michael Asch (Vancouver: UBC Press, 1997).

20. Wilmot to Lords of Trade, March 20, 1764, CO 218/21, 7-8ff., UKNA.

21. Benjamin Green to Board of Trade, August 24, 1766, CO 217/21, Part 2, p. 268, UKNA.

22. L. F. S. Upton, *Micmacs and Colonists: Indian-White Relations in the Maritimes, 1713–1867* (Vancouver: University of British Columbia Press, 1979), 62.

23. Council Minutes, September 10, 1766, CO 217/21, p. 258, UKNA.

24. Council Minutes, July 20, 1773, RG1, vol. 212, p. 180, NSA. For background to this instruction see Margaret Ells, "Clearing the Decks for the Loyalists," *Report of the Annual Meeting of the Canadian Historical Association* 12, no. 1, 1933.

25. Brian Slattery, *The Land Rights of Indigenous Canadian Peoples* (Saskatoon: University of Saskatchewan Native Law Centre, 1979): 250. See also Nancy E. Ayers, "Aboriginal Rights in the Maritimes," *Canadian Law Reporter* 2, no. 1 (1984): 64, who concludes: "There seems to be little doubt that the Royal Proclamation issued by Imperial Crown in 1763 applied to the area now comprising the three Maritime Provinces."

26. Inland Letter Book, Governors and Provincial Secretaries, signed by Provincial Secretary Richard Bulkley, August 14, 1779, RG1, vol. 136, PANS.

27. Governor's Licence Book, August 30, 1783, RG20, Series C, vol. 95, p. 107, PANS.

28. In RS867 is a copy of the 1783 licence of occupation, Provincial Archives of New Brunswick (hereafter PANB).

29. W. D. Hamilton, *The Julian Tribe* (Fredericton, NB: The Micmac-Maliseet Institute of New Brunswick, 1984), p. 9. A document entitled "Petitions for Northumberland County N.B." (PAC MG59 A5 vol. 11, File 1, p. 17), no. 204, reads "Return for a grant of land of 3,033 acres on North west Branch of the Miramichi River for John Julien, Indian Chief of the Miramichi Indians and his Tribe." The original licence of occupation for Eel Ground is not extant. A copy exists in partial form, dated 1896, in the Department of Aboriginal Affairs and Northern Development Canada, (hereafter DAANDC), RG10, vol. 2,522, file 107,222,2.

30. W. D. Hamilton, *The Julian Tribe*, 11–15.

31. For a biography of Sproule, see Robert Fellows, *DCB*, vol. 5, 773–4.

32. In a letter of instruction to Deputy Surveyor James Watson, Surveyor General Sproule commented on Millidge's plan. See George Sproule to James Watson, September 13, 1798, RS637/1a/2, PANB.

33. Ibid.

34. For John (Gohn) Noel, see L. F. S. Upton, *DCB*, vol. 7, p. 443. Chief John Noel, who met with Carleton, may have been the father of John Noel the subject of Upton's biography.

35. George Sproule to James Watson, September 13, 1798, RS637/1a, PANB.

36. Enclosure in Jonathan Odell to Joseph Gueguen at Cocagne, September 12, 1800, MG H54, no. 9, Harriet Irving Library Archives, University of New Brunswick (hereafter HILA). For Gueguen see Régis Brun, *DCB*, vol. 6, 304–5.

37. Order given at Fredericton, June 28, 1788, MG H54, no 1a, HILA and Chief Mathew Andrew and four captains to Governor Thomas Carleton, undated but 1788, Legislative Library of New Brunswick.

38. Joseph Gueguen to Governor Carleton, October 13, 1801, printed in Régis Brun, *Pionnier de la nouvelle Acadia: Joseph Gueguen 1741–1825*, 144. For Gueguen see also Régis Brun, *DCB*, vol. 6, 304–5. Gueguen operated a trading establishment at Cocagne, used by both Acadians and Mi'kmaq, while acting as interpreter for both.

39. Certificate by Jonathan Odell and description signed by George Sproule, January 29, 1802, MG H54 EA1, p. 26, HILA.

40. Moses Perley, "History of Indians of New Brunswick," enclosed with Sir Edmund Head to Earl Grey, 17 1848, CO188/106, 217ff., UKNA.

41. Draft Minutes of New Brunswick Executive, May 28, 1819, MG9 A1, vol. 5, pp. 60–63, PANB.

42. Abstracts of petitions for Kent County, 1819, petition no. 174, MG9, vol. 8, Library and Archives Canada (hereafter LAC).

43. From 1822 Anthony Lockwood began showing signs of mental illness. By 1823 there were spectacular displays of his madness, and he was removed from his office. See "Anthony Lockwood," *DCB*, VIII, 506–8. Lockwood left his office in "perfect chaos," which may at least in part account for the considerable number of documents missing from the surveyor general's office, such as licences of occupation.

44. The reduced acreages come from 1851 surveys undertaken by Captain Peter Merzerall, which are discussed in Chapter 3.

45. Thomas Carleton to Henry Dundas, June 14, 1793, CO217/15, 185ff., UKNA. For Ciquard, see Bruno Harel, "François Ciquard," *DCB*, VI, 145.

46. Petition of Noille Bernard…and John Bapt. Tobic, July 1, 1801, MGH54 EA1. Micah Pawling suggests that the drafter of the petition was a Catholic priest, John Baptist, whose mission included all the Catholic settlements from Madawaska to Fredericton. Micah Pawling, "Petitions, Kin, and Cultural Survival: The Maliseet and Passamaquoddy Peoples in the Nineteenth Century" (master's thesis, University of Maine, 1999), 64.

47. Draft minutes of executive council, September 4, 1801, MG9 A1, vol. 2, p. 998, LAC.

48. George Shore to Lieutenant-Governor George Smyth, August 8, 1818, RS557c, PANB.

49. New Brunswick *Journals of the House of Assembly* (hereafter *JHA*), Appendix 12. The Legislative Library of New Brunswick confirmed with the author that *Journals of the House of Assembly* (hereafter *JHA*) was the correct term for the nineteenth century and into the twentieth century.

50. Moses Perley, "The Indians of New Brunswick," enclosure to Sir Edmund Head, August 17, 1848, CO 218/106, f. 218.

51. Memorial of John Baptiste Pomeville & other Indians, October 1810, petitions RS, PANB. There might be a connection with the appointment as chief, dated November 7, 1810, of John Baptiste Pomeville, Jr., in place of his father, John Baptiste, Sr., MG H54, no. 36, HILA. Smoking the Calumet was a ceremonial practice that signified the creation of sacred kinship and was sometimes referred to as "singing the calument."

52. Order to create Reserve, MG9 A5, vol. 7, pp. 1355–8, LAC.

# CHAPTER 2

# ATTEMPTS TO DEAL WITH SQUATTERS

lthough Maliseet and Mi'kmaq were not permitted to convey lands reserved under licences of occupation except to the Crown, members of the Julian family nonetheless began as early as 1793 to sell lands to non-Natives. Before his death in 1805, John Julian sold a parcel of land in 1793 and another in 1799, both from the Eel Ground Reserve. His son Andrew and successor as "King," or as the government commission stated "Chief of the Tribe of Mi'kmaq in the District of Miramichi," with the consent of three of his brothers, in 1813 sold land from the same reserve to cover debts incurred by him and the band for provisions purchased.[1] After Andrew Julian sold two lots in 1815, other chiefs and tribe members petitioned the government, first to have Andrew Julian removed as chief of the Mi'kmaq because he was a "palpable drunkard" and then to have it intervene to stop any further sales.[2] No action was taken on Andrew Julian's removal, but on October 20, 1815, the executive council issued an order for no "sale or exchange of land reserved for the use of Indians…[and] any person committing a trespass of any of those lands will be prosecuted by the Attorney General."[3] It is uncertain, however, if this order appeared in the *Royal Gazette* as a government proclamation because the issues immediately following the date of the council order are missing.

By 1822 the Julian family's increased indebtedness caused them to come to Fredericton to voice their complaints against their creditors' demands. Attorney General Thomas Wetmore agreed to intervene and arranged a creditors' meeting at the Newcastle Courthouse. In doing so, he notified the creditors that "The Indians being tenants of the Crown, it becomes the duty of Government to attend to their complaints, and to see that justice is done to them and unless it can be obtained in some other way it will be necessary to take steps to vest the profits of the land wholly in the Crown." He managed to scale down the debt owed and reach an agreement, signed by Barnaby Julian and the creditors, on future payment. The agreement was contingent on the sale of a portion of Eel Ground Reserve, which was considered of no use to the tribe but had good value as a mill site. A final clause to the agreement made it provisional unless the government used its "exertions in the protection of the Lands for the use of... [the] Indians to the exclusion of any other person making claims under judgements or otherwise."[4] Wetmore also recommended that it could be necessary to have tribe members confine their trading to one firm whose accounts would always be open to government inspection.

The idea of authorized selling of reserve lands arose again in 1832, but this time it came from the Mi'kmaq themselves. Richard McLaughlin, a deputy commissioner for Crown lands, wrote Surveyor General Thomas Baillie that Barnaby Julian, chief of the Little South West Tribe, and Denny Julian, chief of the North West Tribe, had stated that they wished to relinquish the reserves with the exception of a lot for each tribe member. Their condition was that the money raised be placed in a fund for the support of the sick, aged, and infirm belonging to their tribes. McLaughlin proceeded to call a meeting and, through an interpreter, made known the plan with which the Mi'kmaq "seemed fully satisfied."[5] Three chiefs (one was Barnaby Julian) provided names from the Little South West (fifteen names, of which six were Julians) and North West tribes who would receive lots. McLaughlin, however, never received authority to proceed with the agreed arrangement.

Other than for such uses as mill sites, there was initially not much interest in reserve lands. In 1807, after the British government lifted a ban on governors' granting of lands, there was a rush to obtain grants with river frontage both above the Little South West Reserve on the South West branch and below the reserve on the North West Miramichi. After the Napoleonic Wars, immigration to the Miramichi greatly accelerated with many drawn by the expanding timber trade. By the 1830s immigration and natural population growth had created an increased demand for land by a class of mostly poor settlers.[6] Much of the lands earlier granted on the Little South West and the North West, above and below the Little South West Reserve, had gone to merchants and other speculators with the result that the main portions of these two rivers became closed to settlers who could not afford to purchase.[7] As a result, the river frontage lands of the Little South West Reserve became increasingly attractive. Other than at Red Bank, where Barnaby Julian and about fifteen families lived,[8] these lands were unoccupied and appealing to settlers who were prepared to lease or just squat.

From the autumn of 1833 through to the summer of 1836, the Julians negotiated about twenty more leases for meadow and wilderness properties along both sides of the Little South West River. Annual rents on the leases ranged from £1 to £5 with most payable in cash, though a few were to be paid in cash and produce. Although the Julian family benefitted from the rents collected, they also protested to the government the encroachments made by squatters. When Barnaby Julian came to Fredericton in August 1836 to secure an official commission as successor to his father, Francis, as chief of the Miramichi Mi'kmaq, he brought with him "whole documents relative to the reserve," which he wished to explain to Lieutenant-Governor Sir Archibald Campbell. He contended that his father's incapacity (presumably age) had resulted in settlers encroaching on their lands.

Francis's solution was for government to have "some person in Miramichi appointed to look after their rights so that they will not be taken advantage by intruders."[9] He failed to secure an interview with Campbell and received no encouragement that government would intervene to stop encroachments and act against the squatters. In the next three months after his return to the Miramichi, he put more than one thousand acres of Little South West Reserve under lease to squatters, probably most of whom had been occupying reserve lands for some time. In this he had the assistance of William Park, a schoolmaster, who did surveys and kept accounts. In return Barnaby leased him some land.[10]

By the late 1830s many squatters, some under lease and some not, were occupying lands within the reserve on both sides of the Little South West Miramichi. Among the lands leased were the best meadows and mill sites. Within a few years, almost the whole reserve, except for Red Bank village and back woodlots, would be occupied by settlers who had erected camps, houses, and other buildings as well as a school. One reason for the lack of surveys for lands allocated for reserves and government inaction was that control over Crown lands rested with the imperial government. During the Napoleonic Wars, Britain had applied a preferential tariff on imported foreign timber, which greatly increased the importation of timber from New Brunswick. After the defeat of Napoleon, the tariff was continued for the next twenty years.

New Brunswick's prosperity depended on the timber export trade. As only one-fifth of land was in private ownership, the un-granted Crown lands, reckoned to be around sixteen million acres, provided most of the timber exported from the province.[11] In 1816 the need to reorganize Crown lands administration resulted in the transfer of responsibility for Crown lands to provincial jurisdiction.[12]

The House of Assembly, however, was excluded from a role in the administration of Crown lands. The executive placed a duty of one shilling per ton of wood cut on Crown land as a means of increasing government revenue. However, in 1824 the Colonial Office transferred responsibility for Crown lands from the executive council to a newly created office of Commissioner of Crown Lands and Surveyor General and appointed to the office Thomas Baillie, as noted previously.

Then, in 1827, the Colonial Office introduced a new policy for the sale of Crown lands: the money collected would go into casual revenue over which the executive council had no

Surveyor General Thomas Baillie, ca. 1850
Provincial Archives of New Brunswick P37-112

control.[13] The British government saw the revenue as being used to cover the expenses of the New Brunswick government, which had been paid out of the annual parliamentary grant. In short, New Brunswickers, who had been obtaining grants of Crown lands and cutting timber on them virtually at will, now faced the prospect of having to pay.

Thomas Baillie's determination to make the new policy a success resulted in 694,180 acres being sold by 1837. The amount in the casual revenue had risen to £153,739 by 1835.[14] Government officials were receiving their salaries and so were not overly opposed to the new policy, as long as any transfer of casual revenue came to the executive council. However, members of the assembly were determined to gain control over the casual revenue. Eventually, after much negotiation with the Colonial Office, the assembly got its way, on condition of it assuming responsibility for the salaries of government officials.[15] With it came legislative control over Crown lands, including those set aside for reserves.

Since the 1820s, the government had been appointing unpaid commissioners for each county to administer what funds the assembly annually voted for assisting the Maliseet and Mi'kmaq. These commissioners had no authority over reserve lands and did not involve themselves in any form of administration, except the distribution of relief. At the beginning of the 1838 session, the assembly passed a motion of John Weldon's, a member for Kent County, that information be laid

*His excellency Lieutenant-General Sir John Harvey, KCB, KCH, Colonel of Her Majesty's 59th Regiment and Governor and Commander in Chief of Nova Scotia and its Dependencies, &c.*

James Henry Lynch, after Stephen Pearce, Day & Son, English, 1846–1852. 50.8 × 39.5 cm tinted lithograph on heavy wove paper.

John Clarence Webster Canadiana Collection, W701, New Brunswick Museum

before it on "all tracts of Land reserved for the use of Indians."[16] After the surveyor general submitted a "Schedule of Indian Reserves," Weldon proposed selling various reserve lands in Kent County, which were in an uncultivated state, of no use to the Mi'kmaq, and hindered settlement. Commissioners would use the proceeds for the benefit of those aged and distressed members of the band who had an interest in the reserve lands being sold.[17]

There was apparent disagreement on this course of action. William End, a member for Gloucester County, found Weldon's proposal to sell reserve lands unacceptable. He moved an amendment that struck out Weldon's coplete motion and replaced it with one that emphasized amelioration of the Mi'kmaq and Maliseet living conditions. Commissioners were to report on numbers and their general state. He proposed that money be distributed for bounties and the purchase of agricultural implements to "allure them to the arts of civilized life."[18] However, John Ambrose Street, a member from Northumberland County, which had by far the largest number of reserves, moved to expunge End's entire amendment. Street's amendment called for commissioners in the respective counties to be appointed to report to the governor on what parts of the reserves could be sold, with the proceeds to "constitute a fund for the benefit of the Indians of the County in which such Reserves are situate." In the voting that followed Street's amending motion, the house defeated first Street's and then End's motions, before passing Weldon's. End voted against, but Street had no trouble supporting Weldon's motion—a forecast of future disagreement over selling reserve lands.

A week later, after he had failed to win support for his views on the need to ameliorate the conditions under which New Brunswick's Mi'kmaq and Maliseet lived, William End moved in reference to his own county of Gloucester that: "In order to protect and defend the equitable rights of the Indian tribes in the

County of Gloucester, it is thought necessary that Commissioners should be appointed to superintend their affairs and carry into operation such measures as may be hereafter adopted by the Government for their benefit, to make a report to His Excellency the Lieutenant-Governor, as to their general condition, and in what manner those tracts of Land reserved for their use may be rendered most beneficial to them."[19] This resolution gained the assembly's approval and a committee including Weldon and End waited on Lieutenant-Governor Sir John Harvey to present End's motion. Harvey would take no action on either Weldon's or End's resolutions.

In 1834 the British House of Commons had initiated an investigation into the Empire's Aboriginal peoples. Colonial Office inquiries on the subject to Nova Scotia and New Brunswick had been simply ignored. However, in August 1838 Lord Glenelg, the colonial secretary, specifically directed Harvey to furnish him with a report on the state of the Aboriginal inhabitants in the province.[20] For his reply, Harvey sought the views of the unpaid commissioners. Along with his dispatch, Harvey enclosed the Northumberland and Kent counties' commissioners' reports. The Northumberland commissioners in their report emphasized there were extensive tracts of valuable land reserved by the government for the Mi'kmaq, but these "lands are of little or no use to them, in their present condition, one or two of the Chiefs have leased many parts of these reserves to whites upon small, in many instances at most nominal Rents, which prove of little service to the Indians generally, the Rents go principally to the support of the Chiefs."[21] Squatters occupied other lands not leased, and much remained in a wilderness state and of no use to the Mi'kmaq. The commissioners strongly urged the sale of portions of the reserves to provide a fund for the aged and infirm. Moreover, the Mi'kmaq themselves would gladly sell and the commissioners believed the funds from such sales would do more good than if they retained the lands. They opposed leasing because no persons could be found who would make any permanent improvements under this condition. They also decried the practice as "very objectionable and impolitic of jailing Indians for debt."[22]

The Kent County commissioners, John W. Weldon and William Chandler, reported: "The Reserve upon this River [Richibucto] is Extensive but is…of no use to them. If their Grounds were more confined…it would have a tendency to make them more useful of their crops where growing." On Buctouche, they commented: "Upon the Buctouche River there is a considerable Reserve, only four families remain there, their habits are rather better than those residing on the Richibucto River."[23]

For Gloucester County, the commissioners replied that the Mi'kmaq in the county were in very indigent circumstances, having among them a great number of aged and infirm persons. They were generally not in the habit of cultivating the lands reserved for their use, but devoted their attention chiefly to hunting and fishing. With advancing settlement, however, this was barely sufficient to supply the wants of the younger and more active members of the tribe. As with their colleagues, the Gloucester commissioners noted that the reserve lands remained for the most part unimproved, which arose principally from their natural "disinclination to agricultural pursuits, but also in some degree from the exposure to trespassing and encroachments for which they are unacquainted with a remedy."[24]

Lord Normanby, the new colonial secretary, in his reply, took up the idea of selling part of the reserves for the benefit of the Maliseet and Mi'kmaq. After expressing his great satisfaction in knowing that the New Brunswick legislature was anxious to adopt any measures to promote their welfare, Normanby dealt with the possible sale of their lands by delegating this authority to the province on the grounds that "Your local knowledge and that of the Legislature will enable you to judge so much more correctly than myself of the measures most conducive to the well being of the Indians that I do not venture to give you any instructions on the subject." However, he told Harvey he wished "to commend these people to your careful superintendence and would beg you to consider attentively the suggestions of the Commissioners that the Indian Reserves, or part of them, should be sold for their benefit."[25] Otherwise, he was unprepared to give "any instructions on the subject."[26] After Harvey laid Normanby's dispatch before the assembly, John Ambrose Street moved that because Normanby had given to the government and legislature of the province "the propriety of disposing of Indian reserves" an address be presented to the lieutenant-governor that "reserves in Northumberland County be sold at auction with the proceeds applied to the benefit of Indians in that county."[27]

Harvey, however, who had been appointed lieutenant-governor of Newfoundland in April 1841, took no action and simply left the issue to his successor. Sir William Colebrooke succeeded Harvey as lieutenant-governor in 1842. Colebrooke came to the governorship as a believer in reform and with deep humanitarian concerns.[28] After a military career, he had served in various colonial appointments. As the author of a series of reports on Ceylon, he had advocated far-reaching social, economic, and political reforms, including the abolition of the caste system and all forms of legal discrimination. His last appointments before coming to New Brunswick were in the West Indies, where he had to deal with problems created by the abolition of slavery and had earned a reputation as an enlightened governor.

New Brunswick and her sister colonies were governed by a lieutenant-governor and executive council appointed by the Colonial Office, a legislative council (or upper house) also appointed by the Colonial Office, and an elected House of Assembly. In the 1830s a constitutional struggle had begun in the British North American colonies to achieve responsible government.[29] Responsible government meant members of the executive council were to be drawn from the majority party in the assembly and responsible to that body, and no longer to the governor, for their conduct in office. During his governorship, Sir John Harvey had taken care to appoint men to the executive council who commanded the confidence of the assembly without, however, conceding any constitutional principle. In the 1840s, agitation continued until finally in 1848, the British government formally conceded the principle.

Colebrooke understood he would have to find men for his executive council who had support within the assembly, though not as a cabinet as was the English constitutional practice.[30] He held that responsible government was "manifestly impossible" because executive councillors could not be responsible both to him as governor and to the assembly.[31] Nor did he accept that he could be bound by the executive council's advice. He began his governorship with reformist zeal, proposing measures for desperately needed financial reform, municipal incorporation, and creation of a provincial board of works (i.e., a department of public works). In contrast to previous governors who had not initiated much legislation, Colebrooke had members of his executive council draft bills and present them to the assembly as his government's measures. He immediately ran into fierce opposition in both the assembly and the legislative council, whose members saw these measures as challenging what they viewed in pre-responsible government as their undoubted constitutional rights, particularly to control public expenditures.

None of Colebrooke's reformist bills made it through both the assembly and the legislative council to become law. In a lengthy and in places confusing (Colonial Office officials used "vague") dispatch, Colebrooke told Stanley of the difficulties he was having.[32] Although Stanley agreed to examine the failed bills, he reminded Colebrooke: "Much, however, of the argument for or against these several measures must depend on their adaption to the feelings and wishes, and their applicability to the circumstances of the Province. On these points the local authorities must form their opinion, and by their opinion Her Majesty's Ministers must mainly be guided in determining the course to be finally pursed."[33]

*Sir William MacBean Colebrooke, 1787–1870.*
J. E. Ford, English, 1826, watercolour, heightened
with opaque white on ivory, laid down on
card? Overall (case): 9.7 × 7.2 cm; support:
9.7 × 7.2 cm.

John Clarence Webster Canadiana Collection, W417,
New Brunswick Museum.

From his arrival in New Brunswick, Colebrooke determined to seek permanent betterment for New Brunswick Aboriginal peoples. In Moses Perley, Colebrooke found a kindred spirit and a trusted agent for achieving his goal. As a boy and young man, Perley had spent his summers hunting, fishing, and trading among the Mi'kmaq of the Saint John River and its tributaries.[34] His lifelong interest in their history and his passionate concern for their welfare deepened after he shot and killed one of them in an unfortunate accident. While practising law in Saint John, Perley continued to visit their settlements, becoming the province's most informed individual on the Maliseet and Mi'kmaq. In his paper "The Indians of New Brunswick," written for the British government in 1848, Moses Perley stated that Governor Sir John Harvey appointed him in 1837 "Commissioner of Indian affairs."[35] Although no record of an 1837 appointment has been found, Perley was likely referring to a possible appointment as a commissioner for Saint John County. Such appointments seemed to have been made informally, and no council order has been located for Perley's commission.

Shortly after Colebrooke arrived in 1841, Perley sent him a report on the province's Maliseet and Mi'kmaq with suggestions for improving their conditions. Apparently this report has not survived; however, Alfred Reade, as Colebrooke's private secretary (and son in-law), replied to Perley on June 16, 1841. In his reply, he addressed Perley as "Commissioner of Indian Affairs" and provided a summary of Colebrooke's thinking: "His Excellency desires me to state that… he is convinced of the necessity of securing to them [Indians] their lands, of preventing encroachments on them and of administering them in such a manner as to secure to them all the advantages to be desired from their permanent possession."[36]

Reade's letter also provided Colebrooke's view on the importance of Aboriginal education, reflecting his experience in Ceylon and the West Indies: it was "not desirable for the Indians to bring up their children as an exclusive class or caste, but rather to blend them with others who ought to be taught to regard Indians as their fellow christians [sic] and fellow subjects."[37] Under Perley's influence, and reflecting Colebrooke's reformist ideas, the government adopted as policy the establishment of villages for the Maliseet and Mi'kmaq, and also the allotting of lands for individual use with schools and similar institutions, as part of a settled existence along European lines. The tribes would continue to have a general interest in the remaining reserve lands with the funds arising from leasing or other arrangements used for their benefit.[38] However, as Surveyor General John Saunders informed Colebrooke, "the law has not vested the Indian Commissioners with sufficient power to enable them to exercise authority over Reserves."[39] If he wished to proceed with his plans, Colebrooke needed an act to provide the requisite authority. But first he authorized Moses Perley to visit all the reserves and to report on them, including numbers of squatters.

It had been Perley's idea to visit all the reserves to which Colebrooke gave his full support, providing him with instructions through Alfred Reade. It was advised that Perley should communicate with the other commissioners in the different parts of the province and to visit the reserves for which they were responsible.[40] Most particularly Reade's letter detailed Colebrooke's instructions on what Perley was to tell the Maliseet and Mi'kmaq, with special reference to reserve lands: besides the allotment of land for their individual occupation, it was contemplated to protect their interests in what were commonly called the reserves. "As the product of those lands was timber, it was not desirable that they enter into separate engagements with individuals for the right of occupancy or lumbering in which it is to be feared that advantages are not infrequently taken of them by improper persons to the serious prejudice of the Maliseet and Mi'kmaq."[41]

Once Colebrooke had decided his government's policy concerning reserves, the squatter issue became a foremost concern. Perley urged "that some steps should be taken to drive off the squatters on Indian Lands who from long impunity have become very daring and highly audacious." Moreover, others were constantly following their example and the "evil" was "hourly increasing."[42] Within a month of Perley's urgings, the government issued a proclamation for the removal of squatters, which stated, "persons have, without any authority, taken possession of Lands reserved by the Crown for the benefit of Indian Tribes" and commanded all such persons to quit the land they illegally occupied. Those who continued to trespass on reserve lands would be prosecuted.[43] Six days after the proclamation first appeared in the *Royal Gazette*, four Miramichi chiefs and thirteen captains came to Fredericton as a delegation to represent their condition and "the numerous trespasses and encroachments which have been and are now constantly making [sic] upon their lands."[44] They requested Perley visit them so they could show him the extent of encroachments. It is unknown whether Colebrooke saw the delegation, but Perley was already preparing to visit all reserves in the province and report on his findings.

As a guide for his visits to the various reserves, Perley had a report by the surveyor general on the location and acreage of the reserves for which his office had records.[45] With a few exceptions their boundaries had never been properly ascertained. As described in the previous chapter on licences of occupation in Northumberland County (with the largest acreage), there were reserves at Little South West Miramichi, Indian Point, Eel Ground, Big Hole, Burnt Church, and Tabusintac. In Kent County there were reserves on the Richibucto and Buctouche rivers. In Carleton County there were reserves at Tobique and Madawaska. Further down the Saint John River there was a small settlement at Meductic. Outside of Fredericton there was the Maliseet village at Kingsclear with 158 individuals, making it the most populated reserve on the Saint John River. Pokemouche Reserve was by far the largest in extent in Gloucester County, with the next in acreage situated on the Nepisiquit River, and the smallest was one hundred acres, on the north side of Eel River, occupied by Mi'kmaq from the Restigouche River. Finally, there were three islands in Kennebecasis Bay, known as the Three Brothers.

When Moses Perley visited Tobique in 1841, as the first part of his tour commissioned by Colebrooke, he reported there were 30 families consisting of 123 Maliseet living there, subsisted mostly by "the chase" and by occasional employment in lumbering and in piloting rafts down the Tobique and the Saint John rivers. Because of the advantages of their situation and the value of the salmon fishery, they lived in comfortable houses and appeared to him to be in "easy circumstances" compared to other Maliseet. At Madawaska there was a population of only twenty-seven occupying the reserve, and they lived by hunting.

Perley found a total of 118 squatters on the reserves visited, of whom 16 had cleared and cultivated lots for about 4,827 kilometres above Tobique Rock fronting the Saint John River.[46] Those at Tobique, he reported, paid no rent, acknowledged no title, and "from long impunity have become very insolent and overbearing."[47] In line with his own and Colebrooke's thinking, Perley advised that all the Tobique Tribe should remove to the Maliseet village near Fredericton where they could attend school. The ground they occupied at Tobique would then be leased to settlers "for a very considerable sum."[48] He reiterated this view in a letter to Colebrooke.[49] He envisaged the Tobique area established as a county by itself, with the county town at Tobique Point. Tobique reserve lands would be "judiciously leased, and their numerous resources developed and rendered available, [so that] a Revenue might be derived from them sufficient not only to educate all the children of the Tribe, but also to feed and clothe them during the period of such education."[50]

Perley held his first meeting with Miramichi Mi'kmaq on August 28, 1841, at Eel Ground Reserve, Oxford Brook. He addressed them as his brothers and began by speaking about how the "pale-faces" had spread over the land and destroyed the ancient hunting grounds so they could no longer support their families. It was, therefore, best that they seek some other way of life. Queen Victoria was anxious that "her real children…may have lands secured to them, which they cultivate, and which shall not be encroached upon or taken away by any[body]." The new governor she had sent to help would try to get what they asked for from the House of Assembly. Perley affirmed his belief that they wanted some good land they could call their own to build comfortable wigwams and grow their food on: "You cannot otherwise live among the pale-faces, who are fast clearing the land in your country. To be equal with them you must learn to read and write." Perley called upon them to "teach me your thoughts, that I may know them" and explain them to the governor.[51]

In the printed version of his Eel Ground meeting in the *Journals of the House of Assembly*, however, Perley reported that he met with a very cordial and flattering reception from a large number assembled at Oxford Brook, including most of the chiefs from the other settlements. He explained to the meeting the government's wish to improve their condition by forming them into settlements, establishing schools, and instructing them in trades. The announcement that the executive was about to take some interest in their affairs, "created great satisfaction, and cause [sic] much rejoicing," or so Perley claimed.[52]

When Perley went to Red Bank and the Little South West Reserve, he found Barnaby Julian had assumed the right to lease the greater part of the reserve for personal profit. Perley gave £2,000 (a questionable figure) as the amount in goods and money Barnaby had received from leasing the greater part of the 10,000-acre reserve and from which his family alone had benefitted.[53] Although Perley claimed the tribe had consequently deposed him as head chief and appointed his brother Nicholas, Perley was incorrect. Barnaby Julian remained Red Bank chief until his 1854 death.[54] Barnaby, who resided at "Red Bank," wanted this land secured to him by a grant, but Perley recommended it be reserved for a village and laid out in suitable lots.[55] In the first extract of his report, Perley provided a population count for the different reserves. For Northumberland County he reported 359 individuals—more than a third of the total population residing on reserves for the province, which was 935 individuals.[56]

Perley visited each of the forty-nine squatters he found on the Little South West Reserve and issued them a copy of the proclamation against trespass.[57] Allowing for at least 5 per family, their numbers would have been in the range of 250, compared to the 50 on the reserve. Although Perley was impressed by their improvements, he found in general the squatters had a great deal too much land; he recommended reduction of the quantity. He described the squatters as "a grasping lot," who were striving by every means to extend their boundaries.[58] He recommended a survey of the reserve and proper division of it before any determination could be made of the questions arising between those Mi'kmaq residing on the reserve and the settlers.

According to an 1847 petition by one of the squatters, John Gibbons, Perley had stated "that the Indians should not receive any more rent and in consequence of this some of them [settlers] did not pay their rents when due and they were sued for the same and obliged to pay it by law."[59] Until Perley's visit, probably neither the government, nor Perley, had any true idea of the magnitude of the problem on the reserve, nor that many of these squatters had leases from the Julian family for which they were paying annual rents. As a consequence of Perley's visit, fifteen of the Little South West settlers petitioned to obtain grants or at least have their leases confirmed. They described their leases made with Barnaby, their improvements, and how they had been regularly paying their rents.

In his report, Perley summed up his views of Miramichi Mi'kmaq as not industrious. He noted those on the North West were so crowded upon by squatters, they had only a few acres left for their own occupation. This, with the misconduct of Barnaby Julian, rendered what ought to have been one of the best settlements in the province one of the poorest.[60]

In September, Perley visited Burnt Church and Tabusintac. He reported that Miramichi Mi'kmaq considered Burnt Church Point their "headquarters," and noted that they assembled there annually on St. Anne's Day. He described the various social and religious activities and the transaction of public business that took place. There were at Burnt Church four framed houses and seventeen wigwams. There were no cattle, but some families had pigs. In the winter season, he said, "this settlement is entirely deserted, the inhabitants removing to the

Tabusintac [River] and other places, where they gain a subsistence by lumbering and spearing of Eels through the ice."[61]

At Burnt Church Perley counted 250 Mi'kmaq resident on the reserve; it was by far the largest such settlement in the province. Perley held several councils to ascertain their true sentiments with respect to measures for ameliorating their condition. He reported that they seemed "perfectly willing that their lands should be taken under the sole charge of the government, feeling quite certain that their great Mother the Queen would do what was right and just towards them."[62] Perley found that there was desire among the men to learn reading and writing. Most of them knew the alphabet, could spell a little and write their names. According to Perley, their great ambitions were to possess a framed house and for trades training. From Burnt Church, Perley and his party proceeded up the coast in four canoes to visit Tabusintac where, as expected, in the summer season there were no Mi'kmaq residing there. He noted, however, there was a large reserve.

In the second part of his report, Perley laid out his views on the Burnt Church and Tabusintac reserves. He had already commented on the 240 acres at Church Point but now noted that the 1,400 acres on the north side were in a wilderness state. He found no trespassers, though he recommended that boundaries ought to be defined by a survey. However, he expressed other views on the great reserve at Tabusintac, for which he gave the description prepared by the surveyor general for the 1838 "Schedule of Indian Reserves." Either he had with him or had seen a plan of survey, because Perley noted the reserve contained "by estimation nine thousand acres" and the "greater portion of this reserve appears by the plan to be on the North side of the River."[63] It was probably a plan prepared some years before by Deputy Surveyor Charles Peters.

Perley believed it regrettable that so fine a tract of land, stretching along the tideway and possessing two riverfronts, should have been allowed to remain so long in a state of wilderness, forming a complete barrier to settlement of the country about it. He advocated that the reserve should be divided into small allotments and offered for settlement on liberal terms. He believed this would at once lead to the settlement of the whole river and, in due course, of the adjoining country. It was a "capital place" for shooting wildfowl, and he considered that it would make an excellent fishing station: Cod and other fish abounded at a short distance from it to seaward. Quality lobsters and oysters were in abundance. Haddock were so plentiful that the Mi'kmaq speared them from canoes in passing along the coast.

Joseph André Julian, Chief of the Pogmoclch [Pokemouche] Indians...taken in the act of speaking in council, drawn by Captain Henry Dunn O'Halloran, September 13, 1841. This image was created while the artist was visiting Mi'kmaw villages with Moses Perley or Lieutenant Rolland, or both, in September and October 1841. Chief Julian is shown in right profile, seated, holding a book in his right hand with left arm raised, as if making a point. The two following sketches were also drawn by O'Halloran. These parchment drawings are believed to be among some of the earliest of the New Brunswick Mi'kmaq, with the exception of those of the Reverend Richard Byron, which date from 1764.

Provincial Archives of New Brunswick H. D. O'Halloran fonds MC3302-MS3-A-1

Antoine Misael [Mitchell], ninety years of age, taken in the act of explaining to O'Halloran while at Restigouche in October 1841, the meaning of certain hieroglyphic characters peculiar to the Mi'kmaw tribe. Misael is wearing a fur-trimmed jacket. About this time, O'Halloran compiled a volume of text in Mi'kmaw hieroglyphic or logographic writing.

Provincial Archives of New Brunswick H. D. O'Halloran fonds MC3302-MS3-A-2

Perley and his party next went on to Pokemouche, where they arrived on September 10. They were received "with much firing and great demonstrations of joy."[64] Perley counted the population living on the reserve, who received his party on a piece of vacant Crown land, hastily cleared of trees and underwood for the occasion. A large birchbark wigwam had been erected for him and his party's exclusive use, which they found very convenient and comfortable.

He reported the Mi'kmaq at Poke-mouche subsisted during the summer season by fishing and fowling; during the winter they obtained employment in the woods as lumbermen. They did not cultivate the soil or live in houses, but wandered about in pursuit of game, which on this part of the thinly settled coast was in great abundance and variety. Some, he noted, spoke a little broken French, but very few of them could speak any English. They adhered more closely to the ancient habits, forms, and ceremonies of their fore-fathers than any other of the Mi'kmaq.[65]

In October 1841 Perley arrived in Kent County, where he first met in full council with the Richibucto Band. Chief Noel John and several from the Buctouche Band attended. Perley explained the governor's wishes with respect to the management of reserve lands and the improvement of their condition. He reported the announcement was received with great satisfaction, and they professed their readiness to abide by the decision of the government.[66] On Richibucto Reserve he counted 188 inhabitants

Thoma Barnaby, deposed Restigouche chief, in the act of relating a story of the old Indian times, and drawn in 1841 by O'Halloran. During his three-year posting in New Brunswick, O'Halloran displayed a keen interest in the Mi'kmaq, studying their customs and language. On September 7, 1841, while visiting Burnt Church, both O'Halloran and Roland were chosen to be "Sagamows," or Chiefs, of the Mi'kmaq nation, next in rank to Perley, who was "Wunjeet Sagamow," or Grand Chief.

Provincial Archives of New Brunswick H. D. O'Halloran fonds MC3302-MS3-A-3

and was highly gratified to be able to report on their steady industry and good conduct. Generally, reserve members were living very comfortably. For some years past, they had found employment as labourers for merchants engaged in trade and lumbering, particularly by the principal merchant in the area, at whose wharves and shipyard they had almost constant employment. According to Perley, they were noted for being very strong, as well as active, and would do far more work in a day than the ordinary run of labourers.

From Richibucto Perley continued on to Buctouche Reserve. He noted that its inhabitants had one hundred acres cleared, and in the last year they had raised

10 bushels of wheat and 660 barrels of potatoes. There was only one house at their settlement, that of Chief Noel John, whom Perley considered a man of much intelligence and information, and who owned some property (presumably a reference to a grant he had received in 1820).[67] The Buctouche Band relied more on fishing than their brethren of Richibucto. They met annually with them at Richibucto Island on St. Anne's Day to celebrate the Mi'kmaw festival and regulate their affairs. Three years earlier, John Weldon had reported to Sir John Harvey that there were only four families living on the reserve.[68] In an 1840 petition from the Buctouche Band to Sir John Harvey, they said there were fifteen families and two or three widows with large families almost in a starving condition on the reserve.[69] However, Perley's population count of men, women, boys, and girls totalled ninety-three in the band.[70] When Deputy Surveyor Alfred Layton took a count in 1848, his total came to ninety-six.[71] There seems to be no other explanation for the discrepancy than Weldon was drastically wrong, perhaps intentionally so.[72] Perley described the reserve as containing by estimation 3,500 acres.[73] He considered the soil the very finest quality, a deep rich loam and exceedingly fertile, in a very favourable situation.

The results of Perley's visits to all the principal reserves formed the most comprehensive portrait of New Brunswick Mi'kmaq and Maliseet in the mid-nineteenth century: their population numbers and varied means of existence, from still relying on traditional seasonal migratory habits, for example, at Burnt Church and Tabusintac, to those at Richibucto who had found employment with merchants engaged in the lumbering trades. However, Colebrooke and Perley were in full agreement that the very survival of the Mi'kmaq and Maliseet depended on them adopting a sedentary existence, with establishment of schools and agriculture becoming the principal means of maintaining their families. However, theirs and later such attempts would fail. Until Perley's reports listing the numbers and locations of squatters, the government had no idea of the true numbers or how to deal with them. The squatter issue would dominate the New Brunswick government's relations with the Mi'kmaq and Maliseet, and after Confederation it would dominate the Department of Indian Affairs even more.

NOTES

1. W. D. Hamilton, *The Julian Tribe*, 16.

2. Francis Julian and Luis Ganis to Lieutenant-Governor George Smyth, August 7, 1815, RS557E, p. 35, PANB; and representation from Miramichi Indians, Council Minutes, October 20, 1815, RS6a, vol. 2, 118, PANB.

3. Representation from Miramichi Indians, Council Minutes, October 20, 1815, RS6a, vol. 2, 118, PANB.

4. Ibid.

5. Richard McLaughlin to Thomas Baillie, August 6 and August 23, 1832, MG H54, Items 54 and 57, HILA.

6. For example, see petitions of Jared Tozer, October 9, 1841; John Somers, September 3, 1841; and John Holms, September 3, 1842, found in RS108, Land Petitions Additions, PANB.

7. W. D. Hamilton, in *Old North Esk Revisited* (Fredericton, NB: The Micmac-Maliseet Institute, University of New Brunswick, 1988), 18–24, describes the settlement of North Esk Parish.

8. See above for Barnaby Julian's list of fifteen names for grants in the 1832 arrangement worked out with Richard McLaughlin. If a figure of five members per family were used, this would give seventy-five as the Little South West Reserve population.

9. Memo for Barnaby Julian, MG H54, Item 89, HILA.

10. Petition of William Park, December 21, 1841, RS108, Land Petitions, Additional, PANB. Moses Perley comments on Park's role in Perley to Reade, December 28, 1841, RS557A, PANB. He said that Barnaby should have paid Parks and recommended against Park's petition for a grant to a "valuable piece of land."

11. W. S. MacNutt, "The Politics of the Timber Trade in Colonial New Brunswick, 1825–40," *The Canadian Historical Review*, vol. 30 (1949): 51.

12. Graeme Wynn, "Administration in Adversity: The Deputy Surveyors and Control of the New Brunswick Crown Forest before 1844," *Acadiensis* (Autumn, 1977): 51.

13. See A. W. J. Knight, "Timber, Revenues and Politics in New Brunswick, 1827–1837" master's thesis, University of New Brunswick, 1956, 16.

14. W. S. MacNutt, "Politics of the Timber Trade in Colonial New Brunswick," 54–55.

15. *An Act for the support of the Civil Government in this Province*, passed July 17, 1837, *New Brunswick Statutes*, cap 1, William IV, 1836–1837.

16. JHA, 1837–38, January 24, 87–88. On February 2, a "Schedule of Indian Reserves" prepared by Surveyor General Thomas Baillie was tabled, giving acreages (61,200 acres in total) in Northumberland, Kent, Carleton, and Gloucester counties, JHA, 1838, Appendix 12.

17. JHA, February 23, 1838, 187–9.

18. Ibid.

19. JHA, March, 3, 1838, 219.

20. Glenelg to Harvey, August 22, 1838, CO189/15, 253–54ff., UKNA.

21. Report of the Northumberland County Indian Commissioners, January 14, 1839, in Harvey to Normanby, May 14, 1839, CO188/64, 146–52ff. with enclosure 152–57ff., UKNA.

22. Ibid., 157ff.

23. Report of the Kent County Commissioners enclosed in Harvey to Normanby, May 14, CO188/64, 158–59ff., UKNA.

24. Report of the Gloucester County Indian Commissioners, August 22, 1838 and September 6, 1838, MG H54, no. 67, HILA.

25. Normanby to Harvey, July 27, 1839, CO189/15, 343–44ff., UKNA.

26. Ibid., 344ff.

27. *JHA*, 1840, March 5, 144 and March 9, 158.

28. For a biographical sketch of Colebrooke, see Phillip Buckner, *DCB*, vol. 9, 145–8.

29. See W. S. MacNutt, *New Brunswick: A History 1784–1867* (Toronto: Macmillan of Canada, 1963), 277–314.

30. In fact, Edward Stanley, the colonial secretary, specifically warned Colebrooke against applying the cabinet principle. See Stanley to Colebrooke, April 2, 1842, CO189/16, p. 216, UKNA.

31. Colebrooke to Stanley, March 30, 1842, CO188/76, 447ff., UKNA.

32. Ibid., 434–60ff. For background to the dispatch, see above note 29, MacNutt, *New Brunswick: A History*; and note 28, Buckner, "Colebrooke." Colebrooke's insistence on appointing his son-in-law, Alfred Reade, to the vacant office of provincial secretary created a constitutional crisis for him. Lord Stanley refused to confirm the appointment.

33. Stanley to Colebrooke, June 30, 1842, CO188/76, 294–99ff.

34. For a biographical sketch of Perley, see W. A. Spray, *DCB*, vol. 10, 628–31.

35. Moses Perley, "The Indians of New Brunswick," 1848, 219ff.

36. Reade to Perley, June 16, 1841, in Colebrooke, Letter Book, 1841–47, p. 29, PANB; and transcribed in W. D. Hamilton and W. A. Spray, *Source Materials Relating to the New Brunswick Indian* (Fredericton, NB: Hamray Books, 1977), 105–6.

37. Ibid., Reade to Perley, June 23, 1841, printed in *JHA*, 1842, Appendix: Indian Reports, p. cxxii.

38. Saunders to Colebrooke, June 29, 1841, "Report of the Surveyor General on Indian Reserves," *JHA*, 1842, Appendix, p. cxxvi.

39. Reade to Perley, June 23, 1841, in Colebrooke, Letter Book, 1841–47, p. 30, PANB; and *JHA*, 1842, Appendix, p. cxxii.

40. Reade to Perley, June 23, 1841, in Colebrooke, Letter Book, 1841–47, p. 30

41. Perley to Reade, July 28, 1841, William Francis Ganong Papers, New Brunswick Museum (hereafter NBM).

42. *Royal Gazette*, August 4, 1841.

43. Perley to Reade, August 10, 1841, William Francis Ganong Papers, NBM.

44. *JHA*, 1842, Appendix, Indian Reports, pp. cxxvi–cxxvii.

45. Report of the Surveyor General on Indian Reserves, Indian Reports, *JHA*, 1842, p. cxxviii.

46. "Extracts from Mr. Perley's First Report Respecting The Indians on the River Saint John," August 12, 1841, *JHA*, 1842, Appendix, p. xciv.

47. Ibid., p. xcvii.

48. Moses Perley to Alfred Reade, September 21, 1842, RS557C, PANB.

49. "Extracts from Mr. Perley's First Report Respecting The Indians on the River Saint John," August 12, 1841, *JHA*, 1842, Appendix, p. xcvii.

50. *JHA*, 1842, Indian Reports, pp. xcviii.

51. Address, n.d. (but paper watermarked 1840), assumed to have been given at Eel Ground, August 28, 1841, William Francis Ganong Papers, NBM.

52. "Extracts from Mr. Perley's Report of the Micmacs," December 11, 1841, *JHA*, 1842, Appendix, pp. xcviii–xcix.

53. W. D. Hamilton, *The Julian Tribe*, 26–27.

54. Extracts from Second Part of Mr. Perley's Report of the Micmacs, December 18, 1841, *JHA*, 1842, Appendix, pp. cxi–cxii.

55. "Extracts from Mr. Perley's Report of the Micmacs," December 11, 1841, *JHA*, 1842, Appendix, p. cix.

56. "Extracts from Second Part of Mr. Perley's Report of the Micmacs," December 18, 1841, *JLA*, 1842, Appendix, p. cxi.

57. Ibid., p. cxii.

58. Extracts from Second Part of Mr. Perley's Report of the Micmacs, December 18, 1841, *JLA*, 1842, Appendix, p. cxi.

59. Petition of John Gibbons, October 13, 1847, RS108, Land Petitions Additions, PANB.

60. For example, see petitions of Thomas Blackmore, September 3, 1841; Jared Tozer, October 9, 1841; John Somers, September 3, 1841; and John Holms, September 3, 1842 found in RS108, Land Petitions Additions, PANB.

61. "Extracts from Mr. Perley's Report of the Micmacs," December 11, 1841, *JLA*, 1842, Appendix, p. xcix.

62. Ibid., p. c.

63. Ibid., p. cxii.

64. Ibid.

65. Ibid., pp. c–ci.

66. "Extracts from Mr. Perley's Report of the Micmacs," December 11, 1841, *JLA*, 1842, Appendix, pp. civ–cv.

67. Ibid., p. cv. While at Buctouche Perley presented a medal to Noel John, whom he described to Colebrooke's secretary as "very intelligent, and possesses much influence over the Indians in that quarter." Perley to Alfred Reade, August 9, 1841, Ganong Papers, NBM.

68. Included with Sir John Harvey to Lord Normanby, May 14, 1839, CO188/64, 158–59ff., UKNA.

69. Petition of Buctouche Indians to Sir John Harvey, May 26, 1840, RS557F, Kent County, 1788–1868, PANB.

70. "Extracts from Mr. Perley's Report of the Micmacs," December 11, 1841, *JLA*, 1842, Appendix, p. cix.

71. Indian Population, Province of New Brunswick, Comparison statement of Increase and Decrease at the several Camping grounds between the years 1841 and 1848, RS965, PANB.

72. Perley was also far more positive about the Richibucto Band than Weldon who described them in completely negative terms in 1838.

73. Included with Perley's reports was a Report of Surveyor General on Indian Reserves, which repeated the information given in 1838 on reserve acreages with that of Buctouche given as 3,500 acres. Indian Reports, Appendix, *JHA*, 1842, Appendix, Indian Reports, p. cxxvii, PANB.

# CHAPTER 3

# PASSAGE OF THE ACT TO REGULATE
# THE MANAGEMENT AND DISPOSAL OF
# THE INDIAN RESERVES

After the government received Moses Perley's 1841 report in February 1842, the executive council sought the Crown law officers' opinion on whether the reserves were excluded from the Civil List Act of 1837. The Colonial Office had insisted on such an act to ensure New Brunswick government officials would be paid, thereby relieving the home government of paying them from a parliamentary grant. This transfer of financial responsibility, and the revenue accruing from the sale of Crown lands, meant that the New Brunswick Assembly had gained control over virtually all government expenditures. In turn, this placed severe constraints on Colebrooke's ability to pursue any policy that required expenditures where there was opposition by a majority of assembly members.

The law officers determined the reserves were, indeed, excluded from the operations of the Civil List Act, so Colebrooke had no recourse but to seek assembly approval for his betterment plans. They had also been asked whether any legal obstacles existed for the removal of squatters and whether legislation was needed to dispose of parts of the reserves. The law officers' opinion was that squatters could be legally ejected, but it would have to be done by instituting proceedings through the Supreme Court. They also said: "the Executive Government should not sell any of the Lands thus reserved for the benefit of the Indians except by Instructions from the home Government, but they will be quite justified in Leasing any part or parts thereof at a reasonable rent—And we do not think that they can with propriety be made subject of Legislative Interference."[1]

*New Government House, Fredericton, NB,* 1831. Lithograph by Louis Haghe; artist: Lady Anna Maria Head. Government House was built in 1828 to serve as the official residence of the lieutenant-governor; John E. Woolford was the architect.
Library and Archives Canada, C-23443

This opinion, in itself, is open to interpretation. The law officers were clear that the reserve lands could not be sold without first having the imperial government's approval, though the New Brunswick government could lease them. On the question of "legislative interference," they seemed to be saying that the assembly could not pass a bill disposing of reserve lands. In short, the governor should refuse assent to any such bill, unless the bill had a suspending clause attached so it could not come into operation until it had royal assent. During the colonial period, all legislation passed by assemblies was sent by governors to the Colonial Office for nominal review, but the legislation in question could be put into immediate effect. When, however, a governor considered a proposed act of questionable legality, he could insist that a suspending clause be inserted so the act could not be put into effect until it had received royal approval, that is, until the Colonial Office had so notified the governor.

Colebrooke now ordered the Attorney General to eject those who had petitioned for grants as well as those reported as trespassing in Perley's 1841 report.[2] As far as is known, no squatters were ever evicted. Meanwhile, Perley continued to urge action to deal with the squatter problem. In April 1842 he recommended surveys be carried out for both the North West and Little South West Miramichi reserves to determine the quantity of land held by squatters and the balance be divided into lots for settlement. He also recommended a commissioner should accompany the surveyor to arrange with the squatters the quantity of land each should have and the rent they should pay.[3]

The government was not prepared to proceed the way Perley wanted by having a survey undertaken. Instead, it decided to advertise for persons to apply for leases with their terms and then carry out a survey, presumably at the squatter's expense.[4] In May 1842 the government advertised in the *Royal Gazette* that it was prepared to entertain leases for reserve lands that were not required for Maliseet and Mi'kmaq occupation.[5] Squatters seemed to have completely ignored the advertisement until September 1843, when Thomas Keys sent to the government a sworn statement that he had purchased from a John Murphy lots originally leased by Barnaby Julian.[6] James Holms petitioned to find out the terms if he were to lease two lots.[7] Barnaby Julian petitioned relative to a disputed lease concerning the Oxbow meadow.[8] These petitions seem to have been left to the surveyor general to sort out as best he could. They did demonstrate the confusion existing around leases of reserve lands to squatters.

In the 1842 legislative session, Colebrooke submitted Perley's report of his visits and requested payment of Perley's expenses. Both were referred to the committee on such matters. On March 23, John Ambrose Street reported on behalf of the committee that "your Committee are of opinion that these charges are high and evince very little regard to economy on the part of Mr. Perley, your Committee refer the same to the consideration of the House, as they do not, under the circumstances, feel themselves justified in recommending any specific appropriation thereof."[9] After three votes, and in which the resolutions used the term "Commissioner for Indian Affairs" and "appointed by His Excellency to investigate and report," the House voted £50 for Perley's expenses. Although the assembly committee concluded that the information in Perley's report, for the most part, could have been obtained "through the Indian Commissioners of the respective Counties, with, comparatively trifling expence [sic]" it did not question that Perley had acted properly under the direction of the lieutenant-governor. In fact, Perley simply visited the reserves, reported, and made recommendations, all of which were printed in the *Assembly Journals*. Even in his unpublished speech to the Miramichi Mi'kmaq on August 28 at Eel Ground, Perley made no statements or commitments that went beyond the policy Colebrooke had enunciated in Reade's June letters.

As well as his expenses, Perley further upset assembly members when they found out he had sent a letter to the Speaker of the Nova Scotia Assembly, which, with an extract from his published report of December 11, 1841, had

*View of Province Hall and Public Offices.* Province House, built in 1802 and burned February 25, 1880, held the House of Assembly, Legislative Council, and Supreme Court of New Brunswick. The building to the left, which still stands, was the Provincial Secretary's Office, and the building to the right was the Crown Land Office.

Provincial Archives of New Brunswick Assorted Photo Acquisitions #4 P37-162

appeared in the 1842 *Journals of the Nova Scotia House of Assembly.* In his letter, Perley said his recommendations as given in the extract had "the entire approval of the [New Brunswick] Executive" and could be used in any way the Nova Scotians thought fit. What likely had raised the ire of New Brunswick members was his statement that the "Lieutenant Governor has been pleased to place me in sole charge of the Indians of this Province, and of the Reserves for their use, which amount to Sixty-five Thousand Acres, most favorably situated, and all excellent land."[10] No order-in-council or other document has been found to substantiate Perley's claim. During the 1843 session, a correspondent, "Jacob Hardbuckle," reported for readers that "The wolves and bears [the two parties in the assembly, which after responsible government, became the Liberals and the Conservatives] have made a considerable noise in the lower house to-day on the subject of the Indian Reserves, a document from an appendix to the *Journals of the House of Assembly* of Nova Scotia, purported to have been written by M. H. Perley Esq. created a long debate. It would appear by that document that Mr. Perley considers himself entitled to the sole management of the Indians and their reserves in New Brunswick."[11]

By 1843 Colebrooke had become convinced that he needed legislation to implement his full policy of villages and to create a fund from sales, which meant he had to address the squatter problem and the selling of reserve lands. If he followed his law officers' opinion, this would entail a suspending clause in any legislation. In his opening address to the assembly on January 31, 1843, Colebrooke requested members consider the illegal occupation of Crown lands (which Perley had reported was extensive) and of reserves.[12] The select assembly committee appointed to deal with Colebrooke's request first reported on his wish for the Reverend Michael Egan, one of the Northumberland commissioners, to be paid for his services "to the sick and distressed Indians." It recommended no compensation, while an assembly resolution called for the lands reserved to be made available "for the temporal and spiritual wants of the Indians."[13]

On March 21 and 29 the committee reported on the illegal occupation of reserve lands. Its basic premises were that the reserves had not realized the "humane intentions" of government and the reserves were to a great extent unoccupied, while many of them were adapted to agricultural purposes.[14] Its recommended solution was to have nearly all the reserve lands thrown open to settlement. The remainder of these lands were to be set aside for villages to be occupied by the Maliseet and Mi'kmaq. These villages were to include spaces for town, pasture, and woodlots and be divided into small farm lots for which individuals could eventually obtain freehold. Within the villages, there would be lots allocated for churches, schools, and town commons.

As far as legal and illegal occupation of reserve lands, the committee refused to "discriminate" between these two classes of settlers and held that both should be able to claim for any improvements made if lands were sold. The committee proposed commissioners in each county should undertake surveys and evaluate what lands should be sold at a recommended upset price (i.e., lots could not be sold for less than the lowest price set by the seller), which could be paid off in five installments, what lands could be leased, "and those to be reserved for Indians."[15] The resulting monies were to be paid to the provincial treasurer and placed in an "Indian Fund Account," but accounted for by county with expenditures thus regulated; in short, the committee recommended local control over the principal aspects of the whole. If acted upon, its recommendations would have opened most of the reserve lands to white settlers.

Once Colebrooke decided legislation was necessary to implement his program for the betterment of the Maliseet and Mi'kmaq, he proceeded, as he had done with his previous reformist initiatives, to have a bill drafted within the executive council as a government measure. This task went to Robert Hazen, a Saint John lawyer and member of the council without portfolio. He was to draft a bill for "conferring adequate process on the Gov't for effecting the necessary changes in the management of the Indian Reserves."[16] No such bill has been found. If Hazen did draft a bill, it was not brought to council or tabled in the assembly. It seems that at some point Colebrooke's advisers convinced him such a bill, if presented as a government measure, would meet the same fate as his other reformist measures. Colebrooke apparently decided to act more circumspectly.

In his speech opening the 1844 session, Colebrooke requested the assembly take into consideration the management of reserves.[17] To that end the assembly appointed a committee of seven members, but not including Robert Hazen, who was likely deliberately excluded as a member of the executive council. Two of the committee members and MLAs for Northumberland were Alexander Rankin, the wealthiest and most powerful merchant as head of the firm Gilmour, Rankin and Company on New Brunswick's North Shore, and John Ambrose Street, one of the most prominent lawyers in the assembly who had, in 1838, called for the sale of reserve lands.

Rankin had first entered the assembly in 1827. On trade and commerce matters particularly, he could wield great influence with his fellow members. Street had come to the Miramichi in 1823 and had entered the assembly ten years later with the support of Joseph Cunard, Rankin's bitter commercial rival. But in 1842, Street and Cunard quarrelled, and in the election that year Street went down to defeat, though he had the backing of Rankin. Street successfully appealed to the assembly to void the election. In the ensuing election in January 1843, which he won, there was such violence that one man died and troops had to be sent from Fredericton to restore order. Street believed his life had been in danger and openly blamed Colebrooke for not sending the soldiers sooner; in turn, Colebrooke held Street responsible because of his inflammatory speeches.[18]

There seems to have been major disagreement within the committee appointed to draft the bill and which included both William End and John Ambrose Street. In the 1838 session, as earlier described, End had opposed sales and had clashed with both Street and John Weldon, who was now Speaker. End had also chaired the 1843 committee whose report would presumably form the basis for a bill. However, when a bill was tabled, End would oppose it on the assembly floor.[19] Because Street introduced the bill, he likely was able either to override such opposition within the committee, or more probably, he single-handedly drafted it and tabled it as his own bill. Street was an aggressive and skilled debater. He was determined to dispose of the reserves, while ensuring all the money from sales in Northumberland County remained there.

On February 27, 1844, Street moved leave to bring in a bill on reserves. On March 18, the assembly went into committee of the whole to debate Bill 72: to regulate the management and disposal of the reserves in the province.[20] As its mover, Street led off the debate. Although a copy of his bill has not been found, he explained it in some detail.[21] It provided for the sale of reserve lands with small tracts to be retained and divided into lots for those wanting to settle on them. Because in the past no one had the power to sell any of the reserves, they were regarded as obstructing settlement, and under these circumstances settlers had leased portions from the Mi'kmaq and Maliseet. His bill allowed for these lands to be sold, with the purchasers obliged to pay for any improvements. Money raised from sales would go into an "Indian Fund."

Street's bill ran into major opposition on the provision that all the proceeds from sales remain within the county where the reserves were located and under local control. This restricted its operation to Northumberland, Kent, Gloucester, and Carleton counties and meant there would be no funds for any Mi'kmaq or Maliseet living outside those four counties. The bill also envisaged keeping entirely separate funds for the two tribes. As Northumberland had over half the reserves' total acreage in the province, Street's motive was to ensure the money raised within that county stayed under local control.[22]

Street's bill came under immediate attack from Robert Hazen. As a member from Saint John County, which would be outside the bill's provisions, Hazen held that the principle of keeping the funds within the four counties could not be sustained. Not only should all the Mi'kmaq and Maliseet in the province be able to benefit, but also the government should distribute funds. At the root of his argument was his conviction that the "Indians had no title whatever to these reserves: the title was held by the Crown and for the benefit of all [Indians]."[23] Others rose to support Hazen's arguments. When Lemuel Wilmot, a member of the executive council, pressed home the perspective that title to reserve lands was vested in the Crown, he claimed that a chief in Northumberland—undoubtedly Barnaby Julian—drew an annual income of £200 for rent. When both Rankin and Street objected, Wilmot conceded he might be incorrect. But what brought Street to his feet with a charge of "intimidation" was Wilmot's warning to the house: if members passed the bill as it then stood, Colebrooke would not be able to give it his assent. Later, Hazen reiterated that he and other members of the government were telling the assembly that they knew the "Governor could not assent to [the bill as it stood] without disobeying his instructions."[24]

The only instructions Colebrooke could have quoted were those of Lord Normanby's dispatch, and those encouraged the assembly to proceed with legislation, as Street well knew. Aside from this threat, the government members' legislative strategy became apparent on March 28, when on Street's motion the house again debated his bill.[25] Hazen proposed an amendment that removed any reference to counties and tribes and gave the governor the authority to expend the proceeds from sales by warrant. His amendment passed by substantial majority. For Street, this amendment destroyed the principles on which his bill stood. When it was called up again, he refused to proceed with the bill, and it was generally believed it was lost. But on April 6 Hazen had the house again take up the bill, having ensured the inclusion of two key provisions the government wanted. There was further debate in committee, where it was moved the bill be given the three-month hoist (a parliamentary term for defeating a bill), but this was voted down.

After further amendments, the house divided equally on passing the bill. However, Speaker John Weldon, though he had formerly opposed the bill, sided with those wanting the measure to pass. On April 8, the bill passed third reading without a vote.[26]

Although Hazen had gutted Street's bill, it was Street who took it to the legislative council for approval. After what seems to have been considerable discussion, though unreported, the legislative council on April 11 attached a suspending clause: "[Section] XIII. And be it enacted, That this Act shall not come into operation until Her Majesty's Royal approbation shall be thereunto first had and declared."[27] On the same day, the assembly accepted the amendment. Since Colebrooke assumed the governorship, this was the eleventh time that bills had contained a suspending clause, and before his governorship ended another twenty-eight bills would be reserved for royal approval. Of these, only three were refused royal assent.[28] Both the Attorney General and Solicitor General had advised Colebrooke in February 1842 of the need for a suspending clause to any legislation involving the sale of reserve lands. At issue for Lord Stanley, however, who had been highly critical of the law officers in the advice they had been providing to the government, was whether Bill 72 should be considered solely a matter of local importance.[29] Earlier, in 1842, he had written Colebrooke that the British government was "at all times most reluctant to advise disallowance" of New Brunswick legislation where local matters were concerned.[30]

In requesting the act's confirmation by the colonial secretary, Colebrooke stated that it had been found "impracticable" to proceed without legislation. Although the act might not accomplish all that was desirable, it removed the "chief obstacles to the settlement and improvement of the Indians."[31] Colebrooke also enclosed observations by Perley and an opinion of the Attorney General.

Perley had many "serious objections" to the act and opposed in principle any local legislation dealing with reserve lands. He employed the historical argument of Aboriginal Peoples' possession of their lands:

> Before the coming of the Europeans, the Indians were the rightful possessors and Lords of the soil…they neither sold it nor ceded it, nor was it acquired from them by right of conquest. The Crown of England quietly possessed itself of the Country, setting apart certain portions for the use and benefit of the Indians as their share of what had been taken from them. The Crown declared itself trustee of those portions to be held as the rightful property of the aborigines and their Descendants for ever [sic]. The sovereign of England assuming to be the protector and guardian of the Red men in all time to come…The Indians have been good and faithful subjects and nothing whatever has occurred to justify the alienation of their lands or the last link which binds them to the home of their fathers, and preserves among them the remains of independent feelings.[32]

Perley concluded by stating he adhered to his opinion that no legislative enactment was necessary. The Crown was the guardian and trustee of Aboriginal Peoples' property. No other class of subjects should come between the Aboriginal Peoples and the Crown, which had accepted "a great duty" when they became British subjects. They now complained that "the children of the pale-faces have extinguished their Council fires and ploughed up the bones of their fathers. Let them not add to the complaint that their last acre of land has been sold to gratify the grasping avarice of the white man and they have become outcasts on the land which was once theirs and over which for ages they exercised undisputed sway."[33] In his opinion, the Attorney General dealt with such issues as compensation for improvements and number of commissioners, but he also noted there was nothing in the act that made it obligatory for the government to sell or lease; in short, it remained entirely at the executive's discretion whether any reserve lands were alienated.[34]

A committee of the executive council reported on Perley's criticisms of the act. It disputed what it called the erroneous notion that the act's provisions "require" the government to sell reserve lands. It was not to be supposed the government would use the power of sale to an "extent injurious to the Indians." Moreover, the act gave no power that was not already vested in the local government. If the government exercised its authority "prejudicial to the Indians an appeal to Her Majesty could not fail to restrain the Provincial Government in such a course."[35] Such an opinion seems to have been at direct variance with that given by the law officers in February 1842, which had stated reserve lands could not be sold "except by instructions from the home Government" and had rejected the need for any legislation. However, Colebrooke and his council had felt legislation was necessary to accomplish their policy, and the suspending clause allowed them to obtain the sanction of the British government, whether or not it was needed.

When Stanley wrote to Colebrooke in August with approval for the act, he cautioned, "you are invested with extensive powers in respect to the leasing or sale of the lands of the Indians, I think it right to guard you against giving too great facilities in the alienation of their property."[36] He advised it was in the interests of the Aboriginal Peoples to limit sales to portions of lands not brought into cultivation. Just what Stanley meant by that phrase remained uncertain until 1848, when the Colonial Office agreed "that it could only refer to lands being cultivated by Indians."[37] In a succeeding dispatch, Stanley commented on Perley's observations only to the extent that as royal assent had been given, it was unnecessary "to pursue whether Perley had or had not formed an erroneous opinion on the act's effect on the Indians' welfare."[38]

The 1844 act, "An Act to Regulate the Management and Disposal of the Indian Reserves in this Province," 7 Victoria, chapter XLVII, reflected an uneasy compromise between the government, or more particularly Colebrooke and Perley, on the one hand, and Street and his supporters on the other. It attempted to reconcile the opposing objectives of those who were to be the chief benefici- aries—the Aboriginal Peoples or the squatters. The act provided for reserve lands to be leased or sold at public auction under the direction of local commissioners appointed by order-in-council. Although the 1843 assembly committee report had recommended payment by installments, the bill was silent on mode of payment. After expenses, including 5 per cent commissions to the commission- ers, all monies were to be placed in a special Indian Fund to be applied for the "exclusive benefit of the Indians." Expenditure was to be by governor's warrant made to local commissioners for the relief of the indigent and infirm among the various tribes and to procure seeds and farming implements. Thus, the executive could expend the funds as it considered proper to any needy Aboriginals in the province, but expenditures in any one year could not exceed the sales revenue from the preceding year. The act gave authority to local commissioners to lay off tracts to fulfill the government's policy of establishing villages and providing individual allotments.[39]

The preferred course would have been if the government had been able to deal with reserve lands under the Civil List Act and without new legislation, or have drafted and presented a bill as a government measure. Believing it was unable to do so, it accepted an assembly drafted act whose preamble—"Whereas the extensive Tracts of valuable Land reserved for the Indians in various parts of this Province tend greatly to retard the settlement of the Country, while large portions of them are not, in their present neglected state, productive of any benefit to the people, for whose use they are reserved…"—was the MLAs' primary concern. Although the preamble went on to state that the lands should be put upon such a footing as to render them "not only beneficial to the Indians but conducive to the settlement of the Country," this wording reinforced the emphasis on the disposal of reserve lands for immediate white settlement.[40] Under the Revised Statutes of 1854, the 1844 act would become Chapter 85 and be entitled On Indian Reserves. The language would be simplified; however, the act would not be amended in any of its particulars.

In Normanby's reply to Governor Sir John Harvey's dispatch enclosing reports by the province's Indian Commissioners, he provided the only instructions for dealing with Aboriginal Peoples that Harvey and his successor Colebrooke were to have until Stanley's dispatch of August 1844, which gave assent to the 1844 act. It can be well argued that John Ambrose Street's interpretation was correct, namely, that the British government through Normanby had given authority to the "Local Government and Legislature of the Province," as Street's motion of March 5, 1840, stated. Notwithstanding Normanby's dispatch, the provincial law officers concluded that reserve lands could not be sold without explicit instructions.

If Colebrooke could have proceeded under the Civil List Act, he would have done so. He came to believe it was, as he stated when requesting confirmation from Stanley, "impracticable" to proceed without legislation. Because he wanted to implement his policy and not just sell reserve lands, which was what Street and others wanted, he was probably correct in requiring legislation to support such a comprehensive program, involving particularly the establishment of schools and agricultural settlements. His preference was for a government-initiated bill. However, what he got from the assembly was an uneasy compromise.

Whether the legislative council insisted on a suspending clause because they agreed with the provincial law officers is unknown, as there is no record of their debates extant. Normanby's dispatch of July 27, 1839, apparently delegating to the province the authority to deal with reserve lands, and Stanley's direction to Colebrooke that the British government was most reluctant to disallow legislation of a local character, suggest no suspending clause was necessary. A suspending clause, however, offered Colebrooke, if he believed Bill 72 as passed by the assembly was unacceptable, the more politic opportunity of having the Colonial Office recommend disallowance. On the other hand, a suspending clause followed a pattern in New Brunswick legislation during Colebrooke's tenure that suggests considerable legal confusion and a governor who, though well intentioned, lacked the political skills to deal with the intricacies of New Brunswick politics on the eve of responsible government.

Under Colebrooke's governorship, Moses Perley assumed the role and authority to speak for the government that would have been impossible under any other governor. Nonetheless, with regard to Perley's 1841 visit to the reserves and his statements to the Miramichi Mi'kmaq, he followed his instructions, as given in Alfred Reade's two letters. Perley could, however, exaggerate his authority, as he did in the letter to the Speaker of the Nova Scotia Assembly in which he claimed Colebrooke had placed him in sole charge of New Brunswick's Indians. Because such a claim lacked the authority of an order-in-council, it was of no significance.

Attempts to implement the 1844 act took place when both the Mi'kmaq and the squatter/settlers faced extreme economic hardship in Northumberland County.[41] During the early decades of the nineteenth century, the export timber trade to a protected British market became the mainstay of the New Brunswick economy. By the 1840s, Gilmour, Rankin and Company—headed by Alexander Rankin—and Joseph Cunard's firm came to dominate the timber trade out of the Miramichi, controlling between them nearly 772 square kilometres of timber reserves licensed from the Crown. Their bitter rivalry overflowed into every aspect of life, for nearly everyone in the Miramichi depended on the timber trade for at least part of their livelihood.

The colonial timber trade operated through a chain of debt that linked the great British commercial houses to Gilmour, Rankin and Company and Joseph Cunard, and through them to Newcastle and Chatham merchants, down to farmer lumbermen. Rankin and Cunard often insisted their cash advances to lumbermen be redeemed at their company stores. Other timber trade labourers got their goods on credit in the off-season from local merchants—who were in turn indebted to Rankin or Cunard—and paid for them with their labour and cut lumber during the timber-cutting season. Many became perennial debtors, dependent on the local merchant's goodwill to stay out of debtor's prison and hold onto their mortgaged farms.

Merchants' accounts were kept in pounds, shillings, and pence, but the denominations were in New Brunswick currency (Nova Scotia also had its own currency, referred to as Halifax Currency), which had value only within the province. When New Brunswickers had to pay creditors outside the province, they had to do so in sterling or in some other form of specie. New Brunswick currency could consist of copper coinage, chits issued by a local merchant, much devalued bank paper notes, foreign coinage, or IOUs, but all denominated in pounds, shillings, and pence. Generally no cash changed hands, although merchants kept their transactions in pounds, shillings, and pence. This was equally so with property rents, which could take many forms, mostly in kind, though all calculated in money terms. A case in point was the Julian family's rent roll.

Moses Perley stated that Barnaby Julian had "contrived for some years to draw about three hundred pounds per annum in rents and fines" from the settlers on the Little South West Reserve, which appalled him because Barnaby "squandered it all on himself, his family and dependents" who were an "idle and worthless and troublesome set."[42] If, for example, Barnaby Julian received in sterling £300 annually, he would have been among the wealthiest men on the Miramichi. What rents he did receive, however, would likely have been mostly in kind, bushels of potatoes, etc., or some form of paper that he could use at the local merchant. Barnaby Julian was simply one link in the chain of debt in a largely cashless local economy that began with Gilmour, Rankin and Company, went through Newcastle merchants, and ended with the small farmer and chiefs like Julian himself.

In the early 1840s, Britain began the process of ending colonial preferences for timber imports. In New Brunswick the result was a devastating depression as timber prices collapsed. Firms and merchants that faced bankruptcy sought to recover debts from those further down the chain. Those who could not pay went to debtors' prison, while many lost their farms. At Doaktown, for example, half the farmers, a good number in their sixties and seventies, who had first cleared their land forty years before, lost everything when Chatham and Newcastle merchants foreclosed on them. In these conditions, men such as William Salter, clerk for Gilmour, Rankin and Company and collector of Crown debts, could wield immense influence; they could have debtors thrown into prison and seize almost everything they owned. In 1847 Joseph Cunard declared bankruptcy, greatly contributing to the depressing economic conditions. A series of crop failures in the late 1840s added to the hardships farmers faced.[43]

During the "hungry forties," living conditions for the Miramichi Mi'kmaq reached a nadir in privation and population decline. Until the Great Miramichi

Fire of 1825, they had found work in the timber trade, and the hunting had been comparatively good. But with decline in trade in the 1840s, they found their labour valueless and were unable even to sell the small articles they made. They became almost completely dependent on government for assistance to survive. At Red Bank—even by the 1871 census—the population had only reached fifty-six, six more than what Moses Perley had counted in 1841.[44] By the end of the 1840s there were probably not more than eight to ten families.

Under the 1844 act, the executive council could appoint commissioners for each county to look after the reserves and superintend surveys and land sales. Although a copy of the full instructions sent to commissioners has not been found, a draft warrant for the appointment of commissioners exists. It ignored the wording of the act's preamble and defined the objects of the act as providing for the better administration of the valuable tracts of lands reserved for the Mi'kmaq and Maliseet and to realize a fund from them to be applied to their benefit. As their first duty, the commissioners were to visit the reserves to ascertain the extent of squatter occupation, with or without their consent, and to survey the occupied tracts. They were to report such surveys so advertisements could be issued for the sale at auction or lease. They were also to have surveyed and allotted the portions of the reserves required for Mi'kmaq and Maliseet.[45]

The executive council appointed William Salter as commissioner to administer the act in Northumberland.[46] Salter set to work immediately to have the Northumberland reserves surveyed. He selected for the first surveys the reserves with the fewest number of settlers, leaving to the last Little South West. His activity brought forth complaints to Colebrooke from "certain Indians." Colebrooke had Alfred Reade inform Salter that he desired "the provisions of the Act in all relates to the interests of the Indians and in the Settlement of their locations should be [construed?] liberally."[47]

In July 1845 Salter submitted his first plan of survey, for Indian Point, on which there were fourteen squatters. He reported that the settlers were prepared to put up their lots for auction, subject to improvements paid on date of sale, and a fixed upset price per acre. He wanted instructions on the mode of payment, as to whether the full price was to be paid on sale or could be paid by installments. The act, however, did not require the settlers' permission for their lots to be auctioned. Although it provided for disposal by lease or sale, it gave no direction on the course to be followed by commissioners, nor had Colebrooke's instructions given them direction. In June 1844 the Attorney General had already given the opinion that if a "stranger" paid down, the government had the authority under the act to sell.[49] Then in August the government decided to defer, for the moment, advertising lands for sale or lease. It also ordered that all surveys for settlers were to be a charge of those applying but subject to reimbursement by purchasers at the sale should they be other than the applicants.[50]

In August and September 1845, Salter had David Sadler begin a survey of the lot boundaries in the Little South West Reserve. Salter also sent completed survey plans for Tabusintac and Burnt Church reserves with a memorandum evaluating improvements made by settlers.[51] At Fredericton, Salter's surveys and evaluations were compared with Perley's 1841 report on the Indian Point, Tabusintac, and Burnt Church reserves. The provincial secretary replied, criticizing Salter for numerous failures such as only having surveyed those portions claimed by squatters and overrating (i.e., inflating) the extent of squatter occupation. Moreover, he had overlooked the first clause of the act, which allowed surveys only at the governor's express order and at the expense of the occupants.[52]

As well, Salter had not considered the important claims of the Mi'kmaq themselves, which was his first duty under the act, nor had he entered into communications with them for laying out villages and allotments for them. A delegation of Miramichi Mi'kmaq had come to Fredericton to complain of Salter's doings. His actions had "caused considerable mistrust and just alarm in their minds."[53] He was ordered again to enumerate the Northumberland Mi'kmaq at their several camping grounds and to ascertain how many were prepared to take up land for actual settlement so that the unappropriated portions could be leased to settlers. Furthermore, Salter was to take no action on the settlement of squatters until the Mi'kmaq were satisfied as to their locations. Salter had not received authority for the surveys. Consequently, the government had to find the money to pay for them or collect from the settlers themselves. Salter was referred to his instructions on the cost of surveys: he was to tell the settlers where surveys had been made that they would be held liable for the costs.

In his reply, Salter defended his valuations on the grounds they were made four years after Perley's report. From the government's position, of course, all these post-1841 improvements and new squatters were clearly in contravention of the 1841 proclamation distributed by Perley prohibiting continued squatting. But it was Salter's comments on why he had not consulted the Mi'kmaq that are most revealing about his motives and conduct as commissioner. Had he consulted them as to what part of the reserves they could have chosen, he argued, "the most improved and cultivated spots would [have] be[en] selected."[54] He could not have carried their desires into effect because he had no power to interfere with possession of one settler and hand it over to another; in short, he considered he could not eject settlers and hand the lots over to the Mi'kmaq.

Although Salter had told the "Indians he would lay off [allocate] lots for them, they had stated they have no wish to have it [the reserve] subdivided but allow the land to remain together to be by them appropriated as they deem best."[55] They appeared to prefer that the government "should dispossess the squatters altogether and hand over to them their [the squatters'] labour of years; nothing short of this would please the chiefs," but he knew the government would "never sanction such a spoliation." Salter could do nothing about the villages until the amount of vacant lands was determined. However, should no steps be taken until they were satisfied, then the lands would not be disposed of for some time: "If the settlement should be dependent on the acquiescence of the Indians, or their being satisfied, they never will be, without the alienation to them of the greater part and the most valuable part of the Lands now occupied by the settlers."

Salter was also told there were no funds to complete surveys, but he was to survey portions occupied, beginning with the Mi'kmaq, so that location tickets could be issued to them. As the settlers had received notices in 1841 of their illegal occupation, Salter was to collect the arrears in rent and hand it over to the government for deposit in the Indian Fund. Finally, his instructions referred Salter to Lord Stanley's cautionary dispatch on selling too much Aboriginal Peoples' land, and he was to limit sales to lands not brought under Aboriginal Peoples' cultivation.[56]

The government's answer to the difficulties with Salter over surveys to be carried out under the act and determining Mi'kmaq desires was to send Moses Perley to Northumberland County. Under the 1844 act the executive council, when appointing the "Commissioners for Indian Reserves," had made Perley commissioner for Saint John County.[57] In September Perley also accepted an appointment as a "Commissioner to Act in Conjunction with the local Commissioners in carrying into effect the provisions of the Act."[58] He was sent the government's correspondence with the commissioners and Lord Stanley's dispatch as "explanation of the views of Her Majesty's Government in regard to provisions of the law."[59] As the first point of his attention, his instructions required him to deal with the "settlement and location of the Indians on the Reserves." He was to impress on the concerned parties that the government was precluded under Her Majesty's instructions (Stanley's dispatch) "from alienating the improved [Indian] lands excepting under very special circumstances."

In a letter of September 16, 1845, Provincial Secretary John Saunders informed Salter of the government's decision to send Perley to Northumberland County in order to clear up the difficulties arising from the application of the various details in Mr. Perley's report of 1841. It had been judged advisable by the government "to depute that Gentleman to proceed as Commissioner to the several districts."[60] Salter was to inspect the Northumberland County reserves in conjunction with Perley. After he and Perley had provided for the Mi'kmaq locations, Salter was "to reconsider the details in his several reports in regard to the occupancies of the settlers."

Perley's appointment as commissioner to the several districts and instructions provided him with the authority for the council he called on September 27, 1845, with the Mi'kmaq of the northwest Miramichi. His assignment was to ascertain what portions of the reserves they wished to retain and which portions they were willing to relinquish for sale under the 1844 act.[61] Salter was also present. At first, the Mi'kmaq were not disposed to enter into any negotiations. But after Perley explained his instructions and the view of Her Majesty's Government, as stated in the extract from Lord Stanley's dispatch, and after visiting their settlements, those of the North West Miramichi agreed to meet with him and Salter. At Newcastle on September 27, "a conference then took place with the heads of that Tribe, and a Minute of what passed was drawn up and signed."[62]

Although none of the Little South West Tribe leaders were listed in the minutes as present at this council, agreement was reached for the Little South West Reserve that the tribe retain all the land from an agreed line at Red Bank village, upstream from the Oxbow, as lately surveyed by David Sadler. All the remaining land was to be disposed of by the government and the monies from sales to be equally divided among the tribe.[63] For Eel Ground, it was agreed the tribe would have all the land in the rear of two lots on which resided two settlers. The agreement for Indian Point was mainly for all the lands then occupied by the tribe. For Big Hole it was agreed they would receive three thousand acres.

Perley also visited the Little South West Reserve where Barnaby Julian and two other Julians told him they claimed "the whole 10,000 acres as their sole property."[64] Moreover, the Julians refused to acknowledge that the Crown had any claim to the reserve or that any others could expect a share of the rents. Nearly the whole of the reserve had been leased by the Julians. Notwithstanding the 1841 proclamation, the Julians had continued to sue and compel payment. Perley concluded that these leases would continue in force as long as the Julians had title. He believed it absolutely necessary to put an end to the licence of occupation by proclamation so that the "tenantry" could have a legal defence.

After meeting with the Mi'kmaq of the Miramichi reserves, Perley met on October 2 with the heads of the Burnt Church Tribe at Burnt Church Point. At the conference, the assembly act relating to reserves was first read and explained, followed by the extract from Lord Stanley's dispatch of August 1, 1844, and also Perley's instructions of September 13, 1845. The assembled councillors were asked "to state how much of the land at Burnt Church Point and Tabusintac they wish reserved for the exclusive use of the Burnt Church tribe,"[65] to which the council replied that they wished all the land at Burnt Church Point and also the reserve on the north side of the creek as given them by King George when the French were driven away. They also wished all the Tabusintac Reserve be kept for them, except one and a half miles from the head downstream on both sides. The land at Wishart's Point was to be put under rent and the land at Indian Point was to be held for their sole use—neither to be sold nor leased.[63] The minutes concluded with statements that council trusted in the protection of the Queen and they relied "upon her to do them right and watch over them"; they were eager to have farms and houses. They stressed their need for clothing. Although they were the poorest of the Queen's children they wished to pay their respects to her. In his reporting on the meetings in Northumberland County, Perley stated, "I see no objection to the claims therein [Minutes of the Burnt Church Point conference] made by the Indians and I recommend the whole of the Minute to the attention of His Excellency."[66]

After receiving Perley's report, Attorney General Charles Peters drafted the necessary proclamation annulling the licences of occupation of 1783, 1789, and 1808 for the Julians' title to the Little South West Reserve.[67] Although a year later Perley would still be urging its publication, the government never proceeded. No reason appears in the record, but it is highly probable the government doubted its authority to annul the licences of occupation for reserve lands. If the government had proceeded, the Julians could have appealed to the Crown, as the council committee that dealt with Perley's criticisms of the act had stated could happen.

Meanwhile, Salter discontinued Sadler's survey of the Little South West Reserve. He had not attempted to collect rent arrears for deposit in the Indian Fund because he found the settlers had paid rent "under title from the Indians" and "legal means" used to recover rents, and the settlers could not refuse the Julians "their Landlords title."[68] It would be impolitic to collect twice from the same individuals. If the government should carry out the law and sell leases and not give freehold, there would be great dissatisfaction among the settlers. No applications would be made for leases, as the settlers preferred to remain tenants if they could not have freehold. In Fredericton, the government viewed Salter's report with considerable disbelief because of his overdrawn legalistic language in describing the relationship of the settlers to the Julians. It ordered him to collect the costs of surveys before any action under the act could be taken and to report the names of those not paying.[69]

As a result of Perley's visit, the disagreement widened between him and Salter over the act and how to proceed in Northumberland County, specifically the Little South West Reserve. In a November 1845 letter to the government, Salter argued the settlers gained their lands by sanction of the Julians, and he was at a loss as to how he could satisfy them "without trenching on the rights of the Indians."[70] If their improvements were protected, the settlers would pay for surveys. After providing for the settlers, there would be ample land left for the Indians: "should every one of them still remaining of the Micmac Tribe in this county, at once settle themselves down like Europeans on farms and commence in right earnest to improve the soil, and gain a livelihood thereby sufficient Land of good quality on the Reserves unoccupied and unappropriated, [would] still remain for them without at all interfering with the rights of others."[71]

For the Little South West Reserve, Salter recommended the wishes of the Julian tribe be attended to as agreed with Perley at the September 27 meeting. Barnaby Julian, however, was still claiming exclusive right in opposition to government and was still collecting rents.[72] For Tabusintac, Salter commented that before Perley's arrival, the Gonish Tribe was perfectly willing to relinquish all the reserve, provided the government would give them the exclusive use of all the Burnt Church Reserve. It seemed, however, they had reconsidered and now required not only the Burnt Church tract, but also Tabusintac Reserve. Salter said he could not recommend they have Tabusintac because they were not settled on this reserve but exclusively used Burnt Church, and it would impede settlement. However, he would recommend they have one thousand acres for a camping place.[73]

During his Northumberland County visit, the settlers told Perley they would never take leases, only purchase, and they were confident the Crown would never eject them; however, Perley believed the act gave sufficient authority either "to effect compromises with them, or expel them in a summary manner."[74] His opinion of the squatters was that they were "reckless and troublesome," though the Mi'kmaq were not much better. Sales should be limited to portions not under their cultivation. Perley also reverted to the original idea of managing reserve lands, under the Civil List Act, as Crown lands, and he wanted an annuity established to provide for the old and needy.

The two were interrelated. Under the 1844 act reserve lands could be sold at going prices, which Perley held were far too low to create a fund that could benefit them. If treated as Crown lands under the Civil List Act, reserve lands could be held until their value rose to the point where the proceeds would truly benefit them. Meanwhile, a fund could be created that would be sufficient to provide an annuity, which, coupled with the usual assembly grant, could be distributed annually on an accepted scale. Only by these means would the primary objective of the act—creating a permanent provision for both the Mi'kmaq and Maliseet—be achieved. In February 1846, Perley put these ideas into a draft bill, which entailed repealing the 1844 act and the assembly voting the necessary funds for the annuity.[75]

Around September 1846, Perley visited the northeastern part of the province, apparently in his capacity as government emigration officer. While there, he conferred with the Mi'kmaq he encountered and wrote the provincial secretary on his findings for Colebrooke's information. He reported that those of the North West Miramichi were, as usual, dissatisfied about their land. The morning he arrived at Newcastle, it was stated the Miramichi Mi'kmaq had just sent off a deputation to Fredericton, regarding the reserve on the Little South West. This reserve, he said, ought to be broken up at once and the lands sold to the settlers, as agreed upon at the conference of September 1845.[76]

After his return to Saint John, Perley met with Bernard Julian, son of Barnaby. Bernard told Perley that the Mi'kmaw chiefs had authorized him to apply to the executive council to have northwest Miramichi reserves placed under the chiefs' sole control. The alleged reason was to prevent others from trespassing, but Perley saw it as an attempt by the chiefs to gain entire control for "their individual benefit," which he found "really monstrous."[77] Perley reiterated his recommendation that the licences of occupation "to the Julien Tribes on the North West and Little South West Miramichi should at once be cancelled by Proclamation." Perley offered the opinion that, if adopted, such a cancellation would lead to the settlement of a vexed question for the sake of the Indians, as for the interest of the Province generally.

The government soon learned that William Salter cared nothing for Mi'kmaq. His view was they should become agriculturalists like Europeans, and they should be given even smaller lots of reserve lands than the settlers would receive. Although the government ordered him to consult with the Mi'kmaq, he simply refused. Sending Perley to sort out matters resulted in animosity between him and Salter that would bedevil attempts to implement the act. In 1848, the government summarily ordered Perley not to interfere with the disposal of reserve lands in Northumberland County.

NOTES

1. Opinion of the Attorney General and Solicitor General, February 22, 1842, RS637/29a, PANB; also in CO188/76, 122–23ff., UKNA.

2. Provincial Secretary, Jonathan Odell, to Attorney General Charles Peters, March 2, 1842, RS76, PANB.

3. Perley to Reade, April 27, 1842, William Ganong Papers, NBM.

4. Council Minutes, May 5, 1842, RS6a, vol. 4, p. 32, PANB.

5. *Royal Gazette*, May 11, 1842, p. 127.

6. Sworn Statement by Thomas Keys, September 1, 1843, RS9, PANB.

7. Petition of James Holms to surveyor general, September 10, 1843, RS9, PANB.

8. Petition of Barnaby Julian, October 19, 1843, RS9, PANB.

9. *JHA*, March 23, 1842, p. 215.

10. Nova Scotia, *Journal and Proceedings of the House of Assembly*, 1842, Appendix 49, p. 126.

11. *St. John Morning News*, "Late from Fredericton, Saturday February 10th, 1843."

12. *JHA*, January 31, 1843, p. 8.

13. *JHA*, March 13, 1843, p. 174.

14. *JHA*, March 21, 1843, pp. 206–7.

15. *JHA*, March 29, 1843, pp. 235–6.

16. Council Minutes, June 10, 1843, RS6a, vol. 5, p. 89, PANB. Reade wrote Perley that Hazen would refer to Perley for any information he might need in drafting the bill. Reade to Perley, June 12, 1843, Colebrooke, letter book, p. 92, PANB.

17. For the legislative history of Bill 72, see *JLA*, February 5, 27, 28; March 18 and 28; and April 6, 8, 12, 1844.

18. See W. A. Spray, "John Ambrose Street," *DCB*, vol. 9, pp. 766–7 (Doc. No. P38). For the publication of a relevant document, see W. A. Spray, "The 1842 Election in Northumberland County," *Acadiensis* 8, no. 1 (Autumn, 1978): 97–100.

19. See Monday, March 18, in *Loyalist and Conservative Advocate* (Fredericton), March 25, 1844.

20. Ibid., for newspaper report of the day's debate.

21. Ibid.

22. According to Surveyor General John Saunders, out of 61,273 acres of "Indian Reserves," 33,158 were in Northumberland County. Report of the Surveyor General on Indian Reserves, *JLA*, Appendix Indian Reports, cxxvi, June 29, 1841.

23. Monday, March 18, in *Loyalist and Conservative Advocate* (Fredericton), March 25, 1844.

24. Ibid. For what follows on the assembly debates, see *Loyalist* (Fredericton), April 4, 1844; *New Brunswick Courier* (Saint John), April 6, 1844; and *Loyalist and Conservative Advocate* (Fredericton), April, 10, 1844.

25. *JLA*, March 28, 1844, when the house again debated the bill on Street's motion.

26. *JLA*, April 8, 1844. Weldon's reasons are described in Chapter 5.

27. New Brunswick, *Journal of the Legislative Council*, April 11, 1844, p. 158. For progress of the bill, see pp. 142, 153, 158–60.

28. "The Titles and Dates of Bills passed by the Legislatures of Canada, Nova Scotia, New Brunswick…which have been Reserved by the Governors of those Colonies…and Copy or Extracts of the Terms in which such Refusal was conveyed." House of Commons Papers, 1864, vol. 40, no. 529, 673–7 and 695–7. A title page note states those for New Brunswick and other North American colonies contained "suspending clauses" rather than having been reserved by governors. Most New Brunswick bills with suspending clauses related to incorporation of banks and companies, timber duties, and assembly representation. For a comparable period in Nova Scotia, a suspending clause was inserted in legislation just nine times.

29. Stanley to Colebrooke, August 11, 1842, CO218/16, pp. 306–19, UKNA.

30. Ibid., p. 314.

31. Colebrooke to Stanley, June 13, 1844, CO188/87, 217–20ff., UKNA.

32. Enclosure in Colebrooke to Stanley, June 13, 1844, CO188/87, 229–30ff., UKNA; see also Appendix C, JHA, 1848, Indian Affairs in New Brunswick, Supplemental Report from M. H. Perley…, April 2, 1848, CO188/104, 384–85ff., UKNA.

33. Ibid., 232ff.

34. Enclosure in Colebrooke to Stanley, June 13, 1844, CO188/87, 242ff., UKNA.

35. "Report of Council on Indian Act," July 29, 1844, RS9, PANB.

36. Stanley to Colebrooke, August 1, 1844, CO189/17, 239–41ff., UKNA.

37. Grey to Head, November 10, 1848, CO189/18, 330ff., UKNA.

38. Stanley to Colebrooke, August 24, 1844, CO189/17, 249–50ff., UKNA.

39. Acts of the General Assembly of Her Majesty's Province of New Brunswick, 1845, 7 Victoria, Chapter XLVII.

40. 7 Victoria, Chapter XLVII, preamble.

41. For this section on the "Hungry Forties," see T. W. Acheson, "The 1840s: Decade of Tribulation" in Phillip A. Buckner and John G. Reid, The Atlantic Region to Confederation: A History (Toronto: University of Toronto Press, 1994), 307–23. For a description of Miramichi timber trade and the chain of extended credit, see Graeme Wynn, Timber Colony: A Historical Geography of Early Nineteenth-Century New Brunswick (Toronto: University of Toronto Press, 1981), 113–37.

42. Perley to Baillie, December 30, 1847, RS637/29a, PANB.

43. For the consequences of the crop failure in rural areas, see T. W. Acheson, "The 1840s: Decade of Tribulation," 312–3.

44. New Brunswick 1871 Census, Northumberland County, Sub-District Northesk, Division No. 1, pp. 30–35, PANB.

45. "Draft Instructions for Commissioners under the 1844 Act, May 6, 1845, on which there is a note: Registers, p. 134," MG H54, Item 79, HILA.

46. Council Minutes, April 14, 1845, RS6a, vol. 5, p. 339, PANB.

47. Reade to Salter, July 9, 1845, RS13, Letter Books, no. 5, 1845–47, p. 24, PANB.

48. Salter to provincial secretary, July 28, 1845, RS557E, 1845A, Schedule No. 3, Item 1, PANB.

49. Enclosure in Colebrooke to Stanley, June 13, 1844, CO188/87, 237–43ff., UKNA.

50. Council Minutes, August 27, 1845, RS6a, vol. 5, p. 381, PANB.

51. Salter to Provincial Secretary, August 2, 1845, RS557E, 1845A, Schedule No. 3, Item No. 2, PANB.

52. Provincial Secretary to Salter, August 25, 1845, RS557E, 1845A, Schedule No. 3, Item 3, PANB.

53. Ibid.

54. Salter to Provincial Secretary, September 2, 1845, RS557E, 1845A, Schedule No. 3, Item 5, PANB.

55. Ibid.

56. Provincial Secretary to Salter, September 16, 1845, RS557E, 1845A, PANB.

57. Council Minutes, April 14, 1845, RS6a, vol. 5, p. 339, PANB; and for entry in Record of Commission Books, May 8, 1845, RS538, B. 6a, 1840–1857, p. 34, PANB.

58. Reade to Perley, September 15, 1845, RS13, Letter Books, no. 5, pp. 66–67, PANB.

59. Provincial Secretary to Salter, September 16, 1845, RS557E, 1845A, PANB

60. Ibid.

61. "Minutes of Proceedings of a Council held with the Indians of the North West Miramichi," September 27, 1845, RS557E, PANB.

62. Perley to Saunders, October 15, 1845, RS557E, 1845A, PANB.

63. "Minutes of Proceedings of a Council held with the Indians of the North West Miramichi," September 27, 1845, RS557E, PANB.

64. Perley to Saunders, Provincial Secretary, October 15, 1845, RS557E, 1845A, PANB. His report was read in council three days later without comment. Council Minutes, October 18, 1845, RS6a, vol. 5, p. 414, PANB.

65. Moses Perley to J. S. Saunders, October 15, 1845 enclosing Minutes of Proceedings of a Council held with the Indians of Burnt Church, October 2, 1845, RS557E, PANB.

66. Ibid.

67. Draft Proclamation for Colebrooke, November 1845, RS557E, 1845A, PANB.

68. Salter to Provincial Secretary, October 14, 1845, RS557E, PANB.

69. Provincial Secretary to Salter, October 31, 1845, RS557E, 1845A, PANB.

70. Salter to Provincial Secretary, November 12, 1845, RS557E, PANB.

71. Ibid.

72. Ibid.

73. Perley to Provincial Secretary, October 27, 1846, New Brunswick Historical Society, Shelf 27, Packet 6, No. 9, NBM.

74. Perley to Provincial Secretary, February 14, 1846, RS557A, PANB.

75. "Draft of Bill for the Management and Disposal of Indian Reserves," n.d., but 1846, RS637/29d, PANB.

76. Perley to Provincial Secretary, 27 October 1846, New Brunswick Historical Society, Shelf 27, Packet 6, No. 9 NBM.

77. Ibid.

# CHAPTER 4

# IMPLEMENTING THE 1844 ACT IN NORTHUMBERLAND COUNTY, 1847–1867

he government's failure to proceed with the implementation of the 1844 act resulted during the 1847 session with a committee report that urged sales especially in Northumberland County to proceed with "all allotments at present surveyed, and [they] should be sold under the direction of the Government during the present year."[1] It specifically singled out Tabusintac Reserve of nine thousand acres, recommending that three thousand acres be surveyed and offered for sale at four shillings per acre. The lots were to be sold at the upset prices, subject to value of improvements. Funds derived from sales were to be used to relieve the provincial revenues "from any further charges for the support of Indians."

The government accepted it would have to proceed. In May 1847 the surveyor general Thomas Baillie submitted his recommendations on how the government should proceed with sales of Northumberland County reserves. He recommended at Burnt Church Reserve that 1,640 acres should be wholly reserved for the "Indians because they had made it their Head Quarters."[2] In the case of Tabusintac Reserve, he recommended three or four thousand acres be sold along with small acreages occupied by settlers, from which he estimated £1,640 could be obtained for the projected Indian Fund. For Eel Ground on the North West Miramichi, he recommended the sale of twelve lots occupied by squatters and offered a similar suggestion for the fourteen lots at nearby Indian Point.

On the Little South West Reserve, which totalled ten thousand acres, the surveyor general recommended the commissioners be instructed to demand payment of rent arrears and to report the value of each lot, providing separate values for improvements and for land. He estimated about 6,600 acres or two-thirds of the reserve appeared to be occupied by white men. A tract of about 500 acres of the finest land at the mouth of river was occupied by the Red Bank Band. Of the remaining 2,900 acres, unoccupied in different parts of the reserve, he recommended they be held for the band's general use and the projected 50-acre lots for individuals. He noted experience proved the squatters could not be prevailed upon to become tenants, neither could they be ejected without continual litigation and causing "excitement." The only course now open was to sell the parts occupied by the squatters, reserving the value of their improvements "although many of them are certainly very undeserving of such indulgence at all." For the band, their "reasonable" wants could be fully satisfied by the remaining lands. The commissioners should allocate the 50-acre lots as required under the 1844 act.[3]

There was still the need to raise sufficient money for a viable Indian Fund, for which £10,000 was considered necessary. The surveyor general prepared an estimate of the amounts with upset prices based on prompt payment. For all the reserves in the province, he estimated a figure of £12,482 and for Northumberland County £5,632. On May 14, 1847, the executive council authorized the sale of lots, "expressly on condition of payment down and not by Installments."[4] An advertisement in the Royal Gazette appeared on June 16, 1847, for the sale of lots from the Eel Ground and Indian Point reserves on the northwest Miramichi and Tabusintac Reserve—but not for the Little South West Reserve—to take place at Newcastle on August 18, 1847.[5] Should any persons other than the occupiers become purchasers, they would be required to pay for improvements with the amounts estimated by the commissioners. Of the twenty-seven lots put up for sale, twenty-five sold. These would prove to be the only lots sold while Colebrooke remained governor.

Before the August 18 sale, Colebrooke had asked Perley to review Salter's handling of the surveys leading up to the advertisement of June 16, 1847. Perley found the lands were being offered at very moderate upset prices and without the expense of survey. In some cases where Salter had put up lots for sale, Perley felt it was a "grievous wrong to the Indians." Salter, he suggested, "professes great anxiety for the welfare of the squatters, but I perceive no allusion whatever to the well-being of the Indians, or any suggestion with reference to their Settlement."[6]

Meanwhile, Salter went ahead with evaluating the squatters' improvements on the Little South West Reserve. He reported there was "universal repugnance" to the lease system.[7] He was satisfied that should Colebrooke try to create a fund by leasing the lands, no "sufficient sum could be realized by that mode to benefit the Indians." At present, Salter continued, "a few Indians desire the whole advantage to the exclusion of the most needy of the Tribe." However, were the lands sold he believed "a fund would thereby be at once created, the interest of which could be judiciously directed so as to relieve the necessities of such as were sick and aged, distressed and needy." He held that the great body of valuable land was in the Little South West, and its sale would meet Colebrooke's desire, as well as his own, of creating an Indian Fund. Late in July, Salter sent his report on the Little South West Reserve to the government. His total valuation for improvements came to £2,815 with the rent roll given as £136.8.6.

Salter urged that he be given authority for David Sadler to complete the Little South West survey, begun in August 1845. The settlers were willing to pay any reasonable price the government might fix for their land to enable them to obtain a grant, but they would not lease. They wanted to pay in installments: one-third at purchase, one-third a year later, and the final third the following year. Those settlers on the north side did not wish their lots to run to the rear of the reserve, but wanted them divided to make front and rear lots. If the settlers should run their lines halfway to the rear, Salter said that there would be a "large quantity still vacant more than sufficient for all the Indians in Northumberland."[8] Those residing on this reserve had quite enough firewood to last one hundred years and it was growing faster than they cut it down. As for the vacant lands on the south side, they could be sold at reasonable rates.

At Little South West there were 4,773 acres still vacant, he said, besides the 540 acres he had set aside for the Red Bank Band. He had laid off 3,919 acres on the south side and on the north side 2,189.5 acres. The amount to be realized by the sale of all these acreages would be £2,797, which would yield an annual interest of £167 for the benefit of the band. On October 14, 1847, the executive council's committee on land petitions considered David Sadler's completed survey of the Little South West Reserve and Salter's valuations with his recommendations for sales. It concluded all the other lots occupied by non-band members were to be offered for sale.[9]

Although Salter made no mention of it, when submitting the Little South West survey, he may well have known of petitions by Barnaby Julian and John Gibbons. Barnaby Julian's stated that he and his tribe had made extensive clearances on the Little South West Reserve. It acknowledged the land had been given to Barnaby Julian's grandfather, John Julian, for his loyalty and services to the British Crown and that all the Julian family had unequivocally remained faithful and loyal. In defence of his, Barnaby's, leasing of lands, the petition claimed that leasing part of the land had promoted settlement and that the tenants in most cases were perfectly satisfied to remain the same as covenanted with Barnaby. Moreover, Barnaby and others of his tribe and family claimed the rights and privileges of other British subjects, namely the right of possession. The petition concluded with John Gonishe, chief of Burnt Church and all Mi'kmaq of that place, Nicholas Julian, chief of Eel Ground, and Barnaby Julian, chief of Red Bank, stating that all of them were "agreed and pray that Honourable Council to take into consideration and leave it [reserve lands] as it was given them at first by His Majesty King George the third as they are Aborigines of this land and born here on this ground."[10]

In their petition John Gibbons and thirty-eight others claimed they had legal leases from the Julians and had paid rent. Furthermore, three years of crop failures had greatly altered their circumstances. They requested that Colebrooke allow them a certain portion of the rents they had paid the Julians to be placed against the purchase of their lots and they be permitted to pay by instalments.[11] On October 15, 1847, the council considered the petition but refused it on the grounds that the petitioners' request for installments would defeat the intention of the act for an effective Indian Fund.[12]

Another petition, dated December 9, came from John Ganish, Noel Briot, and Hain Gaish and family, "to whom allotments [reserves] for the Mickmac Tribe [of] Burnt Church, Tabusintac and South West was granted of whom we are the immediate descendants have always been loyal subjects to the crown."[13] They understood that Colebrooke had appointed a commissioner to sell their grants in lots to purchasers, taking all their improvements they and their fathers had made. They hoped that Colebrooke "will take into consideration our distress and that you may in your wisdom do whatever you may see meet [sic] to avert such calamity and further that we your humble subscribers are resolved not to receive any money whatever in recompense for land relying on your Excellency's wisdom in duty bound will ever pray."[14]

In the October 20, 1847, *Royal Gazette* an advertisement appeared for the sale of fifty-one lots on the Little South West Reserve, totalling nearly six thousand acres, with the auction on December 22, 1847.[15] Because Salter had not marked off for the Red Bank Band either individual lots or a village site, the government did not know what other lands could be put up for sale or lease. Consequently, the auction had to be limited to those fifty-one lots known to be occupied by settlers. As Salter had advocated, the advertisement stated that purchase could be by installments. This, however, was contrary to what Colebrooke held to be the government's policy, which was full payment at time of purchase.

According to Colebrooke, in the memorandum he had written on November 15, 1847, the surveyor general had been led to consider Salter's "suggestion" for payment by installments because he believed it "had [been] intended to be adopted in the future sale of Indian lands then to be advertised."[16] In this memorandum to executive council members, Colebrooke had described his reasons for opposing sales by credit. He considered the greatest inconvenience and confusion under the act would now be the consequences of proceeding with the sales on such terms. He noted the object of selling the reserve lands was to realize permanently a fund for the benefit of the Maliseet and Mi'kmaq, after defraying expenses. However, there could be no assurance that this object could be attained by credit sales—he believed the result would be a fund on paper, not in hand. If the 1844 act was to be carried out, there was a necessity for reverting to the resolution of the executive council of May 14, 1847, that stated "payment down, and not by installments." There was no occasion for precipitate sales, he believed, until the settlers could purchase with cash down.

Colebrooke went on to comment in his memorandum that to have sales on credit and put the settlers into legal possession of portions of the reserves, without realizing the fund, could defeat the act's intentions. In other words, this would "expose the Government to a revival of those influences which have heretofore so effectually been exerted to defeat its efforts to protect the interests of the Indians."[17] If, however, the assembly provided a "permanent annuity for the Indians" in exchange for reserve lands not required by them, the settlers should be able to purchase on credit under the same terms as Crown lands. Colebrooke had circulated his memorandum to council members, and he had also ordered the surveyor general to provide an estimate for the contemplated size of the Indian Fund.[18] Baillie's figure was £12,750 with an annual interest income of £750, which can be compared to the annual assembly appropriation for the Maliseet and Mi'kmaq of £360.

The petitions from the Julians and John Ganish were sent to Moses Perley for his comments. Perley had no use for the Julians, especially Barnaby, but he had a high opinion of the Burnt Church Mi'kmaq, who were "generally very intelligent and inclined to industrious habits."[19] Moreover, they had taken the temperance pledge seven years ago and had strictly adhered to it since; their personal appearance and the condition of their families had, in consequence, improved during the period. Perley referred to the 1845 conferences relative to reserve lands where, he said, "a full understanding was had as to what particular portions of the Northumberland reserves they required and what tracts of portions they were willing to relinquish to the control and management of the Crown for their benefit."[20] In Perley's view, the constant difficulties facing the government arose because the terms agreed to at the conferences had never been acted upon. His recommended solution was for the government to grant an annuity to the province's Maliseet and Mi'kmaq, while securing to them certain lands from the reserves, and the remainder would be administered as Crown lands from which an income could be derived.

Salter had continued to argue against the government's direction to obtain Red Bank Band's wishes on what lots should be sold at the planned sale of December 22, 1847. In a letter to Surveyor General Thomas Baillie in late November, he bluntly told him that "were the sale in any one case to be on their [the Indians] sanction, and they understood that to be the determination of the government, their sanction would be withheld."[21] Salter's clear bias led Perley to comment: "I have to regret that on this as on former occasions, I have perceived no illusion in the communications of the Northumberland Commissioner [Salter] to the pecuniary interests or the well-being of the Indians, or anything whatever suggests with regard to their permanent condition or the improvement of their condition."[22] On Colebrooke's instructions, the surveyor general wrote Salter a few days before the advertised sale date of December 22, 1847, stating clearly that the "Government are [sic] precluded from disposing of the lands on credit, and that the parties must depend on the Legislature to whom the question will be referred."[23] However, by then Salter had decided not to proceed with the sale on December 22, presumably because he believed that few, if any, of the settlers would purchase outright.

Colebrooke determined to use the 1848 assembly session to make another attempt to amend the 1844 act; he believed the government could not proceed unless this was done. The assembly refused to consider any amendment and replied in an address to Colebrooke that no time should be lost in proceeding.[24] On March 28, Colebrooke prorogued the legislature in order to give his successor as lieutenant-governor, Sir Edmund Walker Head, time to make the changes necessary in the composition of the executive council with the introduction of responsible government. Then, in early April, Colebrooke presented to the executive council his view that it was impossible to raise an adequate fund from the sale of reserve lands. The necessary amount was contingent on prompt payment and at prices the lands would not now realize after deducting expenses. He hoped the council would concur in deferring sales and that the legislature might still be induced to reconsider provisions of the act to guarantee the Indian Fund. The council minute ends with the notation: "To which the Board record [sic] no reply."[25]

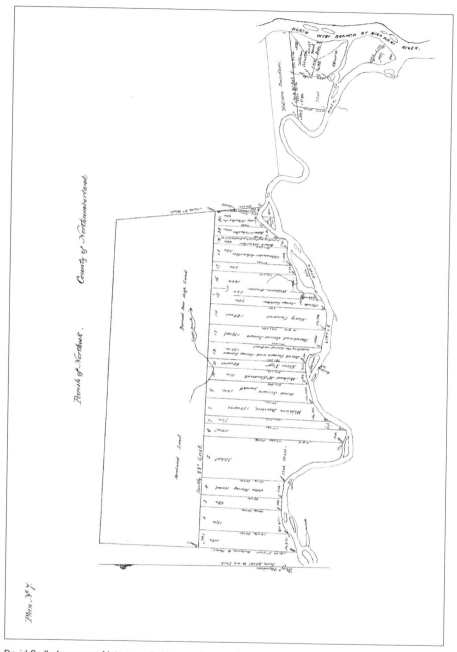

David Sadler's survey of lots occupied by squatters on the north side of the Little South West Miramichi.
Courtesy Natural Resources Canada

Colebrooke also wrote Earl Grey, the colonial secretary, in early 1848, explaining why he believed the lands should be leased, not sold. An official in the Colonial Office in an appended note merely recommended the matter could not be dealt with based on Colebrooke's "cursory" dispatch.[26] Grey sent the dispatch to the commissioners for colonial lands and emigration, who concluded that Colebrooke provided too little information for them to reach an opinion. They recommended that Sir Edmund Head be asked to report on the act, and Grey sent off a dispatch with this instruction.[27]

In one of his last acts as governor, in 1848 Colebrooke had published a pamphlet by Perley entitled "Indian Affairs in New-Brunswick." Perley sent a copy to Nicholas Julian in early April, which he said would teach him and others that the assembly wished to sell their lands. Moreover, Colebrooke had made an order that no more land should be sold until he saw the Queen—"until you are satisfied."[28] Although Colebrooke had in practice suspended further sales by insistence on cash payments and had written a dispatch to London recommending only the leasing of reserve lands, Perley's reference to Colebrooke seeing the Queen was a rhetorical flourish designed for effect. His reference was, in fact, incorrect and misleading, for Colebrooke's days as governor were numbered and he had left the issue to be resolved by his successor and the Colonial Office.

Head assumed the lieutenant-governorship in April 1848. He was the first lieutenant-governor who came to the office without a military background. His instructions were to introduce responsible government, which he did shortly after his arrival. In August Head composed a lengthy dispatch in which he reviewed the issues surrounding the 1844 act, relying greatly on Perley's reports. Head told Grey there were in the province some 1,377 Maliseet and Mi'kmaq and of the 62,223 acres set aside for them, 15,000 acres were occupied by not less than 150 whites under titles of one type or another. Neither Perley nor Colebrooke had ever discussed the trading that went on in reserve lands and that so complicated the squatter issue.

As Head explained, those occupying reserve lands had over and over sold or assigned the lands to creditors as security, a sort of "illegal interest." He was certain that every one of the leases made for these lands was "worthless in the eyes of the law" since the "fee of the Indian lands is vested in the Crown."[29] Nevertheless, many squatters had been occupying lands for twenty to twenty-five years and believed they had title; attempting to eject them would be met with "violent resistance." Moreover, the government had over the years acquiesced in all these transactions involving reserve lands. Although government had issued the 1841 proclamation against squatters on reserve lands, it had done nothing to remove them in succeeding years and instead had left them in "undisturbed possession."

Head likely had read Perley's views on the British government's responsibility for the Aboriginal Peoples. He told Grey that "the aborigines could be treated as persons having legal rights of their own or as wards of Her Majesty's Government."[30] In New Brunswick the policy pursued had oscillated between these two principles. The latter, which he advocated, was the only way to provide protection for them. The strict legal doctrine had been overruled in practice, and the interests of individuals had promoted this compromise.

Although Colebrooke had successfully sought royal assent by a suspending clause, he had afterwards concluded that the 1844 act was defective and impractical to implement. Head next dealt with Colebrooke's two key interrelated concerns: leasing rather than selling and the establishment of a permanent Indian Fund. On leasing, Head explained to Grey that in New Brunswick there was not enough competition for land to allow for settled relations between landlord and tenant. There was much opposition to leasing, and enforcing payment of rents was extremely difficult. The act, as Head further noted, had made no provision for a permanent fund or perpetual annuity in the form that Perley and Colebrooke conceived it.

On the issue of the act's defective character, Head remarked the lawyers in the assembly (including a former Attorney General and John Ambrose Street, QC), who sat on the two committees that replied to Colebrooke's attempts to have the act amended, had stated no amendment was necessary. The telling point for Head was that the act had never been tried, so how could it be declared as inoperative. However, his conclusion was incorrect: sales had taken place for lots at Eel Ground, Indian Point, and Tabusintac reserves on August 18, 1847. After reviewing all the circumstances, Head recommended that the government proceed with the sales, but with revised regulations.

Grey sent Head's dispatch to the committee on colonial lands and emigration. In their report, the commissioners agreed that the executive council would not be justified in setting aside the act, which had been passed into law with a suspending clause. They also agreed with the proposed new regulation to give notice that persons occupying reserve lands, otherwise than under that act, would be ejected. Persons now occupying lands would have to complete their titles under the same penalty and within a specified time. The commissioners had no objection to payment in three installments for lands sold, with the issuing of grants postponed until the payments were concluded. Grey's instructions to Head followed the commissioners' recommendations.[31]

Although Colebrooke and Perley unquestionably believed their policy of establishing villages was for the best, their plans entailed selling substantial parts of reserve lands. Perley's conflict with Salter revolved around ensuring the Maliseet and Mi'kmaq, and not the squatters, became the main beneficiaries of selling land. Perley, no less than Salter, was not prepared to tolerate opposition to the sale of reserve lands.

On the question of whether Colebrooke had the authority to suspend the operation of the act until another reference could be made to the assembly, he had in his favour Attorney General Charles Peter's opinion, given in 1844, that "there is nothing in the act which makes it obligatory on the Government to sell or lease[,] it will remain entirely in the discretion of the Executive."[32] As it turned out, neither at the Colonial Office nor in New Brunswick did Peter's opinion factor into the decisions surrounding the 1844 act. Colebrooke also had held he was not bound to follow advice tendered by the executive council; however, it is a moot constitutional point on the eve of full responsible government whether Colebrooke could have acted as he did without the executive council's consent.

Head's 1848 dispatch was a good analysis of the problems the government faced in its attempt to deal with reserve lands. By then, it was apparent that the uneasy compromise inherent in the 1844 act made it impossible to reconcile the interests of the Maliseet and Mi'kmaq and those of the squatters. In proceeding with sales under the act with revised regulations that still favoured the squatters, Head abandoned Colebrooke's and Perley's policy, not only of villages and eventual Mi'kmaq and Maliseet ownership of remaining reserve lands, but also of an Indian Fund that could truly be of long-term benefit. In its place the only policy Head could recommend was that the "Indians remain wards of Her Majesty's Government."[33]

After Colebrooke's departure, Perley continued to intervene in favour of the Northumberland Mi'kmaq, though he no longer had any authority to do so. He called for a meeting of Mi'kmaw chiefs at Burnt Church on St. Anne's Day. Perley signed himself "Wunjeet Sagamore," or "chief over all," a title to which he had been elected in 1842.[34] In 1844 Colebrooke had submitted to the executive council a letter Perley had written in "his capacity of Supreme Chief of all the Indians in New Brunswick" to Lord Stanley at the Colonial Office. Even at that time, the executive council had ordered Perley be informed that he "cannot be recognized by the Government in this capacity."[35]

Salter's exasperated answer to Perley's call for such a meeting was to request the provincial secretary inform the lieutenant-governor that "Moses Perley Esqr.

the Indian Commissioner for the County of St. John has written the chiefs of the Indians in the County to get up a petition to His Excellency for to send him [Perley] over to Miramichi[.]"[36] Salter added a revealing postscript: "you must be aware by promising a few Beads, Trinkets you may get the Indians to sign any petition."[37]

The government became formally aware of the meeting when Chief John Gonishe, who was facing opposition to his chiefship, wrote on the dissension and difficulties created by some turbulent tribe members. He had summoned a council for St. Anne's Day, July 26, 1848. Gonishe lauded Perley for his faithfulness to the Mi'kmaq and asked Head to send Perley to the council.[38] His petition was written in the hand of Edward Williston, whom Salter described as a "willing tool" of Gonishe. (A year later Williston would be named as the second commissioner in association with Salter to administer the sale of reserve lands in Northumberland County.) Salter criticized Perley as hostile to everything that had been done. He requested the government notify Perley his advice and assistance were not required."[39]

Salter proceeded to organize a conference of Northumberland County Mi'kmaw bands for early June 1848 at Eel Ground Reserve. At the meeting, Salter managed to have the several chiefs express their total trust in him and in the government. According to Salter's meeting minutes, the chiefs stated they had no desire to consult Perley on any matters; they "unanimously" elected Salter their great chief and spokesman. Salter also garnered their support for Noel Brecho's (Briot) appointment as chief in place of Gonishe.

In what was certainly a reference to the 1844 act, the chiefs agreed to abide by the law of the land. Barnaby Julian is not listed as present, but among the petition's signatures was "Barnaby Julien per Rev. M. Egan."[40] The St. Anne's Day council called by Gonishe seems not to have taken place.

When the Eel Ground petition came before the executive council on July 6, 1848, with Head presiding, it ordered "Mr. Perley be informed that his interference in Indian affairs, where he has no direct authority from the Government is only calculated to produce dissatisfaction among many of the Indians and to embarrass the Government in their endeavours to carry out the wishes of the Legislature."[41] Furthermore, it was the opinion of the council that the commissioners for "Indian affairs in their respective districts were the proper organs of communication through which all communications with the government respecting Indian concerns should pass." The council considered the interference of persons calling themselves "Chiefs and Governors only leads to misunderstandings, disunion and embarrassment."

Soon after this reprimand was issued by the executive council, Head informed Grey that Perley's actions precluded him from "employing Mr. Perley in any settlement of these Indian affairs." Although he praised Perley for his knowledge of Aboriginal matters he considered "his zeal on behalf of the Indians had led him to take so active a part in pressing their claims, as to raise a reasonable fear of his wish to step in between the Legislature of this province and the Indians in a manner more consistent with the character of the diplomatic agent of an independent power, than a person subject, like everyone else to the laws of the province."[42] Head used as an example a Burnt Church incident. During an 1845 intervention at the behest of the government because of difficulties with Salter, Perley had visited Burnt Church on October 2, 1845, as part of his duties as provincial government emigrant agent. Head told Grey that Perley, "after reading to the Indians assembled at Burnt Church the act passed in the previous session of the Legislature, and sanctioned by His Majesty in Council, proceeded to read to the same Indians a protest of his own against the act, which was then the Law of the Province." Head told Grey he had explained to Perley "my views as to this matter, and I found him quite prepared to admit that he may have erred in judgement."

When in August 1848, the Miramichi Mi'kmaq heard that Head planned a visit in September, seventeen chiefs assembled in council at Burnt Church. They prepared a petition in which they recorded the tribe was fast fading away, and "the Reserves of land in different sections of the County reserved for the use of the tribe by His Late Majesty King George III…is the only source left to them for a scanty subsistence in their helplessness. And which lands they cling to with the utmost tenacity as hallowed to them by the graves of their ancestors and from which they never wish to be parted in life and from a resting place for their bones in death."[43] Under these dire circumstances, the assembled chiefs implored Head to withhold his assent to any sale or alienation of the several Northumberland County reserves as an act of justice to the tribe. There is no record of a reply from Head.

In the autumn of 1848, Salter heard that John Gonishe had gone to Fredericton along with some Saint John River "Indians sent over by Mr. Perley's influence" to see the governor. He immediately wrote Provincial Secretary John Partelow to warn him. Gonishe had the Mi'kmaq in Gloucester and Kent counties sign a petition in his favour. Salter trusted that "His Excellency will give him [Gonishe] such an answer that he will not again trouble His Excellency[,]" for "if the Indians are encouraged to visit Fredericton that Government House will be visited every week—let them at once know they must apply to the local Commissioner, and His Excellency will save himself a deal of trouble and annoyance."[44] Whether Gonishe ever saw Head is unknown, but Salter now had the confidence of government and was fully in control of Mi'kmaw affairs for Northumberland County.

Salter used his position as commissioner to isolate John Gonishe—a Perley supporter—and draw over other chiefs to accept the sale of lands. Moreover, conditions for the Miramichi Mi'kmaq were becoming desperate. Their numbers had declined to around four hundred, of whom over forty were indigent. The economic depression and crop failures had reduced them to "comparitive [sic] beggary."[45] Appeals to Salter as commissioner had become their only recourse for survival. Although there is no direct evidence, Salter likely used his control over the distribution of provisions to achieve compliance with his wishes.[46]

As agent for Gilmour, Rankin and Company, Salter was in a commanding position to threaten indebted tribe members with jail. For instance, in Perley's 1841 report, when chastising Barnaby Julian for keeping all the rent money, he had claimed that Julian was "so embarrassed in his pecuniary affairs, that he dare not come into Newcastle, save on Sunday, for fear of being arrested by the Sheriff."[47] If debts were with Gilmour, Rankin and Company, which was likely because the firm's store was in the town, this could explain Barnaby Julian's signature (though made "per Rev. M. Egan") on the submission to government drawn up by Salter for the June 1848 Eel Ground chiefs' meeting. At this meeting, the chiefs succumbed to the pressure Salter could exert, but when in September they heard of Head's proposed visit, they returned to their opposition, to no avail.

With new regulations, Lieutenant-Governor Sir Edmund Head hoped to make the 1844 act work more effectively. These regulations had appeared in the *Royal Gazette* of July 11, 1849. The main provisions were that no land could be sold that was occupied by Indians, nor could any Indian lease any lands, and only present occupants could apply for purchase. Most importantly no interest of any kind in reserve lands would be recognized unless it existed prior to the 1844 act.[48]

In regard to surveys and valuation of improvements, the regulations required applicants to bear the costs, and all valuations had to be submitted to the Governor-in-Council for approval. Another provision required that all persons occupying reserve lands, or having made improvements regardless of pretence to title, had to apply before March 1, 1850, to the commissioners appointed under the act; otherwise, they would not be allowed the value of their improvements. (Although this clause did not explicitly state what they were to apply for, it was presumably for survey and valuation.) In the case of the Little South West Reserve, Salter had already submitted valuations, which the government had approved. Purchasers of lots could pay in three annual installments, but no grant was to be issued until final payment. Commissioners were directed to use "their utmost vigilance in protecting all Timber and other rights on Indian Reserves."[49] They were also to recommend portions of the reserves suitable for villages.

The result of a legal opinion by Solicitor General William Kinnear, who believed the act had been "loosely drawn," now required two commissioners for each county.[50] As noted, Edward Williston, who had drafted John Gonishe's petition and who Salter had described as Gonishe's "willing tool," became the second commissioner of Northumberland County.[51] The same issue of the *Royal Gazette* in which the new regulations appeared also published the notice for the sale of fifty-one lots on the north and south sides of the Little South West Reserve.[52] The date set for the public auction was September 12, 1849. The notice listed by lot number the names of the persons in present possession with the acreage and upset price per acre. Despite the new regulation that no application to purchase would be received "except from persons occupying" lots, the notice of sale indicated others could purchase. It stated that if any person other than the occupier became the purchaser, he would have to pay the value of improvements at the time of sale.[53] The regulations came from the provincial secretary's office, whereas the notice was drafted in the Crown Lands office and dated a day later. As during the first attempt to sell the lands in 1847, there was probably a lack of communication between the two offices.

The sale announcement brought forth another petition from John Gibbons, who had earlier sought a lower upset price. This time he wanted the sale postponed because many of the settlers were unable to purchase lots due to crop failures. He warned that if the sale took place, there would be no more than three or four who would be able to purchase. They had nothing left to dispose of that would bring cash. All money they had went for food.[54]

Instead of postponing the September 12 sale, the executive council ordered that purchasers could pay in five installments, as opposed to three, as given in the regulations.[55] How Salter and Williston conducted the sale is unknown. It attracted so little public attention that no mention of it appeared in the Chatham *Gleaner*. What evidence exists from Salter's accounts suggests lots sold at their upset prices (that is, they could not be sold for less), and this in turn suggests little or no bidding for lots took place.[56] However, of the fifty-one lots offered, only eighteen sold: ten on the north side and eight on the south side.

A comparison of the occupant and the purchaser at the time of sale suggests for most of these lots either the occupants purchased at the upset price or reached agreements before the sale to purchase at the upset price. Henry Cunard, brother of Joseph who had gone bankrupt two years previously, purchased the four lots possessed by Joseph. Among Joseph Cunard's were two lots on the south side where he had a double sawmill, the most valuable property by far, which Salter had valued at £1,087. Out of the eighteen lots sold, only five seemed to have gone outright to new purchasers, including a lot to John Ambrose Street. These five buyers presumably paid to the occupants the cost of improvements according to Salter's valuations.

In a highly respectful letter, which Salter signed but left Williston to write, they greatly regretted so few lots had sold.[57] They had delayed reporting for two months in hope many of those who had agreed to purchase, but had not paid on the date of sale, would have come forward with their first installment. They deplored that so few had complied with the "humane intention of the Legislation." Although there were many reasons, the most prevailing one arose from the unprecedented hard times and crop failures. However, in some cases the settlers had disregarded the sale altogether, "depending upon understandings with the Indians and believing that the provisions and purposes of the Act would never be realized."[58] In justice to those who had purchased and to put all on an equal footing, Salter and Williston recommended the unsold lots be advertised again and offered on the same terms. Many, they believed, would come forward if they were convinced the government would compel them to pay rents. This tactic was a complete reversal from Salter's previous opposition to the government collecting rents and arrears from settlers. A second sale would "test their sincerity."[59]

The government approved another round, and a notice appeared in the *Royal Gazette* of January 2, 1850, for the sale of lots offered, but not sold, at the September 12, 1849 sale. The date of public auction was set for January 30.[60] This time, the advertisement stated that any "person refusing or neglecting either to purchase or lease under these arrangements will be immediately prosecuted as an intruder." Ten lots sold, still leaving twenty-three unsold.[61]

All thirty sold lots of the original fifty-one offered for sale eventually sold by installments, with the possible exception of three.[62] Of those sold, only twenty-one had been fully paid for and grants issued by the time the province handed over responsibility in 1868 to the new Dominion Government. Thus, thirty lots remained un-granted but occupied in 1868. In summary, the sale of Little South West Reserve lands under the 1844 act resulted in the alienation by grant of twenty-one lots, totalling 2,248 acres, out of the fifty-one lots put up for sale, totalling 5,954.5 acres; the remaining thirty lots, totalling 3,706.5 acres, were still occupied by squatters in 1868.

For those settlers who had leases from the Julians, the new regulations declared such leases officially illegal. Those who purchased under the 1844 act gained freehold title for their lots and improvements. Those who did not purchase had become truly squatters. For the Julians, not only had they and the Little South West Tribe lost forever most the river frontage lands—the most valuable on the reserve—but also what rents they had previously obtained. Whatever success they had in the past in compelling payment, they could have no legal recourse now, with such leases declared illegal. Moreover, despite repeated declarations of intent, the government had failed to eject a single squatter, so there could be little hope that in future any squatters would be removed. However, there was to be no further squatting. Of the 4,046 acres remaining to the Little South West Reserve out of the original 10,000, most was wilderness and unappealing to white settlers. Although the 1844 act required it, and the government ordered Salter on numerous occasions to have surveyed 50-acre lots for individuals and a village site, this was never done. Consequently, no Red Bank Band members obtained possession of any land by grant.

Whatever the Julians' motives in requesting a grant to the reserve, it would have had the merit of giving them undisputed title and allowed them to sell or lease and thereby gain some income to care for the infirm and aged. Even an application by Francis Julian to cut a quantity of pine and spruce logs, juniper and ship timbers on reserve lands free of any fees to government was refused. From a note on the petition, it seems the executive council declined to allow it on Salter's advice.[63]

In the 1850s sickness became endemic as perhaps never before at Red Bank. Fewer and fewer able-bodied were left to care for the chronically ill, not only among the elderly but also among children whose sufferings were only ended by death at a rate that was "staggeringly high."[64] During the winter of 1854, a deadly fever struck on the Miramichi reserves, killing eight of the approximately sixty Red Bank residents, including Barnaby Julian.[65] With Barnaby's death the near century-long era of Julian leadership came to end. Although he had two sons, the tribe had become so dispirited by the loss of their lands and what income they had derived from them, as well as the endemic sickness, that another chief would not be elected for a decade. In 1864 Salter notified the government that Francis Barnaby Julian, one of Barnaby's sons, had been proposed as successor to his father, though his commission to be "Indian Chief at Red Bank" was not issued until 1866.[66]

At the September 12, 1849, sale of the Little South West lands, seven lots, with a total of 602 acres, of Big Hole Reserve on the northwest Miramichi were also put up for auction. Not all of these sold, and six more sales were held from 1853 to 1863. As early as August 1845, Salter had reported that the squatters (he always called them settlers) at Tabusintac were anxious to see the intentions of the 1844 act carried out. The executive council approved his request to conduct a survey of the lands where the settlers had made no improvements. In November 1847 Salter forwarded a survey plan.[67] He also submitted petitions for a number of lots on the north side, which were advertised for sale with the auction to take place on August 11, 1853.[68]

Again, Salter's plans for selling reserve lands were met with resistance. The then chief of the Burnt Church Mi'kmaq, Noel Briot, petitioned against the sales, and the government ordered that no sales be made while the petition was investigated. Although the document has not been found, we know Salter and Williston were asked to report, as was Moses Perley, because Perley was sent their reply to Briot's petition. Perley reported that Briot's petition had been written by him "from dictation of an Interpreter at Burnt Church, in presence of all the leading men there, and I have every reason to believe that the statements in it are substantially correct."[69] As well, Perley had sent a copy of Salter's and Williston's reply to the petition to Briot, who Perley said was "a man of unimpeachable character and veracity; and if he receives the necessary clerical assistance, I have little doubt he will satisfactorily retract the Statements of the Commissioners."[70]

It seems the thrust of Briot's petition was that the agreements recorded in the conference minutes taken by Perley in 1845 had not been respected. According to Perley, the Mi'kmaq of Burnt Church complained that though attention had been paid to the minutes in nearly every other particular, as regards Tabusintac, exactly the reverse took place of what they had desired. He noted they alleged the upper (northern) portion of this reserve had been marked off for sale as they desired, but the lower portion, which they wished to retain, had been surveyed and portions advertised for sale. Perley suggested the records of Crown lands would show whether they were correct in this statement, and if so, he pointed out, there were certainly reasonable grounds for their complaint. They had always been and were still willing to give up the upper part of this reserve. The charge of caprice made by the commissioners against the tribe was precisely the charge made against Salter in this case.

Apparently, Briot went to Saint John to see Perley, where Perley gave him a letter to take to Fredericton to sustain his petition relating to the Tabusintac lands and answer the commissioners' statement.[71] In this letter, Perley told Surveyor General Robert Wilmot that the "Indians complain greatly of the conduct of Mr. Salter, the Chief [Briot] complains of the insult and indignity to which he has been subjected when calling upon Mr. Salter on business." Although Briot spoke English "very imperfectly," he was assisted by Louis Remi Paul, one the tribe's captains, who travelled with him to see Wilmot. In his letter, Perley assured Wilmot that Briot had his highest respect and he believed him to "be a thoroughly honest, upright man and his character you will find certified by all the Priests to whom he is known."[72] In conclusion, Perley asked Wilmot to give Briot a hearing.

Presumably, as a result of Chief Briot's meeting with Surveyor General Robert Wilmot in Fredericton, Wilmot then met with James Davidson who had done the Tabusintac survey and marked off the lots in 1847. He asked Davidson to report on what lands should be set aside at Tabusintac for the tribe. In April 1854, Davidson made his report. He recommended that seven lots on the north side of the river should be reserved for the tribe; all the other lots on both sides of the river, as surveyed by him, should be sold, unless any the tribe might wish to retain a particular lot for a camping ground.[73] Davidson was of the opinion that the extensive reserve on both sides of the river had impeded settlement and if, as he recommended, part of it was sold then there would still remain more than sufficient land for the tribe for all purposes. He had no doubt they would be averse to such sale, as they had told him so on several occasions. Davidson left for the government's consideration whether this would be sufficient reason to hinder settlement to the extent that this reserve did, in his estimation.

Davidson noted the tribe had not made any improvements on the lands in question, and the greater part of the timber of any value had been cut and hauled away. He acknowledged he was not aware that any part of it has been used by them for any purpose. Wilmot replied that the government agreed with Davidson's recommendation that the lots on the north side of the Tabusintac River should be reserved for the tribe. Also, they could select any lot on the south side suitable for a camping ground.

No lots on the north side were sold during 1853, apparently because of Chief Briot's intervention, but a lot on the south side was sold in that year. Although often unsuccessful, attempts to sell lots on the north and south sides at auctions held between 1853 and 1867 did result in squatters obtaining 1,301 acres through grants and another 204 acres for which the purchasers had not

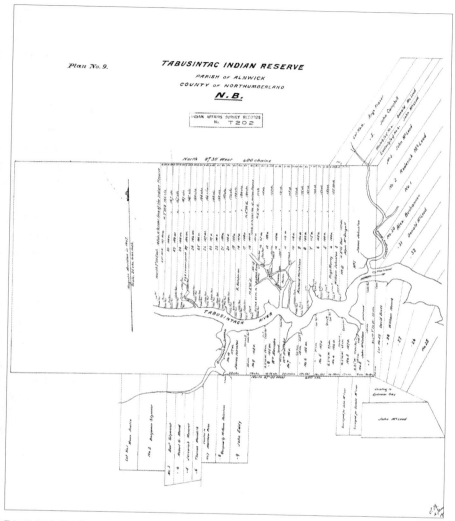

Tabusintac Indian Reserve, survey by James Davidson, 1847.
Courtesy Natural Resources Canada

completed payment. The sum realized for the sale of Tabusintac Reserve lands totalled £211 before deductions by William Salter.

An essential provision of the 1844 act was the establishment of the Indian Fund for the "exclusive benefit of the Indians." The act required commissioners, after deducting for their commission and expenses, to pay semi-annually to the provincial treasurer all sums received. In turn, the treasurer had to keep a separate and distinct account of these sums and show the amount received from each county. While held by the treasurer, the fund would gain interest to be paid by annual legislative grant. Monies from the fund were to be paid out by lieutenant-governor's warrant to county commissioners for relief of indigent and infirm Natives and for procuring seeds, etc. As a result of the accounting procedures established by the act, it is impossible to separate out receipts and expenditures by reserve, only by county. Moreover, after 1851, the printed accounts in the *Journals of the House of Assembly* ceased giving balances by county and just provided the balance for the whole fund. A further complicating factor is that the assembly continued to vote a grant for the relief of the Maliseet and Mi'kmaq. Because commissioners such as Salter drew by warrant from both the assembly grant and from the Indian Fund, determining how much benefit Northumberland Mi'kmaq might have received from the Indian Fund is also impossible to determine.

Notwithstanding Salter's apparent controlling influence as commissioner, the Northumberland County Mi'kmaq could still make their unhappiness with him known, as in an 1862 petition by those at Burnt Church. While noting that both commissioners, Edward Williston and William Salter, resided in Newcastle, some thirty miles distant from Burnt Church, they stated that Mr. Williston "has always given the greatest satisfaction," but "Mr. Salter has not acted in such a way to your petitioners as to gain him their regard or entitle him to your Excellency's confidence."[74]

After the Dominion Government at Confederation assumed responsibility for Indians, Salter wanted to continue as commissioner for Northumberland County, only to find Charles Sargeant of Chatham was assuming the duties. Salter accused Sargeant of using a "noted Indian, Benjamin Christmas from Nova Scotia of disturbing the minds of Indians at Eel Ground."[75] In his letter to Provincial Secretary John A. Beckwith, Salter claimed Sargeant was "not liked by a large majority of the Indians and is a very unfit person to be a Commissioner."[76] However, the contrary was true. In 1872 Indian Affairs appointed Sargeant as Indian Agent whose commission initially made him superintendent of reserves for the whole province. Salter died in 1874, so he did not live to see Sargeant draw an annual salary of $400.

# NOTES

1. *JLA*, April 12, 1847, pp. 357–8.

2. Surveyor General's Recommendations on Sale of Indian Lands in Northumberland County, May 6, 1847, RS637/29a, PANB.

3. Surveyor General's Recommendations to Executive Council, May 6, 1847, RS637/29a, PANB.

4. Memorandum by Lieutenant-Governor Colebrooke, November 15, 1847, RS637/29d, PANB.

5. *Royal Gazette*, June 16, 1847, pp. 3360–1.

6. Perley to Provincial Secretary, July 22, 1847, RS9, PANB.

7. Salter to Saunders, July 6, 1847, RS9, PANB.

8. Ibid.

9. Survey Plan of Little South West Reserve by David Sadler, first begun in September and August 1845 and completed September 1847, Considered by Committee of Executive Council on Land Petitions, October 14, 1847, RS656/20, PANB.

10. RS108, Land Petitions, Additions, dated October 1, 1847, PANB.

11. Petition of John Gibbons and Thirty-eight Others, October 13, 1847, RS108, Land Petitions Additional, PANB.

12. Ibid. It has a notation, in council October 15, and a minute giving reasons for not recommending it.

13. Petition signed by John Ganish to Lieutenant-Governor Sir William Colebrooke, December 9, 1847, RS108, Land Petitions, PANB.

14. Ibid.

15. *Royal Gazette*, October 20, 1847, p. 3509.

16. Memorandum by Lieutenant-Governor Colebrooke, November 15, 1847, RS637/29d, PANB.

17. Ibid.

18. Saunders to Baillie, November 17, 1847, RS637/29a, PANB.

19. Moses Perley to Thomas Baillie, December 30, 1847, RS637/29a, PANB.

20. Ibid.

21. Salter to Baillie, November 30, 1847, RS637/29a, PANB.

22. Perley to Colebrooke, December 13, 1847, RS637/29d, PANB.

23. Saunders to Baillie, December 16, 1847, RS637/29d, PANB.

24. *JLA*, March 13, 1848, pp. 6 and 233.

25. Council, April 4, 1848, RS6a, vol. 6, pp. 210–1, PANB.

26. Colebrooke to Grey, April 8, 1848, CO188/104, 375–87ff., NA.

27. Board's Report in T. W. C. Murdoch and F. Rogers to Herman Merivale, October 14, 1848, CO386/83, 146ff., UKNA.

28. Perley to Nicholas Julian, Chief of the Indians of the North West, April 11, 1848, RS557E, PANB.

29. Head to Grey, August 17, 1848, CO188/106, 180–201ff., UKNA.

30. Ibid.

31. Board's Report in T. W. C. Murdoch and F. Rogers to Herman Merivale, October 14, 1848, CO386/83, 146–53ff.; and Grey to Head, November 10, 1848, CO189/18, 328–31ff., UKNA.

32. Attorney General to Jonathan Odell, June 11, 1844, enclosed in Colebrooke to Stanley, June 13, 1844, CO188/87, 239ff. and 242ff.

33. Head to Grey, August 17, 1848, CO188/106, 180–201ff., UKNA.

34. W. A. Spray, "Moses Perley," *DCB*, vol. 9, p. 629. Spray's biography of Perley is the most comprehensive source on him.

35. Council, May 14, 1844, RS6a, vol. 5, PANB.

36. Salter to Provincial Secretary, June 14, 1848, RS9, PANB.

37. Ibid.

38. Petition of John Gonishe, June 14, 1848, RS9, PANB.

39. Salter to Provincial Secretary, June 29, 1848, RS9, PANB.

40. Salter to Provincial Secretary, June 20, 1848; and enclosing Petition from Indian Chiefs, RS7, vol. 40, pp. 58–62, PANB.

41. Executive Council, July 6, 1848, RS6a, vol. 6, p. 256, PANB.

42. Head to Grey, August 17, 1848, CO188/106, 197–9 ff., UKNA.

43. Council of Micmac Indians assembled at Burnt Church, September 5, 1848, New Brunswick Historical Society, Shelf 27, Packet 6, NBM.

44. Salter to John Partelow, Provincial Secretary, October 2, 1848, PANB.

45. Petition to Salter and Williston signed by Nicholas Julian, Newal Brehous, Barnaby Julian, and Mitchell Sark, January 29, 1850, RS9, PANB.

46. In January 1849 Salter reported that he had drawn on the Receiver General in favour of Gilmour, Rankin and Company for £20 to provide provisions for Chiefs Nicholas Julian and Noel Briot. The accompanying account lists the items provided with prices; the chiefs, of course, never saw the money and were dependent on Salter's goodwill to obtain the provisions from his firm, Gilmour, Rankin and Company. Salter to Provincial Secretary, January 6, 1849, RS9, PANB.

47. "Extracts from Mr. Perley's Report of the Micmacs," December 11, 1841, *JLA*, 1842, Appendix, p. xcix.

48. *Royal Gazette*, July 11, 1849, p. 4649.

49. Solicitor General W. B. Kinnear to Provincial Secretary, March 7, 1848, RS9, PANB.

50. Ibid.

51. The appointment of the commissioners under the act appeared with new regulations in the *Royal Gazette*, July 11, 1849, p. 4649.

52. *Royal Gazette*, July 11 and 18, and August 1, 1849, pp. 4650, 4660 and 4681.

53. Ibid.

54. Petition of John Gibbons, July 28, 1849, RS9, PANB.

55. Council, July 31, 1849, RS6a, vol. 6, p. 374, PANB.

56. Accounts of William Salter submitted to Surveyor General, December 31, 1851, January 16, 1852, and March 7, 1853, RS8, PANB.

57. Williston and Salter to Surveyor General, November 10, 1849, RS9, PANB. The letter is in Williston's hand.

58. Ibid.

59. Ibid.

60. *Royal Gazette*, January 2, 1850, p. 4895.

61. *Royal Gazette*, October 4, 1863, p. 286

62. *Royal Gazette*, September 21, 1859, p. 8758; and November 7, 1860, p. 9156. See also petition of John Payne wishing to purchase the lot, July 16, 1860, RS8, PANB.

63. Petition of Francis Julian, October 4, 1854, RS9, PANB.

64. William Salter to Robert Wilmot, Surveyor General, May 18, 1853, RS637

65. For the condition of Miramichi Indians and especially at Red Bank, see W. D. Hamilton, p. 32.

66. Record of Commissions Book, October 2, 1866, RS538, B.1, 1857–1876, PANB.

67. William Salter to Provincial Secretary, November 29, 1847, RS637/29a, PANB. This is the first known survey of the whole Tabusintac Reserve.

68. William Salter to Robert Wilmot, Surveyor General, May 18, 1853, RS637/29a, PANB; and *Royal Gazette*, June 15, 1853.

69. Moses Perley to Robert Wilmot, September 20, 1853, RS637/29a, PANB.

70. Ibid.

71. Ibid.

72. Ibid.

73. James Davison to Robert D. Wilmot, April 5, 1854, RS637/29d, PANB.

74. Burnt Church Mi'kmaq to Lieutenant-Governor Arthur Hamilton Gordon, March 24, 1862, RS557, PANB.

75. William Salter to Provincial Secretary, John A. Beckwith, May 31, 1869, RS557E, PANB. Salter stated that he had also written Indian Affairs to complain about Sargeant.

76. Ibid.

# CHAPTER 5

# IMPLEMENTING THE 1844 ACT:
# GLOUCESTER, KENT,
# AND VICTORIA COUNTIES

## GLOUCESTER COUNTY

$\mathcal{S}$amuel Bishop was among the commissioners appointed under the authority of the 1844 act.[1] A year earlier, Thomas M. DeBlois, in his capacity as one of the unpaid commissioners for Gloucester County, had reported to Colebrooke that he had received numerous representations concerning trespass upon the Pokemouche Reserve by white inhabitants to the "great injury of the Indians" who were settled on it.[2] Under these circumstances, he requested Colebrooke to direct a survey of the reserve at the government's expense so Bishop could take measures to prevent trespassing. As a result, Deputy Surveyor Alexander McNeil completed a survey of Pokemouche in 1845. He divided the reserve into thirty-three lots running east to west. On this survey he showed eight squatters occupying nine lots—one squatter had taken possession of two lots. When the surveyor general prepared his estimate in May 1847 of the amounts with upset prices, of Pokemouche's 2,600 acres he recommended setting aside 200 acres for the Mi'kmaq inhabitants and selling the remaining 2,400 acres at three shillings an acre for a value of £360. None of the lands to be sold were occupied by squatters with permission of the Pokemouche Mi'kmaq. Although McNeil's survey had shown squatters on lots, the surveyor general's estimate did not have any squatters occupying lots, probably because no decisions had been made relating to the squatters.

In July 1847, Samuel Bishop reported on what lots should be reserved for the Mi'kmaq and what should be sold.[3] When sending McNeil's 1845 survey to the government, he had provided all the information it had asked for on the Pokemouche Reserve, with the exception of the value of lots for sale. Presumably, the surveyor general based his recommendation of May 1847 on Bishop's report. However, in his July 1847 letter to Baillie, Bishop recommended that twelve lots, totalling 596 acres, be reserved for the Mi'kmaq with the remainder to be offered for sale.

The first sale took place on July 7, 1852, when only one lot of one hundred acres sold. Bishop considered it the most valuable because it was a mill site, but it sold for only three shillings an acre. No other sales took place until 1857, when Deputy Surveyor James Davidson conducted the sale of four lots. Before the sale, he inspected the lots and reported he could see no see reason why the land should not be granted. One quarter of the reserve, 650 acres, he thought was quite sufficient for the Mi'kmaq because they scarcely occupied part of it. However, because the adjoining lands were becoming settled, they would require a place to stop during the winter season and also sufficient quantity to plant on for those who wished to do so. Davidson thought even less than a quarter of the reserve would be sufficient because he considered reserves were detrimental to the settlement of the country, wherever they were situated. He added that the Mi'kmaq were fast dwindling, and in his opinion, they would become altogether extinct in the near future.[4]

Other sales followed, with the last taking place in 1861. The total lands lost by sales came to 1,895 acres, for which the New Brunswick government issued grants for 1,277 acres, with the remainder having been sold; however, purchasers had not completed payments. There was considerable confusion over figures, but it seems the combined total acreage for lots sold and grants issued, lots sold but payment not completed, and unoccupied lots came to 1,495 acres. If the unoccupied lots, totalling 560 acres, were intended for the Pokemouche Mi'kmaq, this was neither stated nor implied. An attempt would be made in 1871 to count the number of Mi'kmaq in Gloucester County. The commissioners reported that they believed there were a few residing in the lower part of the county, which probably included Pokemouche and Tracadie, and provided figures of ten men, eleven women, and eighteen children.[5] At the time Canada assumed responsibility for Pokemouche Mi'kmaq, the Crown Lands Office could provide no details of the purchases made and how much money the government had received from the sale of lots because the commissioners had remitted directly to the provincial treasurer for deposit in the Indian Fund. It had no knowledge of remittances made and so had no record of sales.[6] Samuel Bishop, however, had kept a record, which he turned over to Indian Affairs in 1874. Sales came to $998.44 with $146.90 still owing (New Brunswick converted to decimal coinage on November 1, 1860).[7]

## KENT COUNTY

As noted in Chapter 1, around 1822 the government determined, as a matter of deliberate policy, to open up both the Buctouche and Richibucto reserves to settlement. Squatters and potential settlers petitioned for lots on the south side of the Buctouche River in the knowledge that was what the government contemplated. In 1823 both the Buctouche and Richibucto reserves were reduced in size from 40,960 to 4,655 acres in Buctouche's case and from 51,000 to 5,720 acres in Richibucto's. Other than different acreages, the two reduced reserves were virtual twins with their northern or rear boundaries measuring 4.3 miles long for Buctouche and 5.3 miles long for Richibucto and their eastern or front boundaries 2 miles deep. Although an 1824 council minute ordered that a reserve be made for Richibucto Mi'kmaq incorporating the reduced acreage, no similar order seems to have been made for Buctouche. The first description of the reduced Buctouche Reserve was in the 1838 schedule, but it had the wrong acreage. As shall be noted further on, the most definitive document, therefore, for the establishment and confirmation of the Buctouche Reserve is Peter Merzerell's 1851 survey.

What seems to have been the prevailing attitude among officials in Kent County can be gauged from Deputy Surveyor Alfred Layton's report to the surveyor general in 1831 on the Richibucto and Buctouche reserves: "If the Indian Reserves were curtailed in extent to about two hundred acres on each Stream, the original designs of the Government will be fully answered, and the Indians will even have then more than sufficient scope for all their agricultural pursuits and it will be the means of throwing open to the industrious Settlers large tracts of valuable land now as it were locked [?] up from them, in the heart of fine and flourishing Settlements."[8]

Although the government had granted former Mi'kmaq lands on the south and north sides of the Buctouche River, the 1822 council minute, when recommending the grants, had made them conditional on "not interfering with that part allotted to Indians," that is the 4,655 acres.[9] If not already well under way, squatting was soon occurring. In what seems to have been a pattern, non-Natives would squat on reserve land and then offer to purchase it from the band or a band member for cash or provisions.

After the assembly in the 1838 session passed a resolution relating to the sale of reserve lands, which John Weldon had initially proposed,[10] he and William Chandler apparently anticipated government approval for reserve lands at Buctouche being thrown open to settlement.[11] Acting in their capacity as commissioners, they had reserve lands on both sides of a creek, named Mill Creek, surveyed and laid out in lots. Although the government never acted on the assembly resolution, Weldon and Chandler authorized settlers to apply for grants. John MacMillan, for example, applied to them for a single lot in 1838 and two years later for the adjoining two lots for which he received grants. Although the lots were part of the Buctouche Reserve, the grant descriptions were worded so this fact was not mentioned. As well, MacMillan in 1840 signed a lease (drafted by Weldon) for a term of ten years with Chief Noel John and thirteen other band members for a tract of reserve land (though this was never stated in the agreement, nor was the acreage), and he agreed to pay them £150.[12] Weldon and Chandler also authorized in 1840 other land grants for which the descriptions made no reference to the lots being within the reserve.[13] This could only have happened with the collusion of the Crown Lands office.

A similar pattern also developed on the Richibucto Reserve. For instance, the arrangement Joseph Ward reached around 1837 with Paul Athenaise, at the time chief, to be allowed to occupy a lot on the reserve. Ward handed over a paper for Chief Athenaise to sign, which he stated was a lease for six years at an annual rent of £3 payable in produce, and at the end of the six years Ward would agree to yield the lot. But at the end of six-year period Ward refused to do so. Instead, he let his cattle and hogs loose in the neighbouring reserve enclosures to destroy their potatoes and grain. After an official of Crown lands intervened at the request of the band, Ward produced another document, which supposedly entitled him to payment by the band for all improvements he had made before he would give up possession. In their petition describing how Ward was claiming possession, along with his son, who had erected a house on the lot, the Richibucto Band petitioned the government to have the Wards "forthwith put out of the lot" they were occupying.[14] Although the case involving Ward was frequently before the government, he and his sons were still in occupation in 1844.[15]

Another similar case was that of Michael Young, though in this arrangement the lease (drawn up by Weldon) involved Young paying rent to the wife of Pierre

Joseph Augustine, which he had failed to do. Instead, he turned his cattle and hogs into her small patches of grain and potatoes and also abused her, as did his sons, to the point that her life was endangered.[16] In a letter to Provincial Secretary William Franklin Odell, John Weldon commented on the Michael Young case that the statements were true in the Richibucto Band's petition, which has not been found. He noted there were others who had made similar arrangements with band members to settle on their lands. There was, however, "no controlling the Indians and what has been done to them would continue until some regulation was enacted to vest control of the reserves in a recognized body for the use of Indians, but beyond their control."[17]

As Speaker of the assembly, John Weldon presided during the increasingly divisive debate over Bill 72 for management of reserve lands during the 1844 session. He felt so strongly about the issues that he intervened in the debate. He considered the lands held by the Maliseet and Mi'kmaq were injurious to the counties in which they were reserved because they hampered the settlement of the country. He thought something should be done without further delay. In reference to passing the 1838 motion calling upon the government to allow settlement on reserves, he noted still nothing had been done. The lands were "no good to the Indians as they were, for they would never cultivate them."[18] If at any time the house addressed the government on the subject, "the Indians arose in a body and petitioned government not to break up the reserves."

He thought the government should set off sites for villages in small lots on which they might settle. It would do "the Indians good to break up the reserves because it would have the effect of confining them to a small space, where they would have an inducement to cultivate land and fence it in."[19] When Bill 72 came to a vote with John Weldon in the Speaker's chair, the assembly divided equally. Although he had told the house he was opposed to the bill, when its opponents proposed to give it three-month hoist (which would have defeated the bill because it would die at the end of the session), Weldon voted for it and thus ensured its passage.[20]

Deputy Surveyor Peter Merzerall was appointed commissioner for Kent County under the 1844 act.[21] He provided the information on Richibucto and Buctouche reserves to the surveyor general that was incorporated into his recommendations to the executive council on the lands held by squatters under engagements with band members and the estimated sums from sales. For Buctouche the acreage given was 3,500 and for Richibucto it was 4,600 acres. The surveyor general reported that the two reserves included much good land and were a great obstruction to the improvement of the country. Both reserves had been partly divided into lots, and he remarked "that some of the Indians had houses and had made large clearances."[22] He estimated the Buctouche Band members would require eight hundred acres for their own use and those of Richibucto one thousand acres. For both reserves, the surveyor general provided no estimate on the number of acres occupied under agreement with Buctouche and Richibucto bands, presumably because Merzerall had not given him such information.

The surveyor general estimated a value of four shillings an acre, for the total value of lands at Buctouche as £540. But for Richibucto he had a value of five shillings an acre with total value of £900.[23] No estimate of squatter numbers was provided for either reserve. When Perley had visited Buctouche in 1841 he had found five squatters and another eight at Richibucto.[24] Up to 1845, Buctouche Band members had sold land to nine non-Natives, amounting to 388.5 acres. Merzerall may have considered that these sales had permanently alienated the lands and therefore not reported them. His figure of eight hundred acres occupied by squatters without band agreement suggests squatter numbers may have been higher than Perley's count of five.

Although lots were leasing to squatters at Richibucto, there seems to have been less squatting than at Buctouche. Certainly, there was major opposition to the issuing of grants. When Merzerall visited Richibucto in the spring of 1845, he tried unsuccessfully to persuade band members to have the best part of the reserve divided into lots and for them to settle upon the lots instead of moving about. Merzerall found them opposed to his proposition that by leasing or granting the remainder of the reserve they would be able to raise funds to procure their seed and implements for farming: "they would never consent to any part of the Reserve being leased or granted [presumably as envisaged under the 1844 act]."[25] He advised Colebrooke that it was best to grant the portion of the reserve occupied by settlers because they had leased the land in the hopes of obtaining a grant. If they could not obtain a grant it would cause a great deal of trouble because some of the settlers had built houses and barns and would be most unwilling to abandon their improvements.

After the Colonial Office had accepted Sir Edmund Head's recommendations for proceeding with sales, but with revised regulations, the government published the new regulations in July 1849. Both John Weldon and Peter Merzerall were listed as commissioners for Kent County; however, they made no attempt to sell lots in accordance with the 1844 act. Almost certainly their reason was the need for complete surveys of both reserves. In the spring of 1851 Merzerall completed the surveys of both reserves, showing all surveyed lots occupied by settlers and also those still unoccupied. On the eastern side of each reserve, facing on the

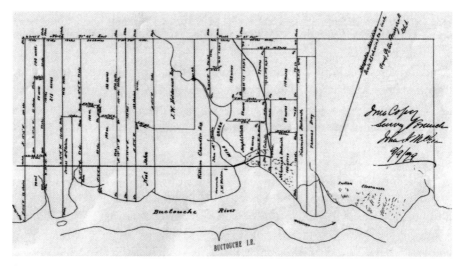

Survey of Buctouche lots occupied by squatters and Indians, based on Peter Mezerall's 1851 survey.
Courtesy Natural Resources Canada

Buctouche and Richibucto rivers, were designated areas described as "Indian encampments or Indian clearances," though no acreages were given.[26] Probably motivated by the survey, Chief Thomas Nicholas of Buctouche petitioned against the squatters. Although the petition has not been found, the government evidently sent it to Merzerall, who immediately went to Buctouche. In response to his explanation to the Buctouche Band about the nature of the act to dispose of the reserve to raise a fund for their use, he "found them very cross and obstinate and refused to listen to any arrangement whatever."[27]

Weldon and Merzerall submitted a report to the government, dated March 27, 1851. Although this report has not been found,[28] a copy of their report was forwarded to Chief Thomas Nicholas,[29] who took issue with its contents. He went to Francis McPhelim, Kent County MLA. Because Nicholas could not write, McPhelim drafted a letter based on what Nicholas told him for submission to the government, refuting statements made in the commissioners' report.[30] In the letter, Nicholas stated the commissioners' claim was incorrect that attributed improvements to a John McMillan who had occupied reserve land. According to Nicholas, the improvements had been made by a previous squatter and the land had been "forcibly taken from us by Mr. McMillan after [the] previous squatter had left." Moreover, the accusation that a former chief, the late Noel John, had received a considerable sum from McMillan was likewise untrue, and

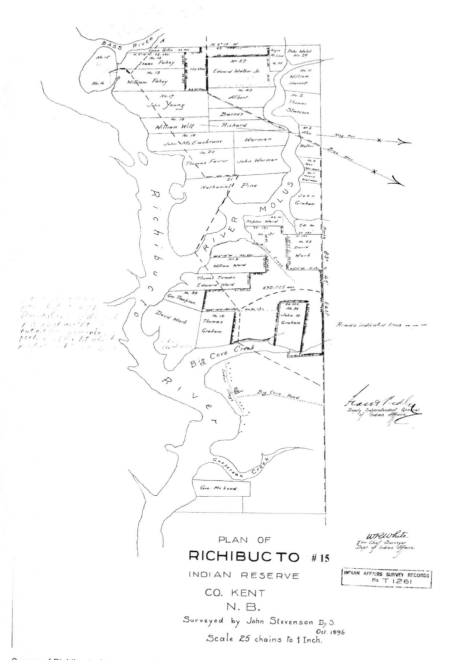

PLAN OF
# RICHIBUCTO #15
INDIAN RESERVE
CO. KENT
N. B.
Surveyed by John Stevenson Dy.S.
Oct. 1896
Scale 25 chains to 1 Inch.

Survey of Richibucto lots occupied by squatters and Indians based on Peter Merzerall's 1851 survey.
Courtesy Natural Resources Canada

the commissioners were "not ignorant of the facts." Nicholas also wrote that according to the commissioners, McMillan had paid a certain sum to the band for the privilege of cutting ship timber; however, he had then taken a ten-year lease, which had expired. Nicholas noted that McMillan was "suffered to trespass and to injure us by these Com[missione]rs contrary to their instructions."[31]

Nehemiah Beckwith had also apparently taken possession of a large tract of reserve land to the east of Mill Creek, which Nicholas stated was supposed to have been reserved for the band by Weldon and Chandler around 1840: "many acres of which had been cleared by the Indians and from which he had driven us, without any consideration whatever."[32] Nicholas described how in the summer of 1850 a yoke of Indian oxen had strayed onto Beckwith's land and his sons had blinded the animals, making them useless, and it was just one of many of the "unfeeling acts perpetuated against us by McMillan & Beckwith." According to Nicholas, Buctouche Band members had often given notice to McMillan not to work on their lands. Nicholas had petitioned against McMillan and Beckwith by going to Fredericton for the "purpose of having justice done to ourselves and our families," only to find his complaint was never looked at, and that "our wrongs are accumulating rather than diminishing." Nicholas's letter stated McMillan and Beckwith had been cutting reserve timber without paying a penny: "first they took our timber now they take our logs, and now lastly our lands."[33] Nicholas concluded his letter by calling on the government to save them from "frauds" that up to now had been concealed from the lieutenant-governor and the executive council both by the commissioners and the trespassers.

Sir Edmund Head ordered John Ambrose Street, whom Head had just appointed to the executive council as Attorney General, to send a copy of Nicholas's letter to Merzerall and Weldon, and it would be necessary to stay the sale of any Buctouche Reserve lands.[34] If the story of cattle was true, Head considered it a "most wicked thing."[35] He wished Street to investigate matters personally when he went to Dorchester, the shiretown of Westmoreland County, and wanted to know if there was "any thoroughly trustworthy person in that neighbour who could be sent over! It must not be a person on the spot."[36] At Dorchester, Street engaged Daniel Kerr, a Justice of the Peace, to undertake an investigation.[37] Daniel Kerr had copies made of Nicholas's letter, which he sent to Merzerall and Weldon; the latter, however, refused to receive it, stating that "the charges in the letter were without foundation and that he should take no notice of them."[38] Kerr opened the inquiry by asking Nicholas if he had written the letter; Nicholas replied that Francis McPhelim had done so on his authority.[39] When Nicholas intimated that he could not speak English, an interpreter was provided. Various witnesses were called, all non-Natives, to testify on each of the charges made in Nicholas's letter.

According to Nicholas's letter to the government, Weldon and Merzerall had reported there were no band members settled on that part of reserve above Mill Creek and only two below Mill Creek. Nicholas claimed in a letter of July 1, 1851, to the Attorney General (no doubt written by McPhelim) there were "exactly now [here] fourteen families numbering seventy-six persons at present, but when all counted will reach to one hundred and twenty persons, so much for the truth of the Report."[40] At the inquiry conducted by Kerr, evidence was given that no reserve families lived above (west of) Mill Creek, and all lived below (east of) Nehemiah Beckwith's grant. Much time was devoted to the blinding of the oxen and whether McMillan paid for the timber he cut. Kerr reported to the government that: "from the fullest enquiry and examination to make I consider that the principal statements made by Nicholas and his charges against the Indian Commissioners, and Mr. McMillan and the Beckwiths are wholly devoid of truth."[41]

That would likely have ended the matter, which had gone entirely against Nicholas, except for Francis McPhelim's second intervention. It seems John Ambrose Street may have had some suspicions that all was not as it appeared, for he met with McPhelim in Buctouche to discuss Nicholas's charges. McPhelim made further inquiries and found that "every accusation set forth can be fully borne out by oath not by the Indians only, but by White men."[42] As he wrote to Street, McPhelim expected that Mr. Kerr would call upon him for information he might require, but in this he was disappointed. He had seen Kerr in Richibucto, but he had mentioned nothing to McPhelim about the matter. He considered that the parties against whom the charges were made might find it their interest to keep him in the background as much as possible, but they would find this difficult.

Further evidence that Nicholas was telling the truth—at least about band members residing above and immediately below Mill Creek with not all living east of Beckwith's grant—comes from a survey plan, which was an exhibit at the Kerr inquiry.[43] On a tract of one hundred acres, fronting on the Buctouche River, bounded on the east by Noel John's grant and to the west land occupied by Charles Miller, is written "occupied by the Indians about 100 acres."[44] At some point, however, the words were crossed out; similarly for a smaller acreage located between Mill Creek and land occupied by Nehemiah Beckwith and fronting on the river.

The first recorded sale of Richibucto Reserve lands at auction was in 1851, when Weldon and Merzerall put up for sale ten lots totalling 661 acres; however, only two lots were purchased and grants issued for them.[45] The sale drew forth a belated petition from Chief Peter Pierre Paul, who claimed as a result of the sale that remaining land was "barely sufficient to afford a settlement for each family."[46] But his main reason for petitioning was that two of the Richibucto Band members had disregarded his instructions about selling lands to whites and had done so to Alexander Glencross. He wanted Head to have the sale declared void. If the sale was nullified, Glencross continued squatting because his lot of one hundred acres, along with three others, was put up for auction on September 3, 1867. Furthermore, the three others would all receive letters patent from Indian Affairs, so Glencross could not have purchased the lot. Although annotated as "Imperfect," the list of Recorded Sales of Indian Reserves to March 14, 1867, prepared by the New Brunswick government for the Dominion government, had no record of any sales of Richibucto Reserve lands.[47] Merzerall's 1851 survey of the 5,720 acres remaining of the original reserve had laid out thirty-seven lots, some occupied and others not. Of all these lots, only two would be purchased and grants issued by the New Brunswick government under the authority of the 1844 act.

By 1860 Chief Thomas Nicholas of the Buctouche Indians wanted to resign because of his age. Supporters of his son, Marin, wanted him to succeed as chief.[48] On their behalf Chief Francis Bernard of Shediac seems to have been instrumental in sending a petition requesting Marin Nicholas's appointment. There was, however, more support for Dominique Bernard, because the priest, Henry L. Berthe, certified that "Dominque Bernard was elected chief of the Indians of Buctouche by a large majority of votes."[49] The election was held in July 1861 in the presence of Francis McPhelim in his capacity as the local MLA.

Dominique Bernard's opponents, however, accused him of taking away their lands and being likely to make false statements; he "possesses no land of his own, and is at variance with all our Tribe he is a person much given to strong drink."[50] Likely connected to the dispute over succession, a deputation from the Buctouche Band complained to Lieutenant-Governor Manners-Sutton: "their present chief [sic] has recently alienated by sale or transfer to persons not belonging to his tribe at least six lots of Indian land, containing nearly 1,500 acres, and that there are not now more than 200 acres remaining reserved for the Indians."[51] The government appointed Henry Livingston, John Little, and David Wark as Indian Commissioners to investigate the matter.[52]

The investigation opened on November 11, 1861, and from the minutes it seems to have been judiciously conducted. Buctouche Band members, including

Thomas Nicholas, described as the old chief, and Dominique Bernard, described as the new chief, attended. In its proceedings, the investigation followed a list of sales prepared by the priest Henry Berthe, and Thomas Nicholas gave his explanation of the sales. The three commissioners also made a series of observations that placed the sales in context. They noted the reserve originally extended nearly four and half miles along the north side of the Buctouche River and contained about four thousand acres. They observed that the "late commissioners [Peter Merzerall and John Weldon] appear to have recommended the Sale of all that part of the Indian Reserve to the West of the Grant to Mr. Beckwith, and they surveyed it, and laid it out in Lots."[53] This was done, the three commissioners "presume[d], with the Sanction of the Government," with parts of the lands granted to five others.[54] Most of the remaining lots had "been taken possession of by the parties to whom they were located [sic] and considerable improvements made. They no doubt Settled on the Land with the Sanction of the commissioners and with the understanding that the Government would Sell it and that on paying the price fixed they would obtain Grants." In addition to this "nearly all of them paid the Indians considerable Sums for their Consent to take possession of it."[55]

Although the commissioners contended that Weldon and Merzerall had intended "to reserve for the use of the Indians all that part of their land being to the East of the Grant to Beckwith they understood that several persons had made considerable improvements on this tract.[56] In their estimate, it contained about 1,200 acres, "and that part unoccupied by these parties and now left for the use of the Indians is Variously estimated at from two hundred to five hundred acres."[57] Most of the squatters had purchased land from the reserve members from 1850 onwards and did so with the sanction of Weldon and Merzerall. The acreage lost to the reserve before 1845 amounted to 388.5 acres, but for the period from 1850 to 1867 the figure rose to 3,045.5 acres. Of the latter figure, 578 acres were the result of sales advertised in the *Royal Gazette* in 1851, 1863, and 1867, and for which either grants were made by the New Brunswick government or by letters patent from the Dominion government. Although sales and leases by Buctouche Band members had long been prohibited, the 1849 regulations for sales and leases under the 1844 act were more explicit and detailed than before. By using phrasing such as "with the Sanction of the Government" the commissioners avoided commenting on the illegality of the sales and the actions of Weldon and Merzerall in authorizing grants while ignoring the 1844 act.

# VICTORIA COUNTY (MADAWASKA AND TOBIQUE RESERVES)

When Moses Perley visited Madawaska Reserve in 1841 he found it occupied by twenty-seven Maliseet. The "Captain of the Madawaska Settlement" was Louis Bernard, who told Perley when he was boy there had been a considerable village. Perley described in his report how a settler, Simon Hebert, had managed to purchase nine acres of land from a Maliseet. On the basis of this purchase Hebert had then acquired from the government a grant for two hundred acres of reserve land.[58]

Further down the Saint John River was Tobique Reserve. Its extensive acreage made it by far the largest reserve outside those of Northumberland and Kent counties, though by no means did all the Maliseet on the St. John River reside there. Kingsclear, outside of Fredericton in York County, was more important. It was there that representatives from the other Maliseet communities gathered in 1843 ito prepare a petition, setting out their concerns relating to the loss of their traditional hunting grounds. Moses Perley's visit in 1841 had given them "great satisfaction," but since then their raised hopes had been deferred. They now felt they must act on their own behalf. Their lands were being daily encroached upon for so long "with impunity."[59] The trespassers had grown "bold in their deeds of plunder, [and] scarcely admit the Indian to have a right to stand upon the Land." The present system of managing the reserves was "inefficient." They sought the "social comforts and individual rights to Educated people." The petition concluded: "Unless an immediate remedy is applied, the result must be the complete dispersion and destruction of the Tribe, the thought of which affects the deepest feelings of Your Petitioners' hearts, and makes them shudder at the possibility of severing that sacred attachment which they bear to the soil and to the graves of their fathers."

Tobique being by far the largest reserve on the Saint John River (and in the province) and having the largest number of squatters were probably key factors in Jeremiah Connell being one of seven members appointed in February 1844 to the committee tasked to draft a bill related to the selling of reserve lands. He had first been elected in 1835 and was one of two members for Carleton County, in which Tobique Reserve was then located. As already discussed, the eventual draft bill was the work of John Ambrose Street, a member for Northumberland County. His bill had run into major opposition with its provision that all proceeds from sales would remain within the county where the reserves were located and under local control. This would restrict its operation to Northumberland, Kent, Gloucester, and Carleton counties and meant there would be no funds for any Maliseet or Mi'kmaq living outside these four counties.

In the ensuing debate, John Ambrose Street contended that the large reserves in the northern counties should be applied exclusively to the assistance of the Mi'kmaq living there, while the "Indians residing on the river Saint John on both sides of the Tobique" be retained for the "benefit of the Milicete tribe, which numbers about 400 individuals."[60] Other than Tobique, with its reputed sixteen thousand acres, Maliseet reserve lands at Madawaska, Meductic, Woodstock, Kingsclear, and "Brothers" Island near Saint John were comparatively insignificant in acreage, so in reality Tobique sales would have contributed almost all the funds for the Maliseet if Street's views had prevailed. In reporting the debate, the *New Brunswick Courier* made no mention of the two Carleton County members, Jeremiah Connell and Charles Perley (first elected in 1843), intervening in it. On division, however, both voted with the majority in defeating John Ambrose Street's proposal on the distribution of funds raised from sales. When it was moved that the bill be given the three-month hoist, Connell (Perley was absent) voted against the motion.

John Dibblee and two others, all of Woodstock, were appointed commissioners for Carleton County in June 1845.[61] In July, Dibblee visited Madawaska and Tobique. He reported to Colebrooke on the squatters present and Maliseet views on the sale of reserve lands.[62] At Madawaska he found only four families that were "averse to being interfered with either as respects the disposal the timber or the occupancy of the land and are desirous of having control thereof in their own hands."[63] At Tobique, he found the band had formed quite a village on the upper side of the Tobique River and had built a chapel, though it was unfinished. The land where the village was located had been little improved, but below the river was a meadow Dibblee thought would cut twenty tons of hay. He believed the band had leased it for too little, and he required the lessee to pay more. There were no settlers from the reserve's upper boundary, opposite the Aroostook River to approximately two miles below the Tobique River. From this point, squatters occupied reserve land down to the lower boundary at Tobique Rocks. Although Perley had stated he found sixteen squatters in 1841, Dibblee on his list had only thirteen, with varying acreages and years in possession.[64] Of the thirteen squatters, nine had been in possession of reserve lands for twenty years or more. In particular, three of the families had intermarried, reinforcing their occupancy.

Dibblee made no recommendations but left it to the government to decide whether it wanted to comply with the squatters' wishes, "well convinced that the desire [of the government] is to protect the interest of the Indians."[65] If

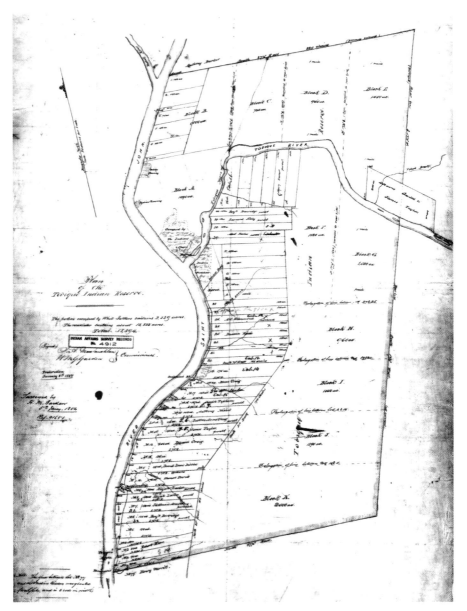

Plan of the Tobique Indian Reserve prepared by Indian Affairs in 1894 from the survey by James Maclauchlan and H. M. G. Garden in 1854 and by Garden in 1867, dividing the rear area into blocks.
Courtesy Natural Resources Canada

the government decided to sell part of the reserve, he recommended that fifty acres to each band member should be a sufficient reservation, and this should embrace the village site. Dibblee foresaw that this plan would be "attended with difficulty," as "the Indians appear much dissatisfied at the Land being taken out of their controul [sic] Either by sale or Lease." He suggested if assistance could be given to finish the chapel, this might remove many of the objections band members had to the "controul [sic] being exercised over their Lands."[66] In making a census of Tobique Band members, Dibblee found there were seventy-six male inhabitants, in which total he included all male children. If each received fifty acres, he calculated that 3,800 acres would be required, which incorporated most of the reserve land north of the Tobique River. This would then leave the lands south of the Tobique River at the disposal of the government to sell to the squatters.

Dibblee proved correct about Tobique's opposition to selling reserve lands. As a result of his visit, a petition was sent to Colebrooke. On learning from Dibblee that it was the government's intention to sell off the "Lands known as the Indian reserve," the petitioners were "very much adverse [sic] to having their lands sold. They had always considered the lands known as the Indian reserve to have been granted by the British Government for the benefit of the Melicite [sic] tribe of Indians."[67] They had settled at Tobique as had their fathers before them. They wished for a grant for the whole tract of land where they were settled, but were agreeable to have the lower tract of land from the Tobique River divided into lots and leased with a competent person appointed to manage the business.

In his May 1847 recommendations to the executive council, the surveyor general had emphasized "The necessity which exists for breaking up this Reserve [Tobique], at least in part is universally acknowledged. Its unimproved wilderness condition, at the very mouth of the large River Tobique, is found to be a serious obstacle preventing the formation of settlements on the banks of the Tobique above it."[68] Yet, the government would not proceed with sales of Tobique lands until 1854. A petition from the Tobique Band in January 1847 complained that parties were cutting and carrying away timber on reserve lands without paying any compensation. Their lands were being trespassed with impunity year after year. They petitioned for the replacement of John Dibblee with Andrew Rainsford, a local justice of the peace, as commissioner for Tobique. Dibblee resided in Woodstock, and the petitioners believed "their affairs [would be] Conducted in a manner more satisfactory to them by the appointment of some person residing in the Vicinity of the Tobique to the office of Commissioner."[69]

On his appointment, Rainsford had sent to the surveyor general a report on Tobique, noting the "Reserve has always been considered as an equivalent to a grant"; he deemed it "unjust now to depose the Indians of it, unless with their concurrence, which cannot be obtained."[70] Rainsford had wanted to have the reserve surveyed and to be able to submit a report showing the boundaries and the number of acres in the occupation of the white people, but he had been unable to obtain a surveyor. He reiterated the necessity for a survey in May 1848, after he had been informed that the executive council would be considering the sale of reserves. As commissioner, he reported, "there will be no objection to selling such parts thereof [Tobique Reserve] as are in the occupation of the whites, as both they and the Indians are anxious to have it done, but before this can be effected it will be necessary to have the Reserve surveyed."[71]

There was, however, an important caveat to the Tobique Band's willingness to have the lands sold to the settlers. Rainsford made clear this was contingent on the Tobique Band members being the sole beneficiary of the sales. Upon "no other Terms would [he] wish a Sale to take place and these he knew would be satisfactory to the Indians."[72] If the act needed to be amended, this should be done. After Head became lieutenant-governor, it was requested Rainsford report on Tobique. He emphasized the part of the reserve occupied by whites was "totally valueless to the Indians," as the settlers paid them nothing, while the uncertain tenure prevented the squatters from making improvements.[73] The money from sales had to be for the benefit of the Tobique Band because this was the only way "to adjust the Matter Satisfactorily—having a due regard for the rights of the Indians, and a fair consideration for the Claims of the Settlers."[74] As in his previous correspondence, Rainsford again noted the need for a survey.

Finally, in late 1853, the government ordered James Maclauchlan and H. M. G. Garden to complete a survey of Tobique.[75] On their arrival at Tobique, they informed the band of their instructions with regard to the squatters occupying the part below the Tobique River's entrance, "which appeared to meet their wishes."[76] Maclauchlan and Garden regretted that the reserve—"containing over 18,000 acres, situated at the entrance of the Tobique River, and extending up and down the St. John River, the former three and latter four miles: also embracing both banks of the Tobique at least five or six miles from its confluence with Saint John"—could only have a direct tendency to hinder settlement without any compensating advantages for the band members.

In their opinion if five hundred to one thousand acres were reserved for them on the upper side of the Tobique and extending back to The Narrows, so called, and the remainder of the reserve sold it would raise a fund of over £2,000. They proposed that the interest on this sum be distributed equally, either quarterly or semi-annually, among those band members who would make the Tobique their place of residence. If carried out, "they were satisfied that such an arrangement would not only add materially to the support and comfort of the tribe, but be very instrumental in facilitating the settlement of the extensive tract of wilderness bordering upon the Tobique River."[77] As well as a survey of the boundaries of Tobique Reserve, Maclauchlan and Garden marked off lots of land fronting on the Saint John River, starting with Lot 1 at Tobique Rocks, the lower boundary line. They interviewed each of the squatters they found on nineteen lots.[78]

Since 1814, when John Larlee Sr. first took possession of lands that became Lot 8 in the survey, members of his family and others had not only squatted at will, but also treated the lands as their own, buying and selling without title. They had ignored with impunity the 1841 proclamation and specific provisions of the 1844 act against squatting on reserve lands. Aside from the actual squatters, others not physically occupying lots had engaged in speculation, including notably Benjamin Beveridge. All told, the squatters had occupied 2,039 acres of the reserve's 18,394 acres as surveyed by Maclauchlan and Garden. Beveridge, a native of Scotland, had first settled on the Perth side before moving across the Saint John River to Andover. He became the wealthiest man in Victoria County (created in 1844 out of the northern part of Carleton County) as the result of his extensive involvement in the timber trade. He was also a Member of the Assembly for Victoria County from 1863 to 1869, when he was appointed to the legislative council.

Initially, the Crown Lands Office scheduled a sale of Lots 1 to 19 and one other lot for June 7, 1854, but postponed it until August 4.[79] Garden conducted the auction, which was held at Beveridge's establishment in Andover. The revised regulations required that only occupants of lots on reserves could apply for purchase, presumably to disallow speculation. Purchase could be outright with a 15 percent discount or in three annual installments. Names listed in the *Royal Gazette* were the occupants, as given in Maclauchlan and Garden's report of January 5, 1854.

Garden reported two days after the auction that all the occupants purchased with the exception of one who did not attend the sale.[80] Eight had paid the first installment, but the remainder had not yet done so. When Garden sent in his return on August 19, 1854, it showed of the twenty lots up for auction that ten sold, but only one was purchased outright by its occupant.[81] After the 1854 sales under the 1844 act, no further attempt was made to deal with the squatter problem until June 1861, when A. C. Hammond, now commissioner for Tobique Reserve, recommended the "Government had better sell that part of the Indian Reserve lying South of the Tobique River to actual settlers and that if it was divided into Lots would meet with ready purchasers."[82] He suggested if government followed such a course it would materially advance Andover and Perth parishes and "secure to the Indians more certain relief...and settle for ever a great amount of trouble and annoyances to the commissioners here."[83]

When the Tobique Band members learned that more squatter lots on the south side of Tobique River might be put up for sale, they submitted a petition signed (marks) by forty-one of them.[84] They did not want what was called the "flat" or meadow to be sold because they claimed they had been cutting twenty to thirty tons of hay on it to feed their cattle; however, they sought to remain part of their reserve a much larger adjoining area than that of the meadow. Hammond reported for "the last thirty years the Indians had not got so much as one hill of potatoes on it, the government acted to protect from sale 200 acres as reserve land on the south side, which included the flat or meadow."[85]

Although not found, petitions from the inhabitants of the Perth and Andover parishes and the settlers up the Tobique River accompanied Hammond's recommendation on the sale of reserve land south of the Tobique River. The executive council approved his report on July 1, 1861. Charles Beckwith was instructed to survey the lots of those applying to purchase them; he began immediately. Among others a Charles McKenize wrote Surveyor General John McMillan that he was one of those who petitioned for land in the Indian Reserve north side. In response to their petitions, the Indians were attempting "to annul the whole transaction."[86]

What likely happened was that the Tobique Band brought pressure on Charles Beckwith to not carry out any surveys on the north side. He confined his surveys to lands south of the river. In all, he surveyed thirteen 100-acre lots, which were advertised to go up for sale on July 1.[87] A. C. Hammond conducted the sale and reported that of the thirteen lots, four were purchased, but only one installment paid for each of these.[88] Hammond wanted to know if he could extend further time to those who had applied for lots but had been unable to pay down anything. At present, he remarked, money "cannot be obtained at any price in this place."[89]

For reasons unclear, but probably related to continued squatting at Tobique and continued complaints from Tobique Band members on receiving stumpage moneys, in May 1865 the government sent D. Wilson to report on both the Tobique Band members and the squatters.[90] He seems to have visited nearly all the squatters, many of whom had paid at least one installment on their lots, but nothing more. He warned all those who had not purchased against their continued squatting. Wilson concluded these squatters, who in some cases also had not paid stumpage, would never do so unless government compelled them. Accompanied by Hammond, John Francis, and other Tobique Band members, Wilson recorded the cultivated and cleared land within Tobique village. On the question of the "great grievance" relating to stumpage and the band members' claims that Hammond was withholding money from them, he personally examined Hammond's account. These showed Hammond could account exactly what he had taken in for stumpage.

It is unclear to what degree the prospect of Confederation caused a renewed attempt to sell more land at Tobique, but it seems to have been a major factor. In May 1867, Benjamin Beveridge and Vital Hebert, Members of the Assembly for Victoria County, wrote the surveyor general on the "necessity" for a survey of lots at Tobique and for a reduction in price per acre.[91] Because of the price differential, no one would apply for reserve land when they could obtain Crown land of equal quality for less. They emphasized that "the tendency is to have persons squatting on the [Indian] Land as has been the case for Years, who never intend paying for the same."[92] If, however, the price was reduced, this would attract a class of settler willing to purchase.

Within a month, this appeal for action resulted in instructions to H. M. Garden to undertake a survey of rear portions of the Tobique Reserve and divide them into lots of one hundred acres each for settlement.[93] Included in the survey was to be whatever space on the north bank was suitable for cultivation. Although he would not complete the survey until January 1868, two lots, each of one hundred acres, were advertised in the *Royal Gazette* on July 10, 1867, for sale on September 3, 1867.[94] At the sale one of the lots was purchased by making an initial payment, but no grant would be issued, and the second lot was purchased for which a grant would be issued in 1869.

In October 1867, Hammond and recently appointed commissioner W. R. Newcomb wrote the surveyor general to request a plan showing the lots surveyed by Garden that were going to be put up for sale. If, however, he could not provide that information, then Hammond and Newcomb stated they would be "obliged to sell the whole, in one Block as there is no time to be lost."[95] By one block, they meant the whole of lands that Garden was surveying lying below the Tobique River, which he divided into Blocks A, B, and C, and Block D above the river, for a total of 7,234 acres.[96] By the time Garden had completed his survey in January 1868, the Department of Indian Affairs in Ottawa had assumed responsibility for Tobique and other reserves. Garden sent his completed survey to Ottawa, and whatever plans Hammond and Newcomb had for a single block sale were never put into effect.

However, the Tobique Band members were certainly aware of plans to sell land north of the Tobique River. In March 1868 they sent a petition to Governor-General Lord Monck in which they first described the creation of their reserve of twenty thousand acres and its extent in about the year 1800. The main point of the petition was that the tribe had derived little or no benefit from the reserve on the lower side of the Tobique River because white settlers had taken possession of it and converted the land and timber to their own use. Indeed, the tribe had agreed that this portion of the reserve should be sold, but "with the understanding that the proceeds were to be applied to its benefit"; the land had now been sold, but the tribe had derived no benefit from the sale.[97] Moreover, encroachments had lately been made on the upper side of the Tobique River, and the tribe feared this land "will be wrested from them, as that on the lower side has been." The petition concluded: "Repeated representations have been made to the Executive of New Brunswick of the injustice done the tribe but to no purpose[;] the tribe therefore now appeal to your Excellency for that justice which has been denied them in New Brunswick and to which they feel they have strong claims having been noted for their loyalty when occasion required."[98]

When Hector Langevin, the secretary of state in the Canadian government, responsible for Indians, requested what information Crown Lands might have in connection with the petition, Richard Sutton, the provincial surveyor general, replied. The reserve, he wrote, comprised nearly 20,000 acres of which 921 acres had been sold and grants issued (grants totalled 931 acres for an estimated value of $1,258). Another 1,244 acres had been sold for $1,679, of which $493.28 had been paid, and 17,673 acres remained vacant. But of these acres, Sutton noted that about 2,000 below the Tobique River were in possession of "white" squatters.[98] All told the amount contributed to the Indian Fund would have been around $1,700. Of the other reserves on the Saint John River, there was only one sale and it was for thirty acres at Woodstock. Although the Tobique Band had in petitions stated they would agree to give up lands south of the Tobique River, they stipulated they would do so only if they received the money from sales. In fact, they never received any compensation for the lands taken from them under the 1844 act.

# NOTES

1. Council Minutes, April 14, 1845, RS6a, p. 339, PANB.

2. Thomas M. DeBlois to William Colebrooke, September 21, 1843, RS9, PANB.

3. S. L. Bishop to Thomas Baillie, July 14, 1847, RS9, PANB.

4. James Davidson to Surveyor General John Montgomery, December 5, 1856, RS637/29f, PANB.

5. S. L. Bishop and James Hickson to Joseph Howe, February 13, 1871, RG10, vol. 318, LAC.

6. Benjamin M. Stevenson, Crown Lands Office, to S. L. Tilley, lieutenant-governor, July 10, 1871, RG10, vol. 1,928, file 3248, LAC.

7. S. L. Bishop to Minister of Interior, December 17, 1874, RG10, vol. 1941, file 4078, LAC.

8. Report and Schedule of the Reserves in the County of Kent...Alfred Layton Reports, June 30, 1832, RS637, 7F 3a, Kent County, PANB.

9. Draft Minutes of Executive Council, February 9, 1822, MG9, A1, vol. 6, pp. 3177–83, LAC.

10. John Wesley Weldon would become the most prominent figure in the story of the loss of Buctouche Reserve lands. He was born in Dorchester, Westmoreland County, and was admitted to the New Brunswick Bar in 1827. He set up practice in Richibucto, where for Kent County he became deputy treasurer, registrar of probate, and clerk of the peace. First elected to the assembly in 1827 he would be re-elected five more times before being defeated in 1850. In 1840 he became a member of the executive council and continued as a member until 1842. He was Speaker of the assembly from 1843 to 1850. In 1857 he moved to Saint John, where he practised law until his promotion to the New Brunswick Supreme Court.

11. "Livingston Report," RS9, January 17, 1862, no. 40.1, PANB. It is uncertain, but Weldon and Chandler may have intended that all the remaining reserve land to the east of these lots on the eastern side of Mill Creek was to be reserved for the Buctouche Band. They, however, took no action, other than not to make any further grants on the eastern side of Mill Creek.

12. Memorandum of Agreement..., January 20, 1840, between John McMillan and Noel John and thirteen other Indians, MG9, A1, vol. 12, pp. 349–50, LAC.

13. See descriptions for grants to Nehemiah Beckwith, April 25, 1840, no. 2086, and to Thomas Dray, December 16, 1840, no. 2586, RS686, PANB. Both were for lots on the east side of Mill Creek.

14. Petition of the Indians of the Richibucto Tribe of Micmas to Lieutenant-Governor Sir John Harvey, October 12, 1837, RS965, PANB.

15. Petition of Pierre Joseph Augustine an Indian of the Tribe of Richibucto Indians to Lieutenant-Governor Sir William Colebrooke, c. 1841, RS965, PANB.

16. Memorial by Deputy Surveyor William James Layton, attached to petition by Pierre Joseph Augustine to Lieutenant-Governor Sir William Colebrooke, c. 1841, RS965, PANB. Layton commented that her husband also threatened and abused her.

17. John W. Weldon to William Franklin Odell, March 7, 1844, RS 965, PANB.

18. Loyalist and Conservative Advocate, March 25, 1844, reported on the debates of March 18.

19. Ibid.

20. JLA, April 6, 1844, pp. 289–90.

21. See list of Indian Commissioners appointed by the executive council under the act, April 14, 1845, RS6a, vol. 5, p. 339, PANB. Only a single commissioner for each county was appointed. Merzerall was appointed after the government's first choice, Dr. McLarne, resigned.

22. Surveyor General to the Executive Council, May 6, 1847, RS637/29a, PANB.

23. Ibid.

24. Return of the Number of Persons who have settled upon and occupy portions of the Indian reserves in the Province of New Brunswick, 1841, *JHA*, 1842, Appendix, Indian Reports, p. cxxviii.

25. Merzerall to Colebrooke, May 27, 1846. Merzerall commented that although the Richibucto Indians did little farming, they preferred working for the merchants and were very well employed in running timber rafts. A number of Buctouche and Richibucto Indians had taken on the loading of a merchant's large vessel for approximately £150.

26. Ibid.

27. Ibid.

28. Daniel Kerr to Attorney General, August 18, 1851, MG9 A1, vol. 40, pp. 329–38.

29. Peter Merzerall to John R. Partelow, Provincial Secretary, April 1, 1851, RS557F, PANB.

30. "Livingston Report," January 17, 1862, RS9 no. 40.1, PANB. Francis McPhelim (1811–1866) had immigrated with his family to Buctouche in 1821. He had prospered as a merchant and in shipping. In 1850 he became an MLA, and six years later he would become the first Roman Catholic to be a member of the executive council. He would gain a reputation as a political moderate and become noted for his ethnic and religious tolerance. As far as is known, he proved to be the single non-Native to seek justice for the Buctouche Band within the prevailing atmosphere of antipathy towards them. Drafting the letter was McPhelim's first intervention on behalf of the band.

31. "Livingston Report." January 17, 1862.

32. Ibid.

33. Ibid.

34. Sir Edmund Head to Attorney General J. A. Street, July 12, 1851, MG9 A1, vol. 40, pp. 344–45, LAC. The reference to staying the sale was to a notice that had appeared in the *Royal Gazette* of June 11, 1851, for the auction of the 350 acres—the leased lands in question. The sale, however, went ahead and William Chandler purchased the land.

35. Ibid.

36. Ibid.

37. J. A Street to D. S. Kerr, July 26, 1851, MG9, A1, vol. 40, p. 346, LAC.

38. Daniel Kerr to Attorney General, August 18, 1851, MG9, A1, vol. 40, pp. 329–8, LAC.

39. Ibid. Kerr does not state on what date he held the inquiry, but it would seem it was early to mid-August.

40. Thomas Nicholas, Indian Chief, to the Attorney General, July 1, 1851, MG9 A, vol. 12, pp. 340–2, LAC.

41. Ibid.

42. Francis McPhelim to J. A. Street, August 16, 1851, MG9 A1, vol. 40, pp. 352–3, LAC. Head's order to Attorney General Street, July 12, supports this was the prevailing attitude and was known to be the case by the government.

43. Daniel Kerr to Attorney General, August 18, 1851, MG9 A1, vol. 40, p. 331, LAC. It was marked (E), which appears on a survey plan (see endnote 44).

44. Survey Plan, entitled County of Kent Buctouche Indian Reserve, MG9, A1, vol. 40, p. 326, LAC.

45. *Royal Gazette*, June 4, 1851. The two grantees were Angus MacLeod, who received a grant dated May 9, 1854, and John Graham, whose grant was dated May 21, 1856.

46. Chief Peter Pierre Paul to Sir Edmund Walker Head, September 20, 1852. The petition was supported by fifty-five Richibucto Band members.

47. Recorded Sales of Indian Reserves to March 14, 1867, RS637/29a, PANB.

48. Petition from the Mic Mac Indians residing on the Big Buctouche River, August 24, 1860, RS55F, PANB.

49. A copy of a document by Henry L. Berthe lists lands sold by Thomas Nicholas and certifies the election of Dominique Bernard, September 1, 1861, RS557F, PANB.

50. Peter Nicholas, Merang Nicholas, and Noel Nicholas to His Excellency Hon J. H. T. Manners-Sutton, August 26, 1861, RS557F, PANB. They may have been brothers or at least close relations of Marin.

51. Memorandum for the Provincial Secretary from Manners-Sutton, September 2, 1891, RS557F, PANB. Those meeting with Manners-Sutton stated that the number of Indian families at Buctouche was twenty-two.

52. "Livingston Report," RG9, January 1, 1862, RS9, no. 40.1, PANB. At the end of the report the three members were listed as Indian Commissioners.

53. Ibid.

54. Ibid. They were apparently incorrect about Charles Miller or John Weldon receiving a grant of reserve lands. No grant was found for Miller. A check of Weldon's grants in the Buctouche area located none involving reserve land. His name, however, does appear as occupying land that later John McMillan would occupy and receive a grant on survey plan. See also Survey Plan, January 17, 1862, RS9, no. 40.3, PANB.

55. Survey Plan, January 17, 1862, RS, 1862, RS9, no. 40.3, PANB.

56. "Livingston Report," RS9, January 1, 1862, PANB.

57. Ibid.

58. "Extract from Mr. Perley's First Report Respecting the Indians on the River Saint John," August 12, 1841, JHA, 1842, Appendix, p. xcvii.

59. Petition of Toma Francis and twelve other Maliseet, January 10, 1843, RS108, Land Petitions: Original Series, PANB.

60. *New Brunswick Courier* (Saint John), April 6, 1844.

61. Bond of John Dibblee as Indian Commissioner, approved in council June 19, 1845, RS9, PANB. The bond repeats provisions of the 1844 act regarding the duties of commissioners.

62. John Dibblee to Lieutenant-Governor Sir William Colebrooke, July 19, 1845, RS557C, PANB.

63. Ibid.

64. Ibid.

65. Ibid.

66. Ibid.

67. The Petition of the Undersigned…, undated, but sent shortly after Dibblee's visit in July 1845, RS557C, PANB.

68. Surveyor General to the Executive Council, May 6, 1847, RS637/29a, PANB.

69. Petition of Lewis De Belmont, Captain…, January 16, 1847, RS9, PANB.

70. A. W. Rainsford to Thomas Baillie, Restook, August 7, 1847, RS637/29b, PANB.

71. A. W. Rainsford to Thomas Baillie, May 1, 1848, RS105 1840–1849, PANB.

72. Ibid.

73. Ibid.

74. A. W. Rainsford to J. R. Partelow, Provincial Secretary, October 30, 1848, RS557C, PANB.

75. Upon an Account of Messrs J. A. Maclauchlan and H. M. Garden Commissioners for Survey and Report of the Tobique Indian Reserve, January 5, 1854, RS9, PANB.

76. Ibid.

77. Ibid.

78. Return Showing the Number of Squatters upon the Tobique Indian Reserve…, January 5, 1854, RS557, PANB.

79. *Royal Gazette*, August 2, 1854, p. 6975.

80. H. M. G. Garden to Surveyor General, August 6, 1854, RS637/29b, PANB.

81. Sale of Lots Tobique Indian Reserve, Andover, August 19, 1854, RS637/29b; and Grant to Anthony Nichol, July 16, 1855, RS686, no. 7071, PANB.

82. A. C. Hammond to Provincial Secretary, June 27, 1861, RS557C, PANB.

83. Ibid.

84. Untitled Petition, Andover, August 8, 1861, RS 108; Land Petition of John Francis et al., PANB. Two justices of the peace witnessed the signing.

85. A. C. Hammond to Crown Lands Office, December 10, 1861, DIAND B8260-108 (NS), vol. 7, Enclosure. Tobique Indians were so unhappy with Hammond as commissioner that thirteen of them petitioned to have him replaced; Untitled Petition, January 31, 1862, RS557C, PANB. However, the government took no action and Hammond remained commissioner.

86. Charles McKenize to John McMillan, April 9, 1862, RS637/29b, PANB.

87. *Royal Gazette*, March 12, 1862, vol. 20, p. 44.

88. A. C. Hammond to Surveyor General John McMillan, July 15, 1862, RS637/29b, PANB.

89. Ibid.

90. D. Wilson, Report on Tobique Indians, May 11, 1865, RS557C, Indian Documentation Inventory, PANB.

91. Benjamin Beveridge and Vital Hebert to Surveyor General, May 17, 1867, RS637/29b, PANB.

92. Ibid.

93. Crown Lands Office to H. M. Garden, June 1867, RS637/29b, PANB.

94. *Royal Gazette*, July 10, 1867, vol. 25, p. 299.

95. A. C. Hammond and W. R. Newcomb to Surveyor General, October 3, 1867, RS637/29b, PANB.

96. Plan of Survey of Certain Portions of the Tobique Indian Reserve as per Order of the Surveyor General, June 1867 and Woodstock, January 18, 1868. Indian Affairs Survey Records No. T1449.

97. Petition (twenty-one names) of that Part Millicete Tribe of Indians Residing at Tobique in the County of Victoria and Province of New Brunswick, March 1868, RS637/29b, PANB. A copy of the petition was sent by Hector Langevin to the New Brunswick Crown Lands Department, March 21, 1868. The reference to their loyalty most likely was to the War of 1812 and but also the so-called "Aroostook War" in 1839 over the border dispute with Maine.

98. Richard Sutton to Hector Langevin, March 31, 1868, transcribed in Memorandum re: Edmundston (Madawaska) and Tobique Reserves, p. 6, DAANDC.

# CHAPTER 6

# "POLITICIANS" AND SURRENDERS OF BUCTOUCHE AND RICHIBUCTO RESERVE LANDS

nder Section 91 (24) of the British North America Act, "Indians and lands reserved for Indians became the exclusive jurisdiction of the new Dominion Government."[1] Responsibility was placed in the Department of the Secretary of State for the Provinces. The Secretary of State also became Superintendent General of Indian Affairs. The small staff of five officials reported to Deputy Superintendent General William Spragge. In October 1867, Hector Langevin, as Secretary of State, wrote to Richard Sutton, Surveyor General of New Brunswick, requesting information on lands that had been set aside for Indians.[2]

Sutton replied the following December and enclosed a copy of the 1844 act; a return of all lands as yet un-granted that were held for "Indians"; a return showing which lots had been sold to non-Natives but were not yet granted; and a list of unpaid commissioners who had been appointed by the provincial government.[3] Langevin next addressed a circular to the various commissioners, requesting "information on Indians concerning numbers and other such matters."[4] Henry Livingston of Richibucto replied, with information for both the Richibucto and Buctouche reserves, but recommended there should be a separate commissioner for Buctouche and Dr. Francis Pouliot be appointed "Indian Agent." Auguste Renaud, the new Member of Parliament for Kent County in the recent 1867 election, also recommended to Langevin Pouliot's appointment. Renaud was apparently from France and a schoolteacher in Buctouche; otherwise, nothing is known of him.[5] Noting there were two recommendations in favour of Pouliot,

Langevin requested his appointment as agent by the Privy Council and it was approved.[6]

Even before Pouliot's appointment was official, Renaud wrote Langevin of the necessity for having a survey completed so the inhabitants of lands they had purchased from the Buctouche Band could obtain title from the Crown on paying fifty cents an acre. As Langevin explained later to Joseph Howe, his successor as "the secretary of state responsible for Indians," he had promised Renaud that "should the settlers on Indian Lands in New Brunswick send me a plan, I would allow each settler to have his land at the price sixty cents I think per acre."[7] Renaud had gone ahead and prepared a plan of the reserve, showing the lots and "settlers," which he sent to Indian Affairs. At Indian Affairs no action was taken until Spragge detailed his concerns in a memorandum. No licensed surveyor had signed and dated the plan. Although the names of those occupying the lots were given, the lots had no numbers. Moreover, a surrender would be required from the band in a manner prescribed in the 1868 act and a proper survey completed. Under this act, no surrender of reserve lands could take place unless assented to by the chief, or if there were more than one chief, then by a majority of chiefs of a band or tribe assembled at a meeting, or council of a tribe summoned for that purpose. A certificate of assent to the surrender had to be signed before a judge by the chief and the agent responsible for conducting the surrender. No surrender was valid unless approved by the Governor-in-Council. Pouliot ordered Deputy Surveyor Robert Douglass to survey only those lots "now occupied by the Buctouche Band." In essence, Pouliot had confined the Buctouche Reserve's limits to 350 acres, which was treeless and not worth more than fifty cents an acre.

Renaud informed Langevin that all the land had been surveyed to "la satis-faction des deux parties"; presumably the expression referred to "Buctouche Band and the non-Indians occupying reserve lands."[8] Pouliot sent a plan of the lands sold by the band and another plan of the reserve lands still possessed by it. Both Renaud and Pouliot seemed to have been under the impression that titles to the lands held by "non-Indians" who had purchased reserve land would be forthcoming without any further action by either of them. However, Joseph Howe informed Pouliot that the band would first have to give up the lands in question before any titles could be issued and sent him a blank surrender form with instructions for completion to make legal the Buctouche Band's surrendering of reserve lands. At the same time, Howe also requested of Surveyor General Richard Sutton maps of the various reserves. Among the twenty plans sent was one that had been prepared in 1851 by Peter Merzerall, showing the Buctouche

The above watercolours, dated 1764, "taken from life," are considered to be the earliest known portrayal of what are most likely Maliseets. They were the work of Richard Byron, who is believed to have been chaplain on the HMS *Fame*, commanded by his brother John, while the vessel was in the harbour of the "River of St. Johns in the Bay of Fundy." Byron was noted as a talented amateur artist among his circle of friends and within his family. The images were done with pen and brown ink and watercolour over traces of pencil, with a pen-and-ink order, on laid paper, with an armorial watermark, unframed. They are reproduced here courtesy of Sotheby's London.

The artist's caption on this painting reads, "A most faithful representation of the Indian Dance at Government House, Fredericton, New Brunswick on the 1st of January 1835…Drawn by Captain J. Campbelll, 38th Regiment, A.D.C. to his father Sir Archibald Campbell…" Sir John Campbell, the son of Lieutenant Governor Sir Archibald Campbell (1831–1837), was an accomplished amateur artist. The Indian Dance at Government House depicts the yearly visit of Maliseets to the lieutenant-governor's residence on January first, a custom which commenced with Sir Howard Douglas. As early as 1827, lieutenant-governors would receive the Maliseets of the region on New Year's Day. The Native guests would arrive in ceremonial dress, meet with provincial representatives and exchange ceremonial dances to the accompaniment of a military band. The chief, or sachum, at this time was Tomah Francis of Pilick (Kingsclear). He is pictured in this painting, standing at the room's right corner, dressed in chief's regalia with a blue peaked headdress.

M978.83.6 | Painting | *Indian Dance at Government House, Fredericton, New Brunswick on the 1st of January 1835 at which Major W. N. Orange was present* ©McCord Museum

This Mi'kmaw Ceremonial Robe was made ca.1841 for Captain Henry Dunn O'Halloran. During his tour of New Brunswick in 1841, he met Peter Gonish of Tabusintac, whom he inspired to go to Britain with a Joseph Dominic to seek financial aid for the improvement and stock of their farms. They travelled to New York, took ship to Liverpool, and there, penniless, were forced to pawn their clothes. They then crossed to Dublin and walked through Ireland to visit O'Halloran. He received them well and sent them to London, where they were helped by, among others, the famous American ethnologist George Catlin. He arranged for the men to redeem their clothes. They were then directed to the Aborigines Protection Society, where they met Alfred Reade, Sir William Colebrooke's former secretary, who dissuaded them from going to Paris to seek assistance from the King of France, as fellow Catholics. He also kept them away from the Colonial Office. They returned to New Brunswick sometime late in 1844. The Canadian Museum of Civilization purchased in 1977 the robe at a London auction.

Mi'kmaq Ceremonial Robe. Canadian Museum of History, III-F, S77-1843-Dp

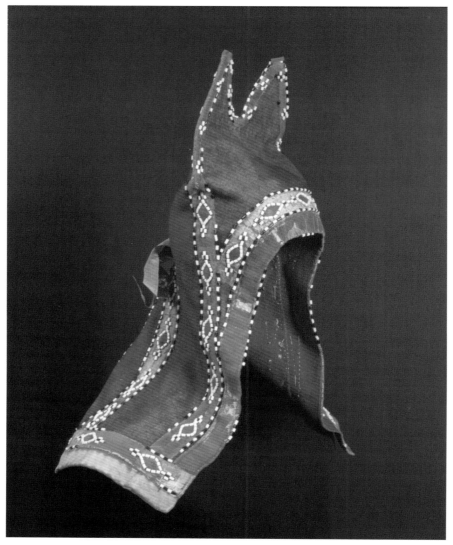

Maker Unknown (First Nations; Wolastoqiyik) Headdress, 1760–1780 wool broadcloth or stroudcloth, silk, and glass beads. Purchased with the assistance of a Movable Cultural Property Grant accorded by the Department of Canadian Heritage under the terms of the Cultural Property Export and Import Act, 1983. Current information indicates that this item originated in the St. John River Valley in the mid-eighteenth century.

1983-47-2-3, New Brunswick Museum, Saint John, NB.

Lieutenant Robert Petley, *Mi'kmaw hunter with fish, spear, musket and paddle*, coloured lithograph, 1837.

Library Archives Canada, C-023349

Robert Petley, *Interior of a Wigwam*, watercolour on wove paper, ca. 1834.

Library Archives Canada C-103533k

Captain R. Levinge, *Salmon Fishing by Torchlight*, New Brunswick, ca. 1840.
Library Archives Canada, C-035960

This coat was collected in 1893 from Chief Frank Francis, Tobique Reserve. Although it was made by a Mi'kmaw woman, the labels bear typical Maliseet beadwork, with its tightly coiled double-curved terminals. It dates from the late nineteenth century and was made of black wool with beadwork and ribbon decoration, black seam, length 106 centimetres (41.75 inches).

© President and Fellows of Harvard College, Peabody Museum of archaeology and ethnology, 94-15/50793.

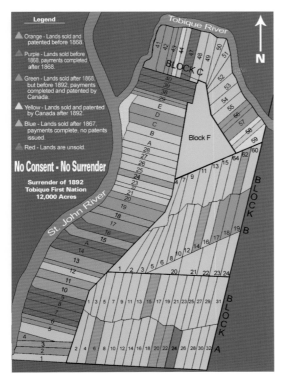

Colour-coded chart prepared by Wayne Nicholas of Tobique First Nation, displaying the various categories of lands involved in the reputed surrender of 1892.

Courtesy Wayne Nicholas

*Fishing scene with Mi'kmaq Guides and Canoes, Miramichi River, New Brunswick*, ca. 1875–1885.
Louise Manny fonds 1989.108.272, New Brunswick Museum, Saint John, NB.

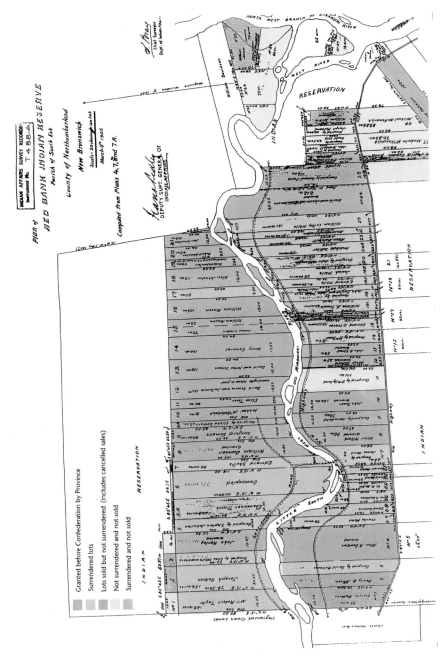

Plan of Red Bank Indian Reserve compiled by Indian Affairs in 1905. It shows the complexity of the various categories of lots, all of which had initially been squatted upon.

Courtesy Natural Resources Canada

Reserve as consisting of 4,655 acres. This figure of 4,655 appeared in a list of acreages of New Brunswick reserves published by Indian Affairs in 1874.[9]

Meanwhile, Buctouche Band members disagreed over who should be chief, and this would have ramifications for the taking of a surrender. Although the priest Henry Berthe had reported the July 1861 election of Dominque Bernard as chief in place of Thomas Nicholas, it seems certain that Thomas Nicholas remained chief for at least some of the Buctouche Band. The provincial secretary did not report until 1868 that Thomas Nicholas had resigned and that his son Marin had been elected in his stead. Henry Livingston described Dominique Bernard to Joseph Howe as a "Self Made Chief." He charged Bernard with disposing of reserve land to white settlers and doing the Buctouche Band great injustices. Livingston sent Howe a petition from Chief Marin Nicholas and sixteen band members.[10] The petition described how Bernard had sold all the block of land where he and his party resided and then left the reserve. However, he returned around 1868 and sold another block of two hundred acres. During that time, Thomas Nicholas had died and his son Marin was appointed chief by a majority.

Moreover, Pouliot was apparently paying all the "bounty money" to Bernard, who was depriving the Marin Nicholas party of any of it, causing great trouble. Pouliot also had secured land for himself within the area set aside for the Buctouche Band. On Marin Nicholas's 1870 petition, the names of four priests appear as witnesses. Such open support for Marin Nicholas and his party suggests the division within the band over the chieftainship had ramifications that extended to any surrender of Buctouche Reserve lands. Pouliot's favouritism towards Dominque Bernard seems to have ensured that Bernard would sign both the surrenders of 1870 and 1871.

In spite of Nicholas's 1870 petition, Pouliot decided to proceed with the surrender. On September 3, 1870, the "Chiefs and Principal Men" signed at Buctouche a surrender instrument, which was also sealed and delivered in the presence of F. E. W. Pouliot.[11] For the required oath, John Weldon, now Justice of the New Brunswick Supreme Court, came to Buctouche. On September 26, 1870, Dominique Bernard and Francis Pouliot made oath before Weldon that the "above release of surrender was assented to and executed by the Chief and principal members of the band of Indians mentioned above, assembled at a meeting of each band or tribe summoned for that purpose and who were entitled to vote thereat."[12]

The Indian Act of 1868 and Joseph Howe's instructions to Pouliot stated that a surrender had to be assented to by the chief, or if there be more than one chief, by a majority of the chiefs of the tribe, band, or body of Indians assembled. However, the surrender document referred to "the undersigned Chief and Principal Men of the Micmac Band owning the Buctouche Indian Reserve." Among the five signatories to the 1870 surrender were Dominique Bernard, Indian Chief, Peter Grims (most likely Ginnis), Deputy Indian Chief. As Marin Nicholas was the only other chief, then Bernard and Grims (Ginnis) were a majority of chiefs for the purposes of the surrender as far as the Indian Act's provisions were concerned. Although for the surrender, Bernard swore that he and four others were the chief and principal men of the band. With Marin Nicholas's petition, sixteen had signed, and none of them would sign the surrender. Those presiding at the surrender, Pouliot and Weldon in particular, had to have known that it had not been assented to by the majority of the Buctouche Band and that the five who did sign could not be realistically described as amounting to all the band's principal members.

Also, the surrender document referred to two different plans for which no distances were given, and the plans did not join up to make a whole of the area to be surrendered. Such a confused description is strong evidence that its author was Pouliot, who sought no professional advice from Deputy Surveyor Robert Douglass;[13] consequently, it seems to have included the whole reserve.

In his covering letter to Howe, enclosing the surrender document, Pouliot confused matters further by stating the two parts designated on the plans as "Indian settlements" were not surrendered like the rest. He reported the "Indians wanted location tickets with the privilege of selling afterwards according to the same rule as the other land surrendered; each Indian having his own right to sell his own share."[14] This suggests that Pouliot realized later that the description had inadvertently included the whole reserve. In his letter to Howe he was attempting to gloss over the consequences for the Buctouche Band. Although Indian Affairs submitted the surrender to the Privy Council for approval, there were doubts about it. In the memorandum requesting approval, Howe stated the department had concluded that the lands described "embraced only a portion of the reserve."[15] The surrender was accepted by the Privy Council.

Indian Affairs, however, had noted a portion of the reserve, which Angus McMillan had sold to J. A. James, had not been included in the September 3 surrender. Howe ordered Pouliot to obtain another surrender of the lot and "any other lot or lots which it may be required to include" in the surrender.[16] Pouliot had the surrender completed on April 24, 1871, signed by Dominique Bernard as Chief, Peter Grims (Ginnis) as Deputy Chief, and Gregoire Biguel, Captain. Judge Blin Botsford certified the required oath on May 4.[17] Although the text read all "the principal Men of the Micmac Band, owning the Buctouche Reserve," there is no evidence that the principal men were ever assembled to give their consent. The new description could be readily followed and was almost certainly drafted by Deputy Surveyor Douglass, part of which read, "including all the Indian land in the Buctouche Reserve, excepting the piece occupied by us at present time." What Pouliot had done, with the apparent consent of Indian Affairs and with the collusion of Justice John Weldon of the Supreme Court of New Brunswick, was to reduce the Buctouche Indian Reserve from 4,655 acres to about 350 acres.

When first replying to Pouliot about obtaining a surrender of Buctouche lands, Joseph Howe had told him he was returning the plan sent to Indian Affairs "in order that the Surveyor may place upon the lots their proper numbers and may also certify the map in the usual way."[18] On the plan provided by Pouliot, the lot numbers had not been inserted, and there had been no attempt to determine ownership of improvements other than by listing names on the lots. Although Indian Affairs obtained Privy Council approval for the two surrenders, it could not proceed to issue patents without at least lot numbers as a means of describing the land for which a patent was desired. In the department's annual report for 1874, Buctouche was still listed as having 4,655 acres, which suggests that issues around providing patents had caused considerable concern.

The documentary record is silent on why there was no further effort to obtain patents. At the time of Pouliot's appointment as agent, the Deputy Superintendent General had advised that his appointment should not be regarded as permanent because of the likely combining of bands in New Brunswick to create more populous settlements. This policy was first announced in the department's annual report for 1869, in which it was presumptuously stated that in regard to social and moral improvements needed in both the Maritime provinces, it would be necessary to prevail upon the small detached bands of Maliseet and Mi'kmaq to consent to be collected in permanent locations and to give up their migratory habits. If this were done, a limited number of more sizable settlements could be formed where comfortable habitations could be provided, schools established, and implements supplied. This, of course, was the policy advocated by Colebrooke and Perley in the 1840s but never implemented. Whatever the department's good intentions, no attempt would be made in New Brunswick to implement such a policy, though it would be tried in the twentieth century in Nova Scotia and proven a major failure.

Meanwhile, Indian Affairs introduced the policy that was followed in the pre-Confederation Province of Canada of appointing paid Indian Agents. In 1872

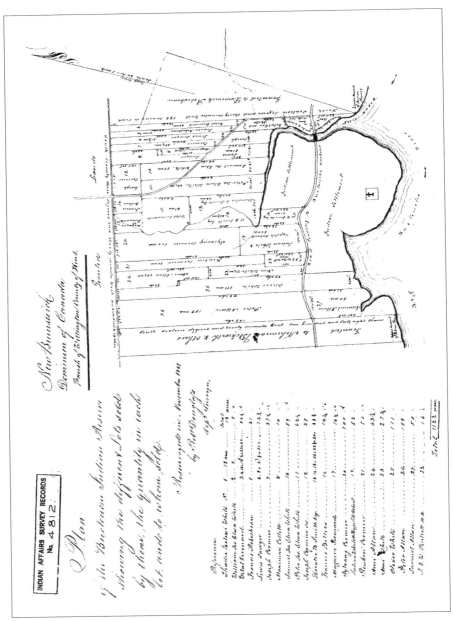

Plan of the Buctouche Indian Reserve, showing the different lots sold, the quantity in each lot, and to whom sold. Resurveyed by Robert Douglass in November 1869.

Courtesy Natural Resources Canada

the department appointed Charles Sargeant of Chatham on the Miramichi as superintendent of all Mi'kmaw reserves in New Brunswick, though his official title was Visiting Superintendent of the North-eastern Superintendency, a part-time position. He would be "for the Indians a sympathetic and energetic agent."[19] Sargeant's initial introduction to the situation at Buctouche arose from a complaint by Chief Thomas Ginnis (Genesse, Guines) and several of his men. They had complained to Thomas Wetmore Blias that Joe White [formerly LeBlanc], Dominique White, and several of the French squatters had taken possession of three lots within the reserve, two of which were occupied by Oliver Nicholas and Andrew Nicholas; the third was vacant. They were accused of having done so "with great violence and disturbed the Buctouche Band members in their peaceable occupation."[20] Blias had agreed to write on their behalf with the complaint. Sargeant wrote to the Whites asking what authority they had for taking possession of the land they were now occupying on the Buctouche Reserve. He warned them they were liable to be prosecuted.

In his reply, Joseph White relayed a convoluted account that in 1870 Oliver Nicholas had killed one of his horses. White threatened to take Nicholas before a magistrate, but relented. Later, he claimed Nicholas had made an affidavit before a magistrate that he had killed the horse and at the same time gave White a quit claim to the lot Robert Douglass had surveyed for him. Nothing more seems to have happened until 1873, when Chief Thomas Ginnis and Andrew Nicholas got involved. What then took place remains confusing, but White received a quit claim deed signed by Thomas Ginnis and Andrew Nicholas for lands on the reserve. White had paid $17 for the land.

Apparently, White's letter was the first knowledge Sargeant had of Thomas Ginnis being a chief, though he doubted that he held any commission. Sargeant then contacted Robert Douglass about the 1869 survey, which he sent to Indian Affairs with other letters showing the state of land matters on the Buctouche Reserve, including the quit claim deed signed by Ginnis and Andrew Nicholas. He wanted to know if the commissioners at that time had any authority to order such a survey.[21] His query had the effect he had anticipated: the commissioners believed they had the right to dispose of the land. At the department, nothing could be found bearing on the case. All it could reply to Sargeant was that the former commissioners, Pouliot and Renaud, appear to have received authority to order a survey of the lands comprised in the Buctouche Indian Reserve, but of course no sales could be legally made by the chief, or by any band member, of lands forming part of a reserve.

Symptomatic of Indian Affairs' lack of knowledge about what had transpired was its reply to a request from Auguste Renaud, now no longer a Member of Parliament, for a "certificate" of Pouliot's 16.5 acre lot of reserve land, for which Pouliot would pay the government. In a note drafted for a formal reply, an official seems to have been totally unaware of Renaud's role in the surrender, when he explained that in 1870 the Buctouche Band had surrendered their lands and in 1871 had surrendered a further portion. He described Pouliot's role as no more than a witness to the surrenders as agent.[22]

In 1877 Marin Nicholas and others of the band called on Sargeant about trouble arising from the division of land made by Douglass in November 1869. One of the band, Thomas Nicholas, had given to a William White what Sargeant called the "shape of a Lease."[23] He informed Indian Affairs that this was one of several cases in which parties had got band members to sell their title and those members had left Buctouche, while those remaining were greatly dissatisfied and, Sargeant thought, had good cause for complaint. In the case of Thomas Nicholas, he had left the reserve, but Noel Nicholas had frequently accosted William White and claimed the land as part of the family lot, which he argued White had no right to take from the Nicholas family. Indian Affairs replied that a lease like the copy Sargeant had sent was absolutely void under the Indian Act of 1876. Sargeant was to so notify White "that he must remove from the premises as soon as possible or proceedings to eject him will be instituted with the costs of which he will be charged."[24] It is uncertain whether William White abandoned the land or was ejected, but Noel Nicholas ploughed it for a year or two before abandoning it. The land in question then became a matter of dispute between Tom Nicholas and Tom Noel, which would be ongoing in 1890. White's removal proved to be the only such case among the sixteen lots of remaining reserve land of which non-Natives gained possession. The other fifteen are discussed later.

During the 1878–1879 winter session of the House of Commons, Gilbert Girouard, Conservative Member of Parliament for Kent County, reached an understanding with Indian Affairs to instruct Sargeant to come to Buctouche and "try to arrange about the White settlers upon the Indian Reserve."[25] At age thirty-two, Girouard, a Buctouche merchant, had defeated the incumbent Liberal and three other English-speaking candidates in the 1878 election to become, after Auguste Renaud, the second Acadian to sit in the House of Commons.[26] The Conservatives had won a decisive victory; consequently, Girouard was in a strong political position with regard to Indian Affairs dealing with titles for the squatters. Sargeant's impending visit to the Richibucto Reserve prompted Girouard's letter to Indian Affairs asking for Sargeant to go also to Buctouche. Indian Affairs instructed Sargeant to visit Buctouche and inspect the improvements made by white men, assemble the band in council, and submit to them the advisability of surrendering the lands occupied by white people on the reserve to be sold for their benefit. If he considered it advisable, he was to undertake a surrender.[27]

On August 6, 1880, a tornado swept through the Mi'kmaw village at Buctouche, leaving nothing but ruin behind. Many of the buildings were demolished, and two band members died. Immediately afterwards, four of the Buctouche Band visited Sargeant. As they most desired lumber, Sargeant made a donation of a full carload, which he sent by rail and schooner to the reserve. While the band members were at Chatham, Sargeant found that "they did not seem disposed to do anything in the land matter."[28] After Sargeant arrived at Buctouche in late August, he had an interview with Girouard on a surrender of Buctouche lands. He found the interest Girouard "took in the matter was all for the settlers, they being a portion of his constituency."[29] Girouard considered that payment of one dollar per acre was quite enough for the land; however, Sargeant believed, since lands recently surrendered at Richibucto had been sold for two dollars an acre, that it should be the same for Buctouche. While at Buctouche, Sargeant found the numbers of the band quite small and procured some papers in the shape of leases, which band members had given the settlers some time ago. In closing his report to Indian Affairs, Sargeant noted, "The Indians however have not referred to the matter [a surrender]" since his last visit, otherwise he would have furnished a report.[30]

Indian Affairs immediately instructed Sargeant "to summon the Indians of Buctouche reserve to consider the matter of a surrender as soon as possible."[31] He was to follow the same procedure as at Richibucto, where in August he had secured a surrender. As instructed, Sargeant notified the Buctouche Band that he would meet with them on a certain date. When he arrived at the reserve, they had not assembled; therefore, he could do nothing. Those present did state they were "willing to make a surrender on the same conditions as the tribe on the Richibucto Reserve,"[32] but he found there were difficulties that did not exist at Richibucto. For this visit, Sargeant reported in particular on the survey Renaud and Pouliot had ordered Douglass to undertake in 1869, dividing up the remaining reserve land into ten- and fifteen-acre lots. Sargeant noted that "many of those lots have been sold or leased to white men, and now they are all mixed, which has a bad effect, while on the Richibucto Reserve the settlers and the Mi'kmaq had no trouble with the white men living above and below them."[33] (See Plan of Richibucto on page 95.) He recommended a surrender of the whole reserve be taken and the matter of each lot in possession of white men be represented to Indian Affairs and the matter could then be settled; "I think, [continued] Sargeant, there [are] some lots which the band should retain, in order to keep them protected." Before replying to Sargeant, Deputy Superintendent General Lawrence Vankoughnet had his staff locate the Douglass survey of Buctouche Reserve. He also obtained information about the situation at Buctouche and a sketch, presumably from Girouard—in Ottawa for the parliamentary session—that showed locations of white settlers within and around the reserve lands. In a reply to Sargeant concerning his recommendation of a surrender, Vankoughnet informed Sargeant he had been advised there were only two or three families resident on the Buctouche Reserve, and there was only one white family within the tract occupied by band families. Other white families occupied a distinct portion of the reserve. In what amounted to a reprimand, he told Sargeant, "if he had authorized any person acquainted with the Buctouche Indians to call them together for the purpose of considering a surrender, they would have had little difficulty."[34]

Sargeant, who was among the most wealthy and influential men on the Miramichi and certainly not dependent on his agent's salary, decided to avail himself of a few facts for Vankoughnet. He was aware there were only two or three families who remained on the reserve, but at certain seasons families moved to where they thought they could make more by their work. His understanding of Douglass's survey, which Vankoughnet seems not to have seen, embraced a tract or portion of the reserve divided into lots. Sargeant enclosed a paper he received from the band that showed how many appeared to be interested. The signatories indicated they were willing to sell a portion of the reserve, but they wanted two dollars an acre and five hundred acres of green woodland to be reserved for the band. Although Dominique Bernard's name was the first signatory, he was not designated as a chief. Marin Nicholas was still considered Chief; in June, Sargeant would write Indian Affairs requesting the department order an election for a new chief in Marin Nicholas's place. In Sargeant's presence, Dominique Bernard would be elected by acclamation on August 13, 1880.

Based on Sargeant's "clarification" for Vankoughnet, it would seem the Marin Nicholas party or faction was not prepared to attend an assembly for a surrender, and unlike Pouliot in 1870 and 1871, Sargeant would not proceed without their presence. Sargeant believed a survey was most necessary in order to prevent trouble. The portion of the reserve surveyed in 1869 was the part, he told Vankoughnet, that he was referring to and where "all the trouble has arisen."[35] The signed paper would give Indian Affairs an idea of what the band members wanted to consider a surrender.

Robert Douglass had never been paid for the 1869 survey, seemingly a result of the unorthodox manner in which the survey had been authorized. In February 1880, Douglass requested Girouard intervene on his behalf with Indian Affairs. Officials at Indian Affairs were confused about whether the survey in question was the one showing the land occupied by the band or another portion, which was occupied by white settlers. Because of Girouard's knowledge of the reserve, Indian Affairs asked him to determine which of the plans was the Douglass survey in question. Officials also found Douglass's original bill, which had been lost, and paid it. Douglass told Girouard he would survey the balance of the reserve for Indian Affairs and give a correct plan of the whole, showing the amount of cleared land and if it was occupied.

Douglass received authority to undertake a survey and completed it in August 1881. Sargeant had instructed Douglass to notify him as soon as the plan was finished, so he could go to Buctouche. But Girouard got involved by writing to Indian Affairs to ask whether the plan should be sent to Sargeant or to the department. He was very anxious to settle the matter of titles as soon as possible. Most of the white people had already paid the band members the value of respective lots, and Girouard considered it would be unfair to force them to pay the full value again. He offered to arrange the matter himself by holding a meeting of whites and band members and proposed a committee would be selected to settle the matter.[36]

A serious falling out between Sargeant and Girouard ensued over this issue. When Sargeant came to Buctouche to collect Douglass's survey plan, he made no attempt to meet with Girouard, much to the latter's consternation. Girouard reiterated to Vankoughnet his idea of appointing a committee to settle the matter; he had seen the band members and white people and was certain it could be arranged without difficulty.[37] Meanwhile Sargeant sent Douglass's survey to the department. He said the plan was quite complete, showing the portion occupied by white men with those lots numbered.[38] But the lots that were not numbered and had been set aside for the band were now in possession of white men, because the band members had sold their claim to the lots. They were anxious, though, to retain a portion of the reserve for woodlots. Only a few lots were vacant; all the rest of the lots had a small portion cleared or nothing on them but small bushes. Because there was no chief, and Sargeant needed Indian Affairs to provide instructions on setting aside a portion of the reserve for woodlots, he considered it inadvisable to take a surrender of the lands.

Indian Affairs now directed Sargeant to secure a surrender, there being no objection to re-surveying a woodlot for the band. The band had asked for a 500-acre woodlot; however, as Sargeant had already told Indian Affairs, there were only four vacant lots left—the total of which came to only 142.75 acres. On October 2, 1880, Sargeant visited the Buctouche Band for the third time to obtain a surrender. He found there were two parties, and it was, he reported, difficult to do anything with them.[39] He ascertained they wanted to keep a portion of the land that had been occupied for some time by white men, having in some instances bought the right from band members. He did not think it advisable to execute a surrender. As some of the lots the band wanted were now occupied and others were claimed by white men, he asked, "What is to be done?"[40] Sargeant enclosed a Memorandum of Land, which described the lots the band was eager to retain. There were problems, Sargeant said, in making complete sense of the bounds given in the memorandum. Also, on Douglass's plan, there were lots occupied by band members that were, in fact, occupied by whites. Hence, it is understandable why Sargeant thought it inadvisable to proceed with a surrender on the Buctouche Band's terms.

In reply, Indian Affairs concluded that although the deeds given to white settlers had no legal force, it would not be proper to disturb them in their occupation of lands purchased in good faith from band members. Sargeant was to prepare a list of lands unoccupied by whites that could be retained for the band. It seems he never did this, likely because Girouard now determined to settle the matter directly by reaching an agreement with the band that would be acceptable to the white occupants.

At Buctouche, Girouard decided to take the initiative and settle the matter along the lines he had been advocating. On October 15, 1880, a public notice appeared with reference to "Buctouche Indian Reserve" that called upon "All those interested in or occupying Lots of land on the said 'Reserve' and desirous of obtaining Grants for the same are requested to meet at Mr. Clement M. Cormier's House" at St. Mary's on October 23. The notice also said, "The Indians are also requested to attend the said Meeting." It was signed by Girouard. At the meeting Onezime Leger was appointed chairman and F. E. W. Pouliot, the former agent, became secretary. Girouard explained the meeting's purpose: to settle the land difficulty with the band members for "All those having bought land from the Indians [and] willing to pay to the Government a certain sum of money for the benefit of the Indians and get a Grant of the Land."[41] He advised the nomination of a committee of seven or more "to meet with the Indians and make them an offer and get them to Surrender the land now occupied by the white people as shown by the Plan of Deputy Surveyor Douglass." (See plan on page 118 dated 1869.)

The meeting accepted Girouard's proposition and appointed a committee of nine with Girouard as honorary president. It was decided the committee would meet on October 28 at Girouard's house. Another resolution passed was for a further general meeting to be held on October 26. At that meeting, the report of the last meeting and those from the committee were read and adopted. It was agreed "to pay for the Indian Fund the sum of three hundred dollars ($300.00) to the Federal Government in order to obtain the Grants [to] their lands." By a unanimous vote of the meeting, Girouard was to present the reports of the meeting, the reports of the committee, and also the petition of all those interested in the Buctouche Reserve to Prime Minister Sir John A. Macdonald, in his position as Minister of the Interior. As a result of a committee meeting of October 28, Girouard telegraphed the Deputy Minister of the Interior to inform him a settlement had been reached with the "Indians of Buctouche Reserve by paying them a sum [as] was mutually agreed upon and also having a surrender." Vankoughnet wired back the same day: "No more than ten per cent of purchase money when paid can under the law be distributed among Indians—the balance will be invested for their benefit."[42]

In protest of the sum offered, forty-five occupants of Buctouche Reserve lands signed a petition to the prime minister stating they had been in possession of the lands for a number of years before Confederation and had made great improvements. Before they came into possession of the lands they occupied, "they had paid the Indians on average $2.00 acre, which was more than the New Brunswick government ever asked for."[43] (Although they did not mention payment under the 1844 act, this reference to New Brunswick could only have been to the act.) They considered "in Equity that they are intitled [sic] to get a 'Grant' of the said Lands." They had made an "offer to the Buctouche Indians of $300 in surplus of what they had already paid." They were willing to pay this sum into a fund if the government gave them grants.

Girouard, who was one of the signatories as an "occupant" (he resided in Buctouche but not on reserve land), sent the petition to Prime Minister Macdonald, stating what the petitioners were asking was just and reasonable. He recommended that while waiting for a final settlement between the petitioners and the Buctouche Band, Onezime S. Leger of St. Mary's be appointed as an agent residing at Buctouche who would be authorized to act in the matter. Apparently, Vankoughnet and Girouard discussed such an appointment to deal with the deeds and other papers given to white occupants; however, Leger's appointment was not accepted. After Girouard had returned to Buctouche, Vankoughnet sent a copy of Douglass's survey to Girouard to facilitate his obtaining the required documents, and there was no mention of Leger's involvement.

It seems some of the Buctouche Band remained unhappy with the offer of $300 for their lands. In April, seventeen reiterated their demand made in February 1880 for at least two dollars per acre for all lands sold at Buctouche, "as it is the best tract of land in Kent County."[44] They also pursued the five hundred acres of green woodland to be set apart for them and their children for firewood. Nine of these seventeen band members listed had signed the previous February 1880 petition. On both, Dominique Bernard was listed as chief. On October 10, 1881, however, Girouard reported by telegram to Vankoughnet that the chief and all others were willing to surrender to the white occupants, providing band members received $70 immediately and the balance of $230 from Indian Affairs, apparently, to be disbursed yearly to the band members. Girouard wanted permission to conclude the bargain reached and collect the money from the white occupants.

Girouard secured an agreement on October 19, 1881, whereby the white people agreed with the band members to pay to the Dominion government, for the benefit of the Buctouche Reserve Fund, the sum of $300 over and above all the money previously paid by them to the band members. In return, the band members agreed to surrender all the lands owned or occupied by the white people. The white occupants also agreed to pay band members $50 immediately, and the agreement was contingent on the $300 being paid by the white people to the Dominion government for the benefit of the Buctouche Reserve Fund. For the band members, this agreement was signed by Dominique Bernard, Thomas Noel, Michael Wilmot, John Noel, and Frank Nowat.[45]

Girouard sent to Vankoughnet all vouchers, deeds, and affidavits concerning the Buctouche Indian Reserve and also "a deed or Surrender signed by the Chief and other member of the same tribe, now residing on the said 'reserve,' to the White People occupants of the said 'Reserve.'"[46] He reported to Vankoughnet that on his return to Buctouche, "they, the Indians, met me and they seemed to be very anxious to have the matter settled. After much trouble I at last succeeded." But he had to pay personally the promised immediate payment of $50 to conclude the whole matter. The band also expected to receive 10 percent on the $300 when it was deposited with Indian Affairs.

Girouard inquired if this percentage could be paid to them at Buctouche. Girouard closed his communication with the hope that what he had done was satisfactory as the matter had taken a great deal of his time, and he "was very anxious this should be [a] closed up affair or arrangement." He hoped that Vankoughnet would "decide now upon the within paper[,] I mean the Deed Executed by the Indians."

That this "matter," "agreement," or "surrender" was concluded in such haste suggests Girouard was under considerable political pressure. In the case of the band members, a statement made earlier that some of them were going away suggests they needed money, and fifty dollars immediate payment was sufficient incentive for them to agree. The document signed by the band members bore no resemblance to a surrender as required under the Indian Act. Furthermore, it had every evidence of being locally drafted in great haste and without the involvement of Charles Sargeant as agent. Whatever may have transpired in conversations between Girouard and Vankoughnet, at no time did Indian Affairs give in writing its explicit approval to Girouard's endeavour to reach an agreement with the band on behalf of the white occupants. The defensive tone of Girouard's letter, when forwarding the agreement reached with the band, indicates he knew Indian Affairs might not approve.

As far as lands given up by the band, it was virtually open-ended in that all lands occupied in any way by whites were surrendered at the signing. Moreover, there was no reference to the previous surrenders of 1870 and 1871. After the agreement and supporting documentation arrived at Indian Affairs, J. V. de Boucherville was tasked with comparing these documents with the previous surrenders. He reported: "I have again tried to compare the Deeds and Lots described therein as well as in what purports to be a Deed of Surrender made by the Indians of Buctouche with Lots described in Surrenders No. 122 & 123 [in 1870 and 1871], but could not do so, for the following reasons. 1st the Tracts of Lands Surrendered as per surrenders No. 122 & 123 are described en bloc. 2nd It is impossible for the want of proper[?] data both on plans and Deeds to identify the lots."[47]

As a result, the department sent Surrenders No. 122 and 123 and a "third informal surrender [author's italics] dated 19 October" to Robert Douglass with a request that he do a comparison by referring to his plans and field notes.[48] The department wanted to know if the lots purporting to be surrendered by the instrument of October 19 were covered by the deeds in Surrenders No. 122 and 123, and whether any lands included in the deed of October 19 had been left out of those same surrenders. If any had been left out, Douglass was to state which ones.

Douglass replied that he had written the description of the first surrender on the margin of the second, No. 123, and for the October 19 deed or surrender, he wrote a description on the last page of the copy sent to him. Douglass offered no clarification as to what lands were to be reserved for the band, though in a sidebar he broke down the total acreage: of 3,278 acres 2,926 acres were held by whites and 352 acres were held by the band. De Boucherville reported that he had examined the descriptions of the lands "comprised in the surrenders made by the Indians to the Crown of Buctouche Reserve & found that the said description covers the land as shown on the plan made" by Deputy Surveyor Douglass.[49] From this statement, Indian Affairs apparently concluded that all lots claimed by white occupants under the 1881 agreement had been previously surrendered. It never proceeded to seek an order-in-council for what it considered "an informal surrender." Payment of the $300 for the Buctouche Reserve Fund was received in April 1882. Beginning in August 1882, the department would issue seventy-seven patents for a total of 3,215.9 acres.

As for the Richibucto Reserve, Sargeant reminded Indian Affairs of the crucial difference between it and Buctouche Reserve lands: at Buctouche many of the lots had been sold to white men and consequently were mixed up, which had a bad effect, whereas on the Richibucto Reserve the settlers and band members had no trouble with the white men living above and below them. (See Plan of Richibucto on page 95.) Presumably, by "bad effect" Sargeant meant there had been trouble on the Buctouche Reserve between band members and squatters. He noted the Richibucto Band resided in a single compact location. Moreover, there was a great disparity in reserve populations: at Richibucto the population was 248, while at Buctouche it was.[50]

In 1876 Sargeant had written Indian Affairs that Chief Louis Nicholas and a few of the principal members of the Richibucto Band had visited him to discuss obtaining the means to construct a church. They proposed to surrender all their reserve of 5,658 acres and use the money to build a church. As far as could be known, there were a few hundred vacant acres and several hundred more on which white men were settled, many of whom had no grant. Some of those had simply squatted; others had partially paid under the provisions of the 1844 act.[51]

Although Indian Affairs replied favourably, no surrender took place. Three years later, the resident missionaries on the reserve informed the department that some thirty-seven white people had been resident on the reserve for periods varying between five and fifty years. Most admitted they had no grants. The department then wrote Sargeant that the Richibucto Band should realize some benefit from the sale of these lands at two dollars an acre and sent him a surrender form. In September 1879, Sargeant went to Richibucto, where he first assembled Chief Noel Millia and principal men. A description of the lands to be surrendered was read and interpreted. The surrender included virtually all the lands occupied by white persons. There being no judge in Kent County, it was necessary for Chief Millia and others to go to Northumberland County to swear before Judge Edward Williston (a former commissioner) that the surrender had been freely assented to at a council assembled for the purpose by a majority of band members.[52]

The 1870 and 1871 surrenders of Buctouche Reserve lands, as undertaken by the MP for Kent County Auguste Renaud and recently appointed agent Francis Pouliot, turned out to be a complete fiasco. Neither had any knowledge of the requirements of the Indian Act or of the critical importance of a complete and accurate survey. Instead, what Pouliot had Deputy Surveyor Douglass produce reduced the reserve lands from 4,665 acres to 350 acres. The document that passed as a surrender ignored the provisions of the Indian Act in every particular. John Weldon again demonstrated, this time as a Justice of the Supreme Court, his animosity towards Buctouche Band members. He, more than anyone else, had to know the law regarding surrenders. In submitting the surrender document to the Privy Council, Indian Affairs at least acted in accordance with the law. Because no proper survey had been undertaken, confusion persisted over white squatters occupying reserve lands.

After Gilbert Girouard became MP for Kent County, he devised a scheme that involved white squatters paying a sum into a fund managed by Indian Affairs. The confusion over occupation of reserve lands was never truly sorted out, other than Indian Affairs apparently concluding that all the lots claimed by white occupants under the 1881 agreement—negotiated by Girouard between the whites and Indians—had been previously surrendered. The department never proceeded to seek an order-in-council for what it considered "an informal surrender," a term Indian Affairs first used in correspondence with Robert Douglass in January 1882.

If departmental officials believed the "informal surrender" meant they could conveniently forget about white squatters occupying Buctouche Reserve lands, they were sadly mistaken. Among the squatters were Sylvain U. Cormier and his three sons who jointly lived on one hundred acres of the Buctouche Reserve.[53] At a date before the 1881 surrender, Cormier mortgaged the land to a person named Gallant, who then obtained a grant to the one hundred acres, under the great seal of Canada, dated August 11, 1882, and described as being part of the Buctouche Indian Reserve. The land in question then came into the possession of a man named D. Burk who brought an action in 1889 to have the Cormier family ejected from the land.

At the trial in September 1889, a verdict was entered for Burk, but with leave to the defendant, Cormier, to enter a nonsuit (stoppage of a suit by a judge when the plaintiff fails to make out a legal case or bring sufficient evidence) if the court should be of the opinion that the title to the land—the Indian Reserve—was in the provincial government; the case depended on that question. In short, the grant of 1882 to Gallant could be questionable.

On June 4, 1890, George F. Gregory moved for a nonsuit—or failing that a new trial—on the grounds that Burk, as plaintiff, could not obtain any benefit from the 1882 Dominion of Canada grant of the land in dispute. He cited the case of *St. Catherine's Milling & Lumber Co. v. the Queen (1)* as placing "the matter beyond doubt, that the title to the Indian Reserves in this Province, vests in the Provincial Government."[54]

In October 1890, in the case of *Burk v. Cormier*, four justices of the Supreme Court gave their opinions on whether the verdict in favour of Burk as plaintiff should stand. Justices Tuck and Wetmore held that in the case it was "not necessary to consider the question of which government has the title to Indian Reserve lands in this Province."[55] Thus, a nonsuit must be refused, and the verdict for Burk should stand.

Chief Justice Sir John Allen, however, went into considerable detail discussing the relevant sections of the British North America Act. In the case of the *St. Catherine's Milling & Lumber Co. v. Reg. (1)* heard before the Supreme Court of Canada, and on appeal before the Judicial Committee of the Privy Council, Allen concurred with arguments advanced relating to provincial rights. Moreover, he held they were "stronger" in the case of New Brunswick.[56] According to Allen, there had never been "any doubt in this Province, that the title to the land in the Province reserved for the use of Indians, remained—in the Crown, the Indians having at most, a right of occupancy."

Allen held that, after Confederation, when the Dominion Parliament legislated on the subject, the "right of the Crown, as represented by the Government of this Province, to manage and sell the lands reserved for the use of the Indians, remained in the Executive Government of this Province."[57] His fellow justice Fraser agreed. As the other two justices had not given an opinion on this question, Allen's ruling stood. Chapter 7 addresses how this ruling of the New Brunswick Supreme Court would shortly come to haunt officials of Indian Affairs.

# NOTES

1.  An Act for the Organization of the Department of the Secretary of State of Canada, and for Management of Indian and Ordnance Lands, Statutes of Canada, 31 Vic., 1868, sec. 3, cap. 42.

2.  Hector Langevin to R. Sutton, October 26, 1867, RS637/29a, PANB.

3.  R. Sutton to Hector Langevin, December 2, 1867, RS637/29a, PANB.

4.  Circular, Department of Secretary of State, Ottawa, November 26, 1868, Indian Affairs Correspondence (Minister's Office Records), RS105, file 1860–1869, PANB.

5.  The Parliamentary Companion for 1872 provides no information other than Renaud was the member for Kent County. He was defeated in 1872 and in 1885 he becomes Buctouche's postmaster.

6.  Copy of Langevin's Recommendation to the Privy Council, July 2, 1869, RG10, vol. 723, p. 126, DAANDC.

7.  Hector Langevin to Joseph Howe, October 28, 1869, RG10, vol. 384, pp. 367–8, DAANDC.

8.  A. Renaud to H. L. Langevin, December 20, 1869, RG10, vol. 384, pp. 365–6.

9.  Indian Reserves in the Province of New Brunswick, Annual Report of the Department of Interior for the Year Ended 30th June 1874 (1875), Pt 2, p. 100.

10. Petition signed by Chief Marin Nicholas to Governor-General Sir John Young, undated but enclosed with Livingston to Howe, December 28, 1870, RG10, vol. 318, B1, 320, p. 113199, DAANDC.

11. "Surrender of Buctouche Indians," Canada Indian Treaties and Surrenders (1894), vol. 1, no. 122, pp. 280–1.

12. Ibid., p. 281

13. I am grateful for the assistance of John Conn, NSLS, of Thompson Conn, Nova Scotia Land Surveyors, Halifax, for a detailed analysis of the description of the lands to be surrendered, which is only briefly summarized here. All conclusions are mine.

14. F. E. W. Pouliot to Joseph Howe, January 2, 1871, RG10, vol. 380, pp. 223–4.

15. Memorandum attached to Order in Council, P.C. 683, March 24, 1871, Registry Document × 014664, Surrender No. 122, DAANDC.

16. Joseph Howe to F. E. W. Pouliot, April 1871, RG10, vol. 381, p. 501, DAANDC.

17. Surrender No. 123, Indian Treaties and Surrenders, pp. 281–2.

18. Joseph Howe to F. E. M. Pouliot, December 10, 1869, RG10, vol. 529, pp. 151–2, DAANDC.

19. For a biographical sketch of Sargeant, see W. D. Hamilton, Dictionary of Miramichi Biography: Biographical Sketches of Men and Women who Played a Part in the Public Life on the Miramichi Northumberland County, New Brunswick, Canada (privately published, 1997), p. 62.

20. Charles Sargeant to Dominique White, December 29, 1874, RG10, vol. 1,949, file 4,337, DAANDC.

21. Charles Sargeant to Deputy Minister E. A. Meredith of the Department of Interior, January 26, 1875, RG10, vol. 1,969, file 4,337, DAANDC.

22. A. Renaud to Superintendent General of Indian Affairs, September 6, 1875, RG10, vol. 1,969, file 5,331, DAANDC, and note attached to Renaud's letter.

23. Charles Sargeant to E. A. Meredith, September 13, 1877, RG10, vol. 1,949, file 4,337, DAANDC.

24. Department to Charles Sargeant, September 20, 1877, RG10, vol. 1,949, file 4,337, DAANDC.

25. G. A. Girouard to Lawrence Vankoughnet, Deputy Superintendent General, July 12, 1879, RG10, vol. 7,612, file 12,162, DAANDC.

26. For Girouard see Della Stanley, "Gilbert-Anselme Girouard," *DCB*, vol. 11, pp. 350–1. Renaud was born in France and was not Acadian, though he has been claimed as such. Girouard died of tuberculosis in 1885, at age thirty-eight.

27. Indian Affairs to Charles Sargeant, August 2, 1879, RG10, vol. 7,612, file 12,162, DAANDC.

28. Charles Sargeant to Lawrence Vankoughnet, January 21, 1880, RG10, vol. 7,621, file 12,162, DAANDC.

29. Ibid.

30. Ibid.

31. Indian Affairs to Charles Sargeant, January 28, 1880, RG10, vol. 7,612, file 12,162, DAANDC.

32. Sir Edmund Head to Attorney General J. A. Street, July 12, 1851, MG69 A1, pp. 344-5, LAC. The reference to staying the sale was a notice that had appeared in the *Royal Gazette* on June 11, 1851 for the auction of the 350 acres, the leased lands in question. The sale, however, went ahead and William Chandler purchase the land.

33. Charles Sargeant to Lawrence Vankoughnet, February 17, 1880, RG10, vol. 7,612, file 12,162, DAANDC.

34. Lawrence Vankoughnet to Charles Sargeant, March 18, 1880, RG10, vol. 7,612, file 12,162, DAANDC.

35. J. A. Street to D. S. Kerr, July 26, 1851, MG9, A1, vol. 40, 346, LAC.

36. G. A. Girouard to L. Vankoughnet, August 7, 1880, RG10, vol. 7,612, file 12,162, DAANDC.

37. G. A. Girouard to L. Vankoughnet, August 17, 1880, RG 10, vol. 7,612, file 12,162, DAANDC.

38. Charles Sargeant to L. Vankoughnet, August 25, 1880, RG10, vol. 7,612, file 12,162. DAANDC.

39. Charles Sargeant to L. Vankoughnet, October 15, 1880, RG10, vol. 7,612, file 12,162, DAANDC.

40. Public Notice, RG10, vol. 7,612, file 12,162, DAANDC.

41. Minutes of a Meeting Called for October 23, 1880, RG10, vol. 7,612, file 12,162, DAANDC.

42. L. V. Vankoughnet to G. A. Girouard, October 28, 1880, RG10, vol. 7,612, file 12,162, DAANDC.

43. To the Right Honourable Sir John A. Macdonald, Minister of the Interior, petition signed and dated November 26, 1880, witnessed by F. E. W. Pouliot, RG10, vol. 7,612, file 12,162, DAANDC.

44. Extract of a Petition from Buctouche Indians, April 4, 1881, RG10, vol. 7,612, file 12,162, DAANDC.

45. Surrender No. 48, Registry Document × 014680, October 23, 1881, DAANDC.

46. G. A. Girouard to L. Vankoughnet, October 31, 1881, RG10, vol. 7,612, file 12,162, DAANDC.

47. J. V. De Boucherville, November 23, 1881, RG10, vol. 7,612, file 12,162, DAANDC.

48. Indian Affairs to Robert Douglass, January 11, 1882, RG10, vol. 7,612, file 12,162, DAANDC.

49. J. V. De Boucherville to Deputy Superintendent General, April 24, 1882, vol. 7,612, file 12,62, DAANDC.

50. Charles Sargeant to Lawrence Vankoughnet, January 21, 1880, RG10, vol. 7621, file 12162.

51. Sargeant to E. A. Meredith, November 25, 1876, RG10, vol. 90, file 7,324, DAANDC.

52. "Surrender of Richibucto Indians," *Canada Indian Treaties and Surrenders* (1894), vol. 2, no. 172, pp. 76–77.

53. Burk v. Cormier (1890), 30 N.B.R. 142 (N.B.S.C.).

54. Ibid. The lawyer for the plaintiff had argued that under the British North America Act the Dominion Government had absolute control of the lands. For *St. Catherine's Milling & Lumber Co. v. The Queen (1888)*, 14 A. C. 46, see Richard H. Bartlett, *Indian Reserves in the Atlantic Provinces of Canada* (Saskatoon: University of Saskatchewan, Native Law Centre, 1986), 37–38. See also Nancy E. Ayers, "Aboriginal Rights in the Maritimes," *Canadian Native Law Reporter 2,* (1984): 10.

55. *Burk v. Cormier (1890)*, 30 N.B.R., p. 145.

56. Ibid., p. 149.

57. Ibid. When discussing Indian interest in reserve lands, Richard H. Bartlett, in *Indian Reserves in the Atlantic Provinces of Canada*, emphasized the importance of Allen's judgment, pp. 41 and 51.

# CHAPTER 7

# AGENT JAMES FARRELL'S 1892
# SURRENDER AT TOBIQUE

At the time Canada assumed responsibility for Indians, most of Tobique's thirty-seven families resided at Tobique Point, on the north side of the Tobique River. Some individuals, such as Newell Moulton, had as much as twenty acres of good farmland cleared. Many residents had teams of horses and some cattle.[1] During the winter, a good number still continued to hunt, but in the next decade the number would drop significantly in the wake of game depletion.[2] In the spring, men found employment in rafting logs, though apparently only a few worked at lumbering; the number would later increase. Fishing for salmon had been a source of profit and a valuable means of subsistence, until the province passed a law prohibiting catching salmon by spearing—the accustomed method at Tobique. The Department of Indian Affairs Report for 1874 commented, the "Indians were prejudiced against any other form of fishing, and also being unable to procure nets, they feel and know that they are deprived of an important source of living."[3]

On the south side of the Tobique River, from The Narrows down to opposite Tobique Village, settlers occupied twelve lots. Four of the twelve lots had been sold under the 1844 act, but money was still owed for them; outright squatters resided on the remainder. Further down and facing onto the Saint John River to Tobique Rocks, twenty or more lots were occupied, of which seven of the settlers had received New Brunswick grants. For the Tobique Maliseet, their major concerns were the continuing squatter encroachments and not receiving stumpage money. They petitioned the new Dominion government in March 1868, stating their reserve had been formed about the year 1800 of twenty thousand acres, but they had derived "little or no benefit from the reserve on the lower side of the Tobique, as it had been taken possession of by white settlers who farmed the land and converted the timber to their own use."[4] Indian Affairs appointed William Fisher in 1873 as South-Western Visiting Superintendent, stationed in Fredericton. Fisher soon found out Tobique's main concern related to stumpage, which led to considerable correspondence with the department. By 1877, with the concurrence of the Tobique Band, Fisher would sell at public auction rights to cut timber on the reserve, and the money obtained was deposited in the band's account at Indian Affairs.[5] There remained, however, the occupation of reserve lands on the south side of the Tobique River by two groups: those who had purchased lots but failed to complete payments and outright squatters. Fisher visited the Crown Lands office in Fredericton and found there "remained upwards of $1,200.00 due by the purchasers to the Indian department."[6] Indian Affairs instructed Fisher to call upon the purchasers to pay up arrears of principal and interest; moreover, it was not the intention of government to remit payment of any portion of the purchase money due on lands that formed part of the Tobique Reserve. Fisher did his best to collect outstanding amounts, but he met with near total refusal.

After Moses Craig succeeded Fisher as agent in 1879, he reported he had been approached by a number of those in arrears to have the department allow them to buy their lands by paying the balance owed without paying any interest. Although Indian Affairs provided him with a list of those in arrears—fourteen in all—Craig had no more success than his predecessor had. Not for the last time, John Costigan, in his capacity as the parliamentary member for Victoria County, wrote the Superintendent General of Indian Affairs that agent Moses Craig, whom Costigan had recommended to become agent, had informed him the "Tobique Indians were willing the government should sell that portion of their Reserve being on the south side of the Tobique River, except that part which they hold as hay land."[7] Costigan wanted Indian Affairs to authorize Craig to have the hay lands surveyed that "the Indians wished to retain and to obtain a surrender from the Indians of the lands on south side of Tobique."[8]

However, when Craig, at the department's order, summoned a council to obtain the views of the Tobique Band on the proposed surrender, he had to report they unanimously refused to surrender any land. Their objection, he said, was that a number of parties living on the reserve were in arrears, and they would not surrender any more until that was paid up.[9] They made their opposition known further by sending a petition to the governor-general, describing how squatters had in the past taken possession of the lands allotted them, and:

> where as squatters are still taking possession of said lands, and will in time if measures are not taken to prevent same unjustly acquire possession of the best and larger portions of such land leaving little or nothing for your petitioners. And whereas it is but just and right that your petitioners should have compensation for the land so appropriated or be relegated [sic] to their right thereto…pray that your Honorable Body will take such measures as will secure to us compensation for our said lands so appropriated as aforesaid, and also such Measures as will prevent any further occupation or appropriation of the lands of your Petitioners.[10]

After John Costigan became a Cabinet minister, he sought again to forward the cause of the settlers and squatters by writing Prime Minister Sir John A. Macdonald, in his capacity also as superintendent general of Indian Affairs, on the question of terms for settlers purchasing Tobique Reserve lands. Costigan's letter led to a memorandum, prepared by the deputy superintendent general, for Macdonald. On Costigan's plea that occupiers of reserve land should not be charged interest, Lawrence Vankoughnet held that they should pay interest, "considering that they have been in occupation of the land for so many years, and the Indians have laid [sic] out of the money for that length of time."[11]

Whether or not at Macdonald's order, Indian Affairs sent J. V. De Boucherville, clerk of land sales, to Tobique for the purpose of settling the matters in dispute between the department and the white settlers. The hope was that the result of his investigations would allow the department to finally settle the vexed questions in connection with the settlers on the Tobique Reserve. De Boucherville and Moses Craig met with the settlers at Perth, where De Boucherville explained the reserve lands could not be treated as Crown lands, and the lands were held in trust by the government for the Maliseet. The settlers had not complied with the conditions of sale originally made to them by the New Brunswick government, and they had to pay interest on arrears due.[12] De Boucherville had the white settlers and squatters on the surveyed portion of the Tobique Reserve sign a Memorandum of Agreement, reflecting what had been agreed to on payments.[13]

Not until 1888, however, did Indian Affairs again take up the issue of squatting at Tobique. James Farrell had just taken over responsibility as agent from

Moses Craig. The department sent to him a copy of De Boucherville's 1883 report, with instructions to notify the settlers and squatters that unless the land they occupied was paid for in full by January 31, 1889, the department would take steps to cancel settlers' sales and to eject the squatters from the reserve.[14] Farrell made a number of determined attempts to obtain the outstanding amounts, but had little success. He recommended the department proceed by process of law.

Elijah Lovely and Daniel Wilmot Larlee, who jointly occupied a lot, absolutely refused to make any payments. After Farrell reported another failure to make either of the two pay, Indian Affairs requested the Department of Justice begin proceedings. Larlee told Farrell that George F. Gregory, a leading lawyer in Fredericton who had acted for the defendant Cormier in *Burk v. Cormier*, had advised Larlee to refuse payment. Gregory had told him also, "your [Indian Affairs patent of 1882 to Gallant; see above] was not worth the paper it was written upon."[15] Gregory had also written Michael Adams, the justice agent designated to pursue the case. In Adams's opinion, the Dominion government could not sell or collect for the land, and their grant would be valueless because of the decisions in *St. Catherine's Milling & Lumber Co v. the Queen* and that of a New Brunswick Supreme Court in *Burk v. Cormier*.[16]

Gregory also wrote Sir John A. Macdonald in his capacity as Superintendent General of Indian Affairs. After stating he was representing Lovely and Larlee, he asked Macdonald to "advise [him] the present claim (by Lovely and Larlee) is distinguishable in principle from the two cases mentioned and sought to be enforced."[17] On behalf of Macdonald, Indian Affairs replied that the Indian Reserve had been handed over to the Dominion.[18] Gregory in turn replied that he was aware of what the department was claiming, but he regretted that:

> your letter does not frankly and squarely deal with these decisions
> [*St. Catherine's Milling & Lumber Co v. the Queen* and *Burk v Cormier*].
> The object of my letter was to call your attention to the adjudicated
> cases in which the same question as it seems to me was involved
> and to get a view of the department on those cases in relation to
> the claims made upon my clients. If however, nothing else will be
> accepted as conclusive but as repetition of those decisions in fresh
> suits to be brought I suppose my clients will have to bear with the
> annoyance of suits. I was aware that the land was supposed to be part
> of the Tobique Indian Reserve but it is not a fact that it was handed
> over to the Dominion by the Provincial government at the date of
> Confederation. Whatever right the Dominion has acquired is derived

*Wolastoqew [Maliseet] Guides at Camp at Two Brooks, New Brunswick*, ca. 1862.
William Francis Ganong Collection 1987.17.416, New Brunswick Museum, Saint John, NB.

from the BNA Act and it has been decided by the highest court [Judicial Committee of the Privy Council] having jurisdiction in the matter that the Dominion can not legally sell or grant the lands.[19]

When the department had a warrant prepared for Lovely's and Larlee's removal, the superintendent general refused to sign after John Costigan intervened on their behalf. Costigan again interceded with the minister to have the department accept payment by Lovely and Larlee of the principal of one dollar per acre and interest only from January 1, 1890.[20] Both eventually paid and received their letters patent in March 1895.

By 1890 the population at Tobique numbered 187 individuals, who were noted for being very industrious.[21] Many were employed by the owners of timber limits, from whom they received lucrative wages. During the winters forty or more of the young and able-bodied men were engaged in the woods. In the spring they were employed in stream driving, rafting, and the running of logs. Building improvements were visible on the reserve. There was a new hall, built at a cost of $800; a new $150 organ had been installed in it, at the band's own expense. New houses were under construction, costing at least $1,000. This new construction, along with repairs, painting, shingling, and interior improvements to the church—payment of which was provided from the band's interest funds—coupled with the neat and painted dwellings of its inhabitants, made Tobique Reserve one of the prettiest situated on the Saint John River, according to James Farrell.[22]

There seems to have been a general satisfaction on the reserve with conditions. Although the continued occupation of reserve lands south of the Tobique River remained a sore point and for Indian Affairs, the refusal of occupants to pay seemed an insoluble problem. With all the lots fronting on the Saint John River occupied, squatters were occupying lands in the interior, which previous surveys had done no more than divide into large blocks. Until the blocks were subdivided into lots, there was no possibility of dealing with the squatting. The department considered that nearly the whole of the reserve south of the Tobique River was to be held for sale, but no sales could take place until there was a surrender of the unoccupied lands.[23]

In an attempt to sort out matters, W. A. Austin, surveyor and chief draftsman in the department, prepared in 1892 a new plan, incorporating past surveys (see Plan of Tobique Reserve on page 102). In the same year, Farrell prepared an up-to-date statement of sales. According to his calculations, there were twenty-six defaulters still owing for their lots, of whom ten he classed as squatters. Three sales dated to before Confederation, while the remaining sixteen had been made by him and previous agents. For the department, however, there remained George Gregory's reference to the *Burk v. Cormier* ruling. Gregory had drawn Farrell's attention to the ruling in his capacity as counsel for Rainsforth Lovely, who had inherited his share of the jointly held lot. Farrell had sent to the department a newspaper report of the judgment, commenting that it was hoped the "judgement will not affect the further collecting of arrears from squatters and settlers occupying Tobique Indian lands."[24] In referring Farrell's letter and newspaper report to the Department of Justice, Vankoughnet noted that because the court had ruled the "beneficial interest[s] in the Indian reserves were vested in the Legislature of the Province," the department saw this as a most important question.[25] It appeared the decision could involve the "rights of Indians in every province except Manitoba to the land that formed at one time part of their reserves, but which had been placed on the market for disposal in the Indians' interest."

Moreover, it also appeared there had been no formal surrenders taken by New Brunswick and Nova Scotia of the lands that had been sold. Vankoughnet had been an official in Indian Affairs since the formation of the department, but it seems that no one in Indian Affairs knew that neither province had an act similar to the Province of Canada's, and they didn't know of New Brunswick's 1844 act, though agents had been reporting about lands sold before Confederation.

Deputy Minister of Justice R. W. Sedgewick replied on behalf of his department. Because the New Brunswick case "went off upon another ground," his department considered there was not any call for action at the present time.[26] However, he was authorized to state that a grant of land issued by the Government of Canada conferred good title, notwithstanding the judgement of the Supreme Court of New Brunswick. If Indian Affairs believed that there was no further need for concern, it soon learned otherwise. Within two months of the New Brunswick Supreme Court's decision the province's lieutenant-governor forwarded to the secretary of state in Ottawa a minute approved by the province's executive council, with reference to the sale of the reserve at Tobique.

The document revealed the council had contemplated for some time approaching the Dominion Government to take measures that would lead to the opening up of this tract of land for settlement. As the present time seemed "opportune," the executive council had chosen to submit a brief statement of its views on the subject of the reserve lands.[27] The minute described the reserve as fifteen or sixteen thousand acres, of which less than five hundred acres was believed to be occupied by the "Indian inhabitants." The remainder was wilderness, much of it cutover but otherwise unused. The reserve's location was most detrimental to the surrounding country and greatly hindered settlement in the immediate neighbourhood.[28] Because the land was suitable for settlement, it was believed homes for at least 120 families could be laid out. The New Brunswick government was prepared, if the "Indian title to these lands could be extinguished, and the title thereto acquired by the province upon reasonable terms, to take responsibility of arranging for the introduction of a body of immigrants."

If the tract reverted to the province, the government would pay fifty cents an acre for the lands fit for settlement. The proceeds realized would yield a higher interest return than was now received from the tract in its present condition, besides removing what the executive council deemed an eyesore from this section of the country, with respect to its settlement. It proposed "leaving 500 acres to be occupied by the Indians," which would be located so as to leave lots fronting on the Tobique River and in the neighbourhood of the Tobique River Bridge, for white settlement. Finally, the minute stated that the "province wished it understood that it was not waiving any rights in respect of these lands, which upon proper construction of the British North America Act might be found to remain in the Government of this Province."[29]

On receipt of the minute, the Privy Council office forwarded it to Indian Affairs for reply. However, Vankoughnet sent it to the land branch with a request for information, where, by mistake he later claimed, a clerk simply filed it. In a letter of apology to the superintendent general, Vankoughnet explained that the minute had escaped his attention until he was reminded of it by the Privy Council over a year later. A report on the minute was hurriedly drafted and forwarded to the Privy Council office. New Brunswick's request came before Cabinet in March 1892, when the superintendent general submitted for consideration a report on the minute.

The department's report took issue with nearly every aspect of New Brunswick's proposal. On the reserve's acreage, the report stated that originally the tract had consisted of 18,394 acres of which 2,113 acres had been sold, with the quantity remaining unsold being 16,281 acres. The report also took issue with New Brunswick's minute on the amount of acreage needed by the Tobique Band. Because the band consisted of 189 individuals, or around forty-eight families, with about four individuals to each family, the report considered that such families should not be limited to less than one hundred acres each; consequently, the extent of the reserve needed by the forty-eight families would be around five thousand acres. This would leave 11,281 acres for sale, if it were decided to proceed with sales.

With regard to New Brunswick's belief that homes for at least 120 white families could be laid out, the report noted that after the five thousand acres for the "Indians had been deducted," it was improbable that so large a number of immigrant families as the minute mentioned could be accommodated on the tract in question. As for New Brunswick undertaking to settle the proposed immigrants, the department's report to Cabinet commented it was desirable that the "Indians should, if possible, be persuaded to relinquish title to all of the lands, excepting the 5,000 acres to be reserved for them and their posterity"; there was no reason "why these lands should not be disposed of through the Indian Agent at Fredericton in the same manner as other surrendered lands on their reserve have already been sold and which are now occupied by settlers."[30]

The report from Cabinet also disputed the sale of lands at fifty cents an acre, as suggested by New Brunswick, noting the price received by Indian Affairs on the same tract, of which the "Indian title had already been surrendered" and which had been sold by the Department of Indian Affairs, had averaged $1.15 per acre. If the residue of these lands were brought into market, there seemed to be nothing preventing that department from obtaining as high, if not a higher, price for the same.

*Wolastoqew [Maliseet] Guides and Canoes along the Tobique River, New Brunswick,* ca. 1862.
William Francis Ganong Collection 1987.17.418, New Brunswick Museum, Saint John, NB.

In consideration of the facts given in the report, the superintendent general recommended to his cabinet colleagues it would be advisable to endeavour to obtain "from the Indians a surrender of all the land remaining not surrendered in the Tobique reserve," excepting five thousand acres, which would be held "for the Indians and their posterity."[32] Cabinet accepted the recommendation, and the secretary of state was authorized to forward a copy of the resulting minute to the New Brunswick government, once it was approved by the governor-general in council, which was done on March 4, 1892.[33] Whether or not the superintendent general knew it, the report deliberately misrepresented circumstances surrounding the selling of Tobique Reserve lands before and after Confederation, as the following analysis of the report details.

When, in his correspondence, George Gregory had pressed his argument that the *St. Catherine's Milling & Lumber Co v. the Queen* and *Burk v. Cormier* cases meant the Dominion government could not sell or collect for Tobique Reserve land, Indian Affairs had replied it claimed this right because the Tobique Reserve had been handed over to the Dominion by the provincial government at Confederation. As Gregory noted, the department had not dealt "frankly and squarely" with the court decisions of the two cited cases.[34] When New Brunswick, in its minute of December 19, 1890, made reference to the possibility of it having rights in respect of Tobique Reserve lands, the superintendent general, in his report to Cabinet, did not deal with this aspect of the minute, though he dealt with all other matters raised by New Brunswick.

In the superintendent's key recommendation of his report to Cabinet, he proposed the surrender of the reserve's southern portion, with the remaining recommendations following from it. He stated that for lands already sold in the southern portion, "Indian title had already been surrendered."[35] However, from 1873 to 1892 the department had sold twenty-nine lots without a surrender, and it had issued letters patent for fifteen lots before 1892 to those who completed their payments. When, at the instigation of John Costigan, Moses Craig had summoned a council at Tobique in October 1880 to determine if there was support for a surrender, it was "unanimously refused."[36]

Moreover, the Department of Indian Affairs had sent a copy of the March 4, 1892, order-in-council to James Farrell because he had inquired whether there was any record of previous surrenders. In his reply to Farrell's inquiry, Vankough-net had stated that in the matter of the March 4 order-in-council "relating to the settlement of Indian Reserve lands at Tobique, I have to inform you, that so far as can be ascertained, no surrender was ever obtained of the portion of the Tobique Reserve south of the Tobique River."[37] At the time of Confedera-tion, Vankoughnet said the New Brunswick government had handed over the reserve to the Dominion government with a schedule showing a number of sales made of land south of the Tobique River, and Department of Indian Affairs had continued to sell to the squatters there on the same basis, but there was no reason why, Vankoughnet said in conclusion, that "a surrender should not be taken of the portion south of the River, as well as the portion north of the River less 5,000 acres."[38]

That there had been no surrenders was further confirmed in 1898, when John Costigan sought from Indian Affairs "a copy of [the] Treaty with the Tobique Indians."[39] W. A. Orr, officer in charge of the land and timber branch, reported to the department's secretary that Tobique Reserve had been handed over after Confederation by the provincial government and "this department carried out sales entered into by the local authorities as well as making subsequent sales of portions of the reserve not occupied by the Indians, situate south of the Tobique River."[40]

As deputy superintendent, Vankoughnet would have approved the wording for the minister's report to Cabinet on the New Brunswick 1890 minute. His correspondence shows that he was familiar with the Tobique file and should have known that there had been no surrenders under the Indian Act. The inclu-sion of the words in the superintendent's report to Cabinet—"Indian title had already been surrendered" and in the recommendation to obtain "a surrender of all the land remaining unsurrendered in the Tobique reserve"[41]—did not correctly portray the true situation relating to Tobique. There had never been any surrender(s) under the Indian Act. For over twenty years, the department had sold lots and issued letters patent for Tobique Reserve lands in absence of any surrender. The department's justification for selling and issuing patents lay in its claim that "the land in question as part of the Indian Reserve was handed over to the Dominion by the Provincial Government at the date of Confederation."[42] But it was just this claim that New Brunswick was, at least implicitly, contesting in 1890 and that George Gregory had explicitly called into question.

As mentioned, in his letter of May 30, 1892, Vankoughnet had told Farrell though no surrender had ever been obtained for the sale of Tobique lands, "there is no reason why a surrender should not be taken of the portion south of the River as well as the portion north of the River less 5,000 acres."[43] Farrell seems to have assumed this was authorization to undertake a surrender.

The regulations governing surrenders were first defined in 1876. Over time changes were made. By 1892, a completed surrender document consisted of two printed forms with set wordings applicable to all surrenders and spaces for insertion of the particulars of each surrender. Form 65 contained a description of what was being surrendered and by whom. The surrendered lands were entrusted to the department to sell and credited with interest "to us and our descendants as to the Department of Indian Affairs may deem right." This was followed by a witnessing clause to be signed by the agent and the list of signatories and dated. Form 66, annexed to Form 65, required the agent and a band member, usually the chief, to sign that the surrender document had been assented to "by a majority of male members of the said Band of Indians of [band name inserted in blank space] the full age of twenty-one years then present." Their signatures had to be witnessed by a magistrate and dated.

Farrell was certainly unaware of the need to use Forms 65 and 66, because the department never sent him the forms required under the act. Instead, Farrel seems to have retained the services of a local lawyer to draft three separate documents, which in total took the form of a property sale indenture between the Tobique Band and the Department of Indian Affairs. The first document contained the wording for the release and surrender of the described lands to the Crown by the Tobique Band. In part it read: The indenture witnessed that the band had released and surrendered as required under the Indian Act a certain part of the Tobique Reserve at the confluence of the Tobique and Saint John rivers and a tract of two hundred acres on the southern side abutting on the Tobique River.

The second document was witness of the male members of the band who were of the full age of twenty-one years old and Chief Frank Francis. In addition, seventeen others were allegedly also signatories, with all their names written out and an "X" made between the first and surnames. There were two exceptions, "S. F. Francis Francis" [sic] and John Moulton, for whom no Xs appear. In the case of Chief Francis his name was written Francis "X" Francis. A following document was an affidavit by James Farrell that he had been duly authorized by the superintendent of Indian Affairs to attend a meeting of Indians on Tobique Reserve.[44] This of course was blatantly untrue.

In a further document, Farrell certified that at the meeting a majority of the male members of the band of the full age of twenty-one years had assented to the surrender. Chief Frank Francis apparently swore a similar affidavit before a magistrate.

However, closer scrutiny of these oaths reveals the number twenty-one upheld as a majority appears suspect. In the 1891 census, thirty-three males residing on the reserve were enumerated who would be twenty-one years or over in 1892. Another seventeen were allegedly signatories to the 1892 surrender. When these seventeen are added to the thirty-three in the census, the total male population, twenty-one years and over, must have been around fifty or more in the 1890s at Tobique. This would have been a quarter of the population of near two hundred at Tobique, which supports a figure of between fifty and sixty. Moreover, the Indian Affairs report to Cabinet of March 4, 1892, had stated the band consisted of forty-eight families. Virtually all these families would have been headed by an adult male; as the censuses show, many families also had sons or lodgers over twenty-one years of age.

In the sworn statements quoted above, it was stated that a majority of the male members of the band assented to the alleged surrender. This could mean that the eighteen alleged signatories were the only ones who made their marks, though a majority of eligible voters were in attendance. In other words, of those in attendance, a majority gave their assent. It could also mean that the eighteen were a numerical majority of all those in attendance. If so, then there would have been no more than thirty-five of the eligible voters in attendance, out of a possible fifty or more.

Of the alleged signatories to the 1892 surrender, a number were young enough to have received some schooling at the Tobique school, which had first opened on January 31, 1881.[45] When De Boucherville was at Tobique in April 1883, he visited the school and reported "how agreeably surprised at finding such a good attendance, there being not less than 22 boys & girls present."[46] He requested a few of the children "to read and cipher of which they acquitted themselves most satisfactorily… Indeed this school is far ahead of a number of schools in white settlements where the teacher receives higher remuneration." Moses Craig reported in 1884 that the school, which "has been taught continuously at Tobique for the last three years and a half, has been a success."[47] The teacher, Miss Hartt, Craig said, "possesses the esteem and confidence of the band, and the children have made good progress under her tuition." Indian Affairs' statistics on schools for 1884 record for Tobique twenty-two students reading and spelling and fifteen writing.[48] Of those signatories to the 1892 surrender, some at least would have attended the school and have gained sufficient schooling to read and write with a degree of proficiency. Yet no signatures appear on the 1892 surrender. The names listed were all done by the same hand, presumably Farrell's.

The only extant documentation for Farrell's 1892 surrender are the three documents Farrell had a Fredericton lawyer draft. Moreover, no documentation has been located instructing Farrell to undertake a surrender. Rather, when Farrell inquired about any previous surrenders, he was told no surrender had ever been obtained, but there was "no reason why a surrender should not be taken of the portion South of the River, as well as the portion north of the River less 5,000 acres."[49] Here the use of the word "surrender" clearly referred to surrenders under the Indian Act. But the department's use of it, in its reply to New Brunswick's minute of 1890, referred to "Indian title having been already surrendered."[50] This was its standard response, the Tobique Reserve had been turned over at the time of Confederation. When, however, in its recommendations to Cabinet it used "a surrender of all the land remaining unsurrendered in the Tobique Reserve,"[51] this begs the question: if the department from Confederation held title, then what land remained "unsurrendered"?

In fact, nowhere in the surviving documentation, and it is voluminous, has been found a single reference—other than Farrell's three documents—specifically citing an 1892 surrender. That the department never sent to the Privy Council any documentation relating to a surrender in 1892 can be demonstrated from an examination of the deputy superintendent general's private letter books. Into these books a clerk copied the deputy's outgoing correspondence and maintained a complete index of this correspondence sent to the Privy Council office and to the superintendent general, with page numbers where a copy could be found in the letter books. When a surrender was sent to the Privy Council office, this was recorded in the index for the Privy Council, the superintendent general, and the relevant band. For the deputy's letter book, dated June 20, 1892–December 29, 1892, though there were numerous surrenders of reserve lands recorded in the index entries for the Privy Council, superintendent general, and the relevant bands, none was so recorded for Farrell's surrender of August 17, 1892.

That no such surrender ever received departmental sanction or was sent for Privy Council approval is borne out by a letter of William Orr to the department's secretary. It was in regard to John Costigan's request for a copy of the "Treaty with the Tobique Indians," in which Orr provided the usual answer of the handover at Confederation. But, he also stated that the "only surrenders given by this Band were ones of the March 21st, 1893, covering parts of Lots, A, B, C, and D on the Tobique Reserve and the other, dated the April 15th, 1896, covering four acres opposite Lot 28 on the reserve."[52]

If any official at Indian Affairs should have known the true status of Tobique surrenders, it would have been Orr, an employee since 1883, a former registrar of patents, and, from 1894, officer in charge of the land and timber branch. This branch was responsible for publishing a section on Land Statements. In this section during the 1890s, Indian Affairs in its reports only provided figures by reserves of land sold and acres remaining for Quebec, Ontario, and the West, but it published also in 1898 and 1899 a "Schedule of Indian Reserves in the Dominion." For Tobique the acreage was 18,500 acres, a figure that had first appeared in the 1874 *Indian Affairs Report*.[53] In the "Schedule of Indian Reserves" in the 1900 *Indian Affairs Report* for Tobique, the figure appears as 5,766 with an explanatory note that reads: "Transferred to the Dominion Government at Confederation. The Reserve originally contained 18,500 acres approximately. The land reserved for the use of the Indians consists of a small tract containing 81 acres situated at the mouth of the Tobique River, on its south bank and nearly the whole of the land lying north of the same River. The remainder of the Reserve has been subdivided and is being sold for the benefit of the Indians."[54]

Further evidence that Indian Affairs had chosen to ignore Farrell's surrender document comes in a departmental reply to the councillors and chiefs of the Tobique Band concerning "our forest land on the South side of Tobique, about four thousand acres more or less."[55] They were "willing [to] sell the land to the Government if this money should be expended towards building and repairing our houses otherwise if it can't be expended that way we shall not sell." To which the assistant deputy and secretary, with no mention of any 1892 surrender, replied: "this Department does not require any consent of the band to dispose of the land; the control of it was given over by the Provincial Government at Confederation."[56] This statement was, of course, in complete contradiction to the provisions of the Indian Act relating to surrenders.

There can be no other conclusion drawn from the Indian Affairs report to Cabinet on New Brunswick's request to purchase Tobique Reserve than it deliberately deceived the Cabinet over the true status of Tobique Reserve lands. Certainly, Vankoughnet believed the *Burk v. Cormier* decision could result in questioning the right by Indian Affairs to sell reserve lands. He would have drafted his minster's recommendations to Cabinet, which were based on a gross misrepresentation that there had been a surrender of Tobique lands under the Indian Act.

When Farrell queried Vankoughnet on the matter, he was told that no surrender had ever been obtained for the sale of Tobique lands. Farrell's motives in proceeding with a surrender were probably related to the intervention by George Gregory in advising his clients to refuse to make the payments Farrell had been ordered to collect. If Gregory was offering correct advice, then the payments collected by Farrell from other squatters could have been declared as illegal. Faced with that possibility, he seems to have decided to undertake a surrender without advising Indian Affairs. When Indian Affairs received Farrell's surrender document, it could have instructed Farrell to obtain a surrender in accordance with the provisions of Indian Act. Likely because the department feared that doing so could raise the question of legitimacy revolving around the whole surrender issue, it chose to ignore the very existence of the document, especially by not submitting it to the Privy Council for approval.

In 1958 the Governments of Canada and New Brunswick signed a Memorandum of Agreement that made it legally possible for Indian Affairs to accept surrenders of Indian land in New Brunswick.[57] However, it did not apply to previous surrenders.

The question remained of whether a surrender of some form had taken place. Farrell had entitled the surrender document "Release of part of Tobique Indian Reserve in Victoria Co. N.B. to the Crown etc." Around 1971 Tobique First Nation raised the matter of the surrender, which Indian Affairs was then alleging had taken place, but no Privy Council order could be found. A document search turned up Farrell's 1892 surrender, though it was not then attributed to him. Apparently, consideration was given to submitting the document to the Privy Council for retroactive approval. That course of action was not pursued. Instead, the decision was made to register it in the Department of Indian Affairs Land Registry, No. 7234-234, dated June 24, 1971, and titled "Surrender."

In 2003 a joint committee made up of Indian Affairs officials and Tobique First Nation members engaged Brian Cuthbertson to research the "alleged surrender," the results of which appear in a condensed form in this chapter. Tobique's solicitor, Harold Doherty, submitted the research with a set of allegations. In 2010 the Department of Justice validated Tobique First Nation's specific claim for compensation. An appraisal firm, de Stecher Appraisals Ltd., was contracted to determine loss of use of some twelve thousand acres. Negotiations for the amount of compensation are continuing.

NOTES

1.  D. Wilson, Report on Tobique Indians, May 11, 1865, RS557C, PANB. Bill Parenteau and James Kenny have commented that the most substantial agricultural production on New Brunswick reserves took place on the Kingsclear, Tobique, and Big Cove reserves. See their "Survival, Resistance, and the Canadian State: The Transformation of New Brunswick's Native Economy, 1867–1930," *Journal of the Canadian Historical Association*, (1992), New Series, 13: 53.

2.  Franck G. Speck, "A Report on Tribal Boundaries and Hunting Areas of the Malecite Indians of New Brunswick," *American Anthropologist*, New Series, 48 (1946): 361.

3.  *Annual Report of the Department of the Interior for the Year ended 30th June, 1874*, Part 2, p. 50. In reporting on the provincial prohibition, William Fisher, agent, called for a "change to be made in some ways advantageous to the Indians." See also Parenteau and Kenny, "Survival, Resistance and the Canadian State," p. 61.

4.  Petition of that Part of the Milicite Tribe of Indians Residing at Tobique in the County of Victoria and Province of New Brunswick, March 1868, RS636/29b, PANB.

5.  *Report of the Deputy Superintendent of Indian Affairs for 1878*, pp. 42–43.

6.  William Fisher to Minister of Interior, July 28, 1873, RG10, vol. 1,940, file 3,945, DAANDC.

7.  John Costigan to Superintendent General of Indians, April 23, 1880, vol. 2,110, file 20,295, pt.1, DAANDC.

8.  Ibid.

9.  Moses Craig to Superintendent General of Indians, October 1, 1880, RG10, vol. 2,110, file 20,295, pt. 1, DAANDC.

10. Petition of the Undersigned Members of the Melicite Band of Indians of the County of Victoria in the Province of New Brunswick, undated, but late March or early April, 1881, sent to Moses Craig by the department, April 5, 1881, RG10, vol. 2,110, file 20,295, pt. 1, DAANDC.

11. L. Vankoughnet to Sir John A. Macdonald, November 30, 1882, RG10, vol. 2,110, file 20,295, pt.1, DAANDC.

12. Report by J. V. De Boucherville to Deputy Superintendent of Indian Affairs, April 14, 1883, RG10, vol. 2,273, file 54,570, Part 1, DAANDC.

13. Memorandum of Agreement consented to by the White settlers and Squatters on the Surveyed Portion of Tobique Indian Reserve with the Department of Indian Affairs, March 29, 1883, RG10, vol. 2,110, file 20,295, pt. 1, DAANDC.

14. Draft to James Farrell, November 8, 1888, RG10, vol. 2,110, file 20,295, pt. 1, DAANDC.

15. James Farrell to L. Vankoughnet, August 11, 1890, RG10, vol. 2,110, file 20,295, pt. 1, DAANDC.

16. Copy of letter from George Gregory to Michael Adams, November 18, 1890, RG10, vol. 2,273, file 54,570, DAANDC.

17. George Gregory to Sir John A. Macdonald, November 18, 1890, RG10, vol. 2,110, file 20,295, pt.1, DAANDC.

18. Draft to George Gregory, November 25, 1890, B8260-108 (NS), vol. 7, Enclosure, DAANDC.

19. George Gregory to Lawrence Vankoughnet, November 28, 1890, B8260 (NS), vol. 7, Enclosure, DAANDC.

20. Reply of Deputy Superintendent to Hon. John Costigan, MP, May 21, 1894, RG10, vol. 2,273, file 54,570, DAANDC; J. D. M. McLean to the Deputy, January 9, 1896; and W. A. Orr to Deputy Minister, January 24, 1896, RG10, vol. 2,273, file 54,570, pt. 2, DAANDC.

21. *Indian Affairs Annual Report*, 1890, p. 25.

22. Ibid.

23. Memorandum to Deputy Minister from Samuel Bray, October 13, 1890, RG10, vol. 2,298, file 59,299, DAANDC.

24. James Farrell to L. Vankoughnet, November 27, 1890, RG10, vol. 7,612, file 12,162, DAANDC. Farrell named the newspaper as the *Saint John Daily Times*. No such newspaper is listed in the *New Brunswick Directory of Newspapers*. Nor is there any report on the case in other Saint John newspapers or those of Moncton.

25. L. Vankoughnet to R. W. Sedgewick, December 5, 1890, vol. 7,612, file 12,162, DAANDC.

26. Copy of a Minute of the Executive Council, approved by His Honour the Lieutenant-Governor on December 19, 1890, B8260-108 (NS), vol. 7, Enclosure, DAANDC.

27. Ibid.

28. Ibid.

29. Ibid.

30. Ibid.

31. Ibid.

32. Ibid.

33. Certified Copy of a Report of a Committee of the Honourable the Privy Council, approved by His Excellency the Governor General in Council, on the March 4th, 1892, B8260-108 (NS), vol. 7, Enclosure, DAANDC.

34. George Gregory to L. Vankoughnet, November 28, 1890, B8260-108 (NS), vol. 7 Enclosure, DAANDC.

35. Ibid.

36. Moses Craig to Superintendent General, October 1, 1880, RG10, vol. 2,110, file 20,295, pt. DAANDC.

37. Deputy of the Superintendent of Indian Affairs to James Farrell, May 30, 1892, B82860-108 (NS), vol. 7, Enclosure, DAANDC.

38. Ibid.

39. W. A. Orr to the Secretary, March 21, 1898, RG10, vol. 4,252, file 1,945, DAANDC. Formerly Orr had been Registrar of Patents. In the department's reply to Costigan, it said that "the Department has no further title to the reserve than the schedule which was furnished by the Province after Confederation, under the provisions of the British North America Act." James Smart to Hon. John Costigan, March 22, 1898, RG10, vol. 4,252, file 1,945, DAANDC.

40. W. A. Orr to the Secretary, March 21, 1898, RG10, vol. 4,252, file 1,945, DAANDC. As Registrar of Patents, Orr would have drafted the patents.

41. Certified Copy of a Report of a Committee of the Honourable the Privy Council, approved by His Excellency the Governor General in Council, on the March 4th, 1892. B8260-108 (NS), vol. 7, Enclosure, DAANDC.

42. Ibid.

43. Deputy Superintendent to James Farrell, May 30, 1892, B8260-108 (NS), DAANDC.

44. Instrument Number 7234-234, dated 17 August 1892, Land Registry, DAANDC.

45. Moses Craig to Superintendent of Indian Affairs, March 20, 1881, RG10, vol. 2,903, file 15,769, DAANDC.

46. Report by J. V. De Boucherville to Deputy Superintendent of Indian Affairs, April 14, 1883, RG10, vol. 2,273, file 54,570, Part 1, DAANDC

47. Moses Craig in a written statement attached to De Boucherville's report.

48. Report by De Boucherville, pp. 176–7.

49. Deputy of the Superintendent of Indian Affairs to James Farrell, May 30, 1892, B8260-108 (NS), vol. 7, Enclosure, DAANDC.

50. Certified Copy of a Report of a Committee of the Honourable the Privy Council, approved by His Excellency the Governor General in Council, on the March 4th, 1892. B8260-108 (NS), vol. 7, Enclosure, DAANDC.

51. Ibid.

52. W. A. Orr to the Secretary, March 21, 1898, B8260-108 (NS), vol. 7, Enclosure, DAANDC.

53. *Indian Affairs Annual Report*, 1874, p. 100; *Indian Affairs Annual Reports*, 1898 and 1899, pp. 336 and 396.

54. "Schedule of Indian Reserves," *Indian Affairs Annual Report*, 1900, p. 465.

55. Councillors and Chief of the Tobique Reserve, January 12, 1913, RG10, Vol. 2,448, file 94,059, DAANDC.

56. Assistant Deputy and Secretary to the Councillors and Chief of the Tobique Reserve, 27 January 1913, RG10, vol. 2,448, file 94,059, DAANDC.

57. For an analysis of the Memorandum of Agreement, see Richard H. Bartlett, *Indian Reserves in the Atlantic Provinces of Canada*, pp. 65–71.

# CHAPTER 8

# THE 1895 RED BANK SURRENDER

hen Barnaby Julian died from fever in 1854, a near century-long era of Julian family leadership at Red Bank came to an end. So dispirited had the band of around sixty become by the loss of their lands under the 1844 act and their dreadful suffering from poverty and disease, members did not elect Francis Barnaby Julian as chief until 1864. However, his commission to be "Indian Chief at Red Bank" was not issued until 1866.[1] The census did not list him, so by then he likely had died. Of Francis Barnaby's two sons, Sock Francis (sometimes Francis Sock) and Peter Francis, the choice for chief fell on Sock Francis. In the 1871 census, Francis Sock (Sock Francis Julian) and his wife Mary Catherine (Moll Magalene Pier Paul) with three children, along with the family of Joseph Dominic, appear living at Red Bank in a single household.

As already noted, Indian Affairs appointed Charles Sargeant as agent in 1872.[2] He opened at Chatham Head in 1876 a large-capacity and admirably equipped sawmill. At his mill he became the largest employer of Mi'kmaw labour in the province, paying wages equal to whites', and a number earned premium wages because of their abilities as mill workers. Although Sargeant enjoyed excellent relations with both leading Mi'kmaw and government officials,[3] he had little respect for Francis Sock as Red Bank's chief, who he said had made himself "obnoxious" to his own band.[4] Moreover, Sock had lost the confidence of Newcastle's police magistrate, John Niven, and of Justice of the Peace William Masson, who would not listen to him. Sock was in very poor health and likely for this reason Sargeant endeavoured to mediate and persuade the band "to be quiet for a while."[5] Sock probably died by 1881 as he does not appear in the 1881 census. His brother Peter Francis assumed the chieftainship. When he died in the winter of 1893–94, there was apparently no obvious successor, and Indian Affairs took no action to have one appointed.

The Roman Catholic missionary, Reverend William Morrisey, ministered to Red Bank and Eel Ground, and at the request of the deputy superintendent general provided a brief picture of these reserves.[6] Of the two, Red Bank was the most important at that time. According to Morrisey, the wages band members earned merely supplied them with the bare necessaries of life. All they did by way of farming was tilling small gardens. In the last few years, males from Red Bank had found work in nearby sawmills, but the wages were low. Morrisey believed that a change was taking place with higher wages in prospect. In this he proved correct, for certainly by the 1890s, according to Sargeant's reports, life at Red Bank had greatly improved, as it had at Tobique.

In Sargeant's first separate report of 1889 on Red Bank, he noted it had many advantages over the other reserves. It was at the junction of the North West and Little South West rivers, and these rivers were particularly good for fishing. Moreover, a nearby mill and lumbering establishment provided ample employment for the younger men. They worked in the woods in the winter and drove logs on the river in the spring, for which they received high wages. Sargeant ranked the reserve's land as good and reported most of the band raised crops, which materially helped them through the winters; however, there was not a single plough, or rake, or mower on the reserve.[7] In general, Sargeant's reports during the early 1890s suggest the fifteen or so families on the reserve lived reasonably comfortably. Although they had a neat church and a resident priest, unlike the more populous Eel Ground and Burnt Church reserves, they had no school.

Charles Sargeant died in 1893. The *Union Advocate*'s obituary noted that "in him the Indians have lost a friend whose hand was ever ready to help them from his own means when there was no government funds available."[8] Superintendent General T. Mayne Daly recommended the appointment of William Doherty Carter, a Richibucto lawyer, to succeed Sargeant.[9] Carter had begun his professional life as a teacher but then enrolled in Dalhousie Law School where he led his class in 1884 and was granted an LL.B. two years later, before being admitted to the bar in 1887. He entered into practice in Richibucto.[10] His appointment, like Sargeant's, was for all the Mi'kmaq reserves in the province. Though nearly half the Mi'kmaq lived in the area of the Miramichi River, there was also a settlement at Richibucto, so there was no reason why the superintendent should not come from outside the Miramichi.

Almost immediately on appointing Carter, Indian Affairs instructed him to ascertain all the names of whites occupying reserve lands within his superintendency and report whether any of these whites were married to Aboriginal women. Although there is no extant documentation, there was probably political pressure on behalf of the squatters occupying lands on Red Bank Reserve in particular to obtain title. In December, Carter reported on that reserve, listing the settlers by lots on which they resided for the north and south sides.[11] The lots he did not list were either vacant or had been granted under the 1844 act. As Indian Affairs would not be able to determine which lots had been so granted until 1898, Carter must have relied on what the occupants told him and also probably on David Sadler's 1845/47 survey.[12]

On the north side Carter found four lots occupied, which had been put up for sale but not sold. Their occupants claimed either to have inherited or purchased the lands, or simply occupied the lands for many years. On the south side, matters were even more confused. In the case of three lots, the occupants made similar claims as those on the north side; however, not only did the twelve occupants make the same claims, but also Carter found they occupied without regard for any dividing lines between properties. They also occupied an adjoining lot, which had been vacant at the time of David Sadler's survey. At another six lots, the occupants claimed long occupancy, though in all cases the lots had been sold under the 1844 act with payments never completed. Occupants of two of the lots knew of the sales and that only portions of the purchase money had ever been paid.

Indian Affairs replied immediately to Carter's list, instructing him to inform the squatters to obtain title to the lands they occupied. Carter was to determine the price per acre that he considered should be charged in each case. Also, he was to establish if the Red Bank Band would be willing to surrender the land.[13] Meanwhile, Carter had to be careful that no more whites took up lands, and if they did, he was to advise the department so that steps could be taken for their eviction. Carter replied early in 1894 that two dollars an acre would be a reasonable price, and they would be willing to surrender the land. Indian Affairs now ordered Carter to notify all who owed for back installments and accrued interest that they would have until June 1894 to pay or the 1849 sales would be cancelled and the land otherwise disposed of. For the remainder, Carter was to inform them they had one month after notification to make payment at two dollars an acre. At the end of the one month Carter was to report the result of his notifications.

Indian Affairs apparently deemed the whole matter dealt with by no later than the end of June 1894—the final date for payments of installments and accrued interest—while the remainder, it assumed, would have already been paid within the month of Carter's notification. When, by early July, no report arrived from Carter, the deputy superintendent general wrote him, requesting the anticipated information.[14] Although he gave no dates, Carter responded that he had notified the white trespassers that they must either pay for their land or vacate.[15] Some trespassers had complained that the rate of two dollars an acre was too high. Others said they would pay, but so far had not. At this point, Indian Affairs seems to have realized that the provisions of the Indian Act had not been followed to obtain a formal surrender. If, of course, any of the squatters did pay but the band had not formally consented to a surrender, then Indian Affairs would not be able to issue a patent. Indian Affairs lost no time informing Carter

William Doherty Carter, Class of 1886.
Courtesy Dalhousie Law School

of the necessity for obtaining a surrender, but first he must ascertain whether the band members would be willing to surrender the land occupied by the squatters, to be sold to them at a fair price.[16]

After visiting Red Bank, Carter reported, "Red Bank Indians or a number of them had expressed themselves willing to surrender part of reserve squatted upon by whites."[17] The department sent him a surrender document, presumably Form 65, in which he was to insert the different lots to be surrendered with necessary descriptions to identify the lots. Given the information at Carter's disposal, this was to prove a practical impossibility. Meanwhile, a completely unforeseen complication arose when Chief Peter Julian of Eel Ground wrote the minister of Indian Affairs, informing him that no Red Bank lands were to be sold without his, Chief Julian's, consent. Peter Nicholas Julian traced his descent through his father, Nicholas Julian, and his grandfather, John Julian (ca. 1783–1868), to his great-grandfather also John Julian (ca. 1720s–1805), whose loyalty during the American Revolution, as described in Chapter 3, had resulted in his being made "Chief or Sachem in & over and among the Indians of said River of Merimichy [sic] & its dependencies."[18]

When Moses Perley first visited the Miramichi in 1841, Nicholas Julian was chief of the Eel Ground Band. At that time, Nicholas was party to an attempt to depose Barnaby Julian of Red Bank as "King" of the Miramichi Mi'kmaq. Barnaby held a New Brunswick government commission, dating from 1836, as "Chief [or King] of the Micmac Indians of Miramichi and its Dependencies." Moses Perley, who had taken a strong dislike to Barnaby Julian because of his leasing of Red Bank lands to white settlers, mistakenly reported that he had been stripped of his kingship. In fact, Barnaby Julian remained king until his death in 1854. Certainly, since Barnaby's death, Eel Ground had surpassed Red Bank in numbers and importance. Closer to Newcastle, its young men could find work loading ships. As well, there were a number of sawmills within three miles of the reserve. For their work at shipping stations and in the lumber industry they received good wages, and Sargeant described them as "fairly well off."[19] With forty families Eel Ground was a comparatively large reserve (Red Bank had fifteen), and this had made it eligible for a school with a full-time teacher in Michael Flinne, paid by Indian Affairs.[20]

When Joseph Howe, as the superintendent general of Indian Affairs in 1871, appointed John Nicholas Julian as chief, he followed precedent by not attaching any term to his commission, i.e., John Nicholas became chief for life. He was one of the last so appointed as Indian Affairs began attaching three-year terms and insisting on elections for chiefs.[21] During most of John Nicholas's time as chief, band members questioned his authority and wanted him removed, but he survived in office until his death in 1884.[22]

In 1888 Eel Ground held its first election with all male members over twenty-one years eligible to vote. Thomas Barnaby won by a single vote for a three-year term.[23] When Thomas Barnaby's term expired, as there was no apparent opposition, he just continued as chief with Indian Affairs' compliance. Trouble erupted in October 1893. Carter found much division over Barnaby continuing as chief, with the opposition led by Lemuel Renou. Following agreement to hold an election, Peter Nicholas Julian entered the scene, denouncing Barnaby's detractors.[24] In a petition to Indian Affairs two weeks before the election to be held April 12, 1894, Peter Julian used his family lineage in an attempt to convince the department that he should be made chief—without any election—not only of Eel Ground, but also "Chief of the Micmac Band of Indians of Miramichi." He cited the loyal conduct of his family during the American Revolution. As well, he claimed a "peaceable state of affairs" had prevailed when the Julians held office, and his own policy would be "to follow in their footsteps."[25]

*Running the Dawsonville Rapids, the Worst on the Restigouche River, New Brunswick*, c. 1900, accoding to W. F. Ganong.

William Francis Ganong Collection 1987.17.669, New Brunswick Museum, Saint John, NB.

When Indian Affairs refused to appoint Peter Julian without an election, he stepped forward to oppose Barnaby. Julian won handily, receiving thirty-five of the fifty votes cast. Under Section 76 of the Indian Act, bands could have an order-in-council passed allowing for chiefs and bands to make regulations governing such matters as schools, health, and the levelling of poll taxes. Once chief, Peter Julian had such an order passed, which gave him added legitimacy and influence as chief.[26]

Emboldened by his election victory and the apparent support from local white officials, Peter Julian now laid claim to Red Bank lands and those of reserves on the North West Miramichi as belonging by right to the Julians. In September, Peter Julian had magistrate John Niven write a letter for him to the minister of Indian Affairs, as he understood that Carter "had been making application to the Indians of the Red Bank Miramichi to get them to consent and sign a paper authorizing him to be allowed to sell the Indian Reserves on the North West Miramichi."[27] Also, he informed the minister "that tract of Land was granted to my forefathers the Jullians [sic] by King George the III of which I have all the grants and papers shewing my direct claim from my people down to this day." He would not allow it to be sold. If Carter proceeded, Peter Julian indicated he would at once proceed to Ottawa "to see my rights are properly looked after and protected." The minister was to let him know if Carter had been authorized to sell any such lands and "to deprive me of the last piece of Indian territory on the Noble Branch of the North West Miramichi which was granted to my forefathers the tribe Jullian" for their loyalty to the British Crown.

In Ottawa officials had no knowledge of the 1783 licence of occupation issued to John Julian for 20,000 acres on the North West Miramichi and to which Peter Julian was referring. Indian Affairs assumed his reference was to Red Bank lands and, moreover, that those lands belonged to his band at Eel Ground. Consequently, the Indian Affairs September reply—most likely drafted by a clerk employing set phrasing—concerned Carter's instructions to obtain a surrender of Red Bank lands "with a view to a settlement being made with the White Squatters on the Reserve, who have been there for a number of years, & to the land being sold to them at a fair valuation, the proceeds of which will be funded, for the benefit of your band."[28] If Peter Julian had not already declared his ownership of Red Bank lands, he had no hesitation in doing so now. In his response, also penned by magistrate John Niven, he told the deputy superintendent general that he was quite willing for the land belonging to his band located on the Little South West Miramichi to be sold, but he did not want sold on any terms Indian Point Reserve or Big Hole Reserve.[29]

Peter Julian requested that Carter be instructed to not sell any of the stipulated lands, nor the reserve on the Little South West Miramichi until October 1, as he, Julian, would be in Ottawa by that time. Indian Affairs' confusion over Peter Julian's claims resulted in a letter to Carter, enclosing a copy of Julian's letter stating his willingness to give up lands at Red Bank. As far as the department understood, only Red Bank lands were being considered for surrender. In a subtly sharp (though completely unfair) reminder to Carter, the deputy superintendent went on to remark, "I am not aware that it was the intention of the Department to dispose" of the other reserves mentioned by Julian.[30] His letter concluded by chastising Carter for not reporting on whether there were any trespassers on the Indian Point Reserve.

Carter was not long in replying to the department. He began by making it clear that Red Bank Band did not acknowledge Peter Julian's authority. They had had no voice in his election, and Red Bank and Eel Ground were separate bands. When, after his election, Julian had tried to interfere in Red Bank concerns, some Red Bank members had complained to Carter, who had been forced to settle matters by directing Julian to refrain from interfering. Since then, there had been no trouble, "though he noted from Julian's letter that he still claimed

Red Bank Indians as belonging to his Eel Ground Band."[31] Carter also reported that he had further investigated the basis for Peter Julian's claim. He found that all the Miramichi bands had formerly belonged to one band under hereditary chiefs. Whoever were his informants still believed all the reserve lands in the Miramichi had been granted to a Pierre [John] Julian and his band. Later the band had divided into two with their chiefs elective.[32] Red Bank members, as well their own reserve, claimed Indian Point and Big Hole, while Eel Ground claimed, in addition to its reserve, the Renous Tract and Indian Town lands on the upper North West Miramichi.

On the Red Bank vacant chieftainship, Carter remarked that during the previous winter a John Dominic had asked to be appointed chief, but the majority of the band appeared to think they could do very well without a chief.[33] He intended to visit Red Bank in the following week to learn if they were prepared to surrender the Big Hole lots on which there were squatters, if it was the intention of the department for him to do so.[34] Earlier in the month, Carter had reported fifteen squatters at Big Hole, but he had been unable to determine what lots they occupied.[35]

Although previously Indian Affairs had reprimanded Carter for not confining to Red Bank his attempts at obtaining surrenders of reserve lands, it now directed him to deal with squatters at Big Hole. He was to ascertain whether the Big Hole members were willing to surrender the lots in question.[36] Carter probably had not received this latest instruction when Peter Julian arrived at Richibucto to hand over a letter claiming the Big Hole Reserve for Eel Ground. In this case, it appears from the handwriting that Michael Flinne, Eel Ground's schoolteacher, had penned the letter, which he also witnessed. All the revenues from Red Bank were required by Eel Ground because it had a church, a school, and a lock-up and needed an additional source of income. Moreover, there were sixty families at Eel Ground and only fifteen at Red Bank, so it was obvious the former had greater expenses. In conclusion, where one senses Flinne's likely hand, the letter asked Carter to consider "whether it would not be something like even-handed Justice in annexing said Block of land to the Eel Ground Reserve."[37] Carter was less than impressed with the claim, informing Deputy Superintendent Hayter Reed that Big Hole had in the past been recognized by both Charles Sargeant and himself as belonging to Red Bank. As far as he could learn, Eel Ground had never laid claim to it until after Peter Julian had been elected chief.[38]

While dealing with the consequences, in Ottawa and at Red Bank, of Peter Julian's claims, Carter had pressed forward with attempting to secure Red Bank approval for a surrender of those lots occupied by squatters. Early in September, he went to Red Bank, where he held a meeting to receive "assent to the Surrender of a portion of their reserve to be sold [for] their benefit."[39] On the reserve there were twenty plus members above twenty-one years of age. Of these only one man was absent. Carter assembled all the "principal" men and explained the object of the proposed surrender. They wanted to have the lots in question leased, but Carter said the lots had to be sold. According to Carter, "Each Indian then came forward and signed his mark to the assent to surrender." John Dominic proved to be the single dissenting band member. But, as Carter explained later to Indian Affairs—and this was not in his initial report of September 11—what band members signed was not an official surrender form. Instead, Carter had obtained signatures to a document giving him power of attorney to sign their names to a surrender form. Carter never explained why he believed he needed power of attorney. Because he did not deem this document "a sufficient execution," he presented to the band a surrender form, which "they nearly all refused to sign."[40]

Shortly after Carter's visit, Joseph L. Ginnish called a meeting on the reserve. He was a lifelong member of Red Bank Reserve and had married into the Julian family. Out of this meeting came a set of minutes protesting the signing of the document presented by Carter. Because nearly all band members, with the exception of four, had refused to sign what they believed was the surrender document, the band protest must have been referring to the signing of the power-of-attorney document. The minutes, which in form are one long single sentence, appear to have been written by a person who knew a bit of official jargon but was no more than semi-literate. It is possible that John Dominic and Joseph Ginnish may have drafted them, along with one or more of the squatters. W. D. Hamilton considers John Dominic to be among the most politically active members of the Red Bank Band in the 1890s when, as we shall see, for a brief period he served as chief and acting band manager.[41] From the 1820s there were schools in the immediate area of Red Bank.[42] John Baptiste Dominic may well have attended one of these schools, for he seems to have obtained sufficient schooling so that he could write letters, which he was to do, causing greater confusion, if that was possible.

The meeting asked that Carter's actions be "reconsidered" in reference to "the selling and leaseing [sic] of certain parts of said reserves."[43] It was claimed that Carter had taken "undue advantage" because he had not called a council first, which should have been held, and due notice had not been given. What the band wanted was "to hold their reserves as heretofore held by their forefathers." Finally, the minutes recorded that the band had "appointed John Dominick [usually Dominic] as chief for the term forwarding the same to the Commissioner

Deputy Superintendent Hayter Reed, 1893–97.
M965.97.4 | Painting | *Mr. Hayter Reed* ©McCord Museum

of which no notice has been taken." Indian Affairs simply ignored the minutes sent.

In the matter of John Dominic, Carter believed him to be behind the protest. Dominic had come to see Carter during the previous winter to say he wanted to be chief of Red Bank. Carter's response was that there were only a few in the band, which had been without a chief for years, so Carter saw no necessity for a chief. However, if band members were unanimous for the appointment of any one of the band, Carter had no doubt Indian Affairs would confirm their choice. Dominic then sent Carter a petition with the names of all but one of the band members calling for him to be chief. Before Carter could take any action, he received word from several at Red Bank that they did not desire a chief. Moreover, they were particularly opposed to Dominic and he "had obtained their names to the petition by representing it as a different document."[44] Carter reported in October that after three attempts to secure a surrender at Red Bank, he regretted he had been unsuccessful and returned the blank surrender form to the Department.[45] Several of the squatters had applied for patents. The way it now stood was the squatters continued their occupation, with the band members receiving no returns.

Indian Affairs made no direct reply to Carter's report on his failure to obtain a surrender. It would seem that the department decided to drop the matter for the time being in light of Chief Peter Julian's visit to Ottawa in November 1894. Julian and second chief Lemuel Renou had arrived with the 1805 licence of occupation, issued to John Julian and the Mi'kmaq to occupy tracts on the North West Miramichi consisting of what would become Big Hole and Indian Point reserves (see Chapter 4). Indian Affairs raised the issue of Red Bank lands and band members. Julian gave assurances that he had no desire to interfere in their affairs, and he now agreed they should be recognized as a separate band. Although never explicitly stated by Indian Affairs, officials and Julian seemed to have reached an informal agreement: in exchange for Indian Affairs giving

Big Hole and Indian Point reserves to Eel Ground, Julian agreed on behalf of Eel Ground to surrender the lands on the three reserves occupied by squatters. Carter was now to ascertain definitely the names of the squatters and lands occupied by them on the three reserves of Red Bank, which Indian Affairs continued to accept belonged to Eel Ground, Big Hole, and Indian Point, so the surrender could take place as soon as possible.

Carter told Indian Affairs he could see no objection to the proposed division, "though the Red Bank band will no doubt feel very sore and do some vigorous kicking."[46] He enclosed a list of the squatters on Big Hole and Indian Point and noted there were no squatters on Eel Ground Reserve—a fact Peter Julian must have known but had not told Indian Affairs. By laying claim through the Julian lineage to Red Bank, Big Hole, and Indian Point, Peter Julian obtained Indian Affairs' acceptance of his claim to Big Hole and Indian Point, which in fact had belonged to Red Bank. In exchange, he gave up his claim to Red Bank and agreed to surrender lands that two months previous had belonged to Red Bank and for which, moreover, Eel Ground should now receive the full financial benefits. In his letter, Carter also reiterated that Red Bank had positively refused to surrender any of the land claimed by them in possession of white settlers.

If Indian Affairs believed that all was settled to its satisfaction, it was soon disabused of this notion when a letter from John [Baptiste] Dominic arrived. Apparently, Hayter Reed not only wrote Carter on November 16 about Peter Julian's Ottawa trip and the decision to hand over Big Hole and Indian Point reserves, but also he notified Red Bank. Dominic then had someone, likely a magistrate or a lawyer, write, including signing for Dominic, the following rejoinder: "I received your Letter of the 16th instant and Beg to Inform you that the Indians of Red Bank Have a written Claim from King George III of the Big Hole and Indian Point Reserves, which they can produce at any time. I think that is all the Claim that is necessary."[47] When Indian Affairs asked Dominic to send the documents mentioned, he replied that "they had got lost or strayed." He also mentioned what was the major factor in the dispute over Big Hole.

In 1892 Charles Sargeant had arranged for Red Bank Indians to surrender fishing rights at Big Hole in the form of a lease in return for an annual rent of $150. The surrender document explicitly stated Red Bank ownership of Big Hole as: "We, the undersigned Chief [Peter Francis Julian] and Principal men of the Micmac tribe of Indians at Redbank Owners of the Reserve on the Main North West Miramichi River known as the Big Hole Reserve...hereby release...that certain fishing station...in the Big Hole Reserve."[48] Dominic said Red Bank had received two payments, but none had come in the autumn of 1894. He wanted to know why. In February 1895, Lemmie Pierre Paul, who also was active in Red Bank's affairs, came to Richibucto, bringing a petition signed by all the Red Bank Band requesting that all proceeds from the fishing lease be divided among them. Carter had already received a cheque from the lessee for $150, and he advanced a portion to help the band out of some difficulties they were in. Since his visit to Ottawa, however, Chief Peter Julian had also applied for the funds to be used for the Eel Ground church. Word of this had likely reached Red Bank and was the immediate cause of Lemmie Paul's visit. From Red Bank Band's point of view, obtaining rent from the fishing lease had become intricately tied to the government's persistent pressure to have members sign a surrender. Lemmie Paul told Carter the band "had reconsidered their decision to refuse a surrender of the lands settled on by Whites and they were now ready and anxious to surrender."[49] They wanted Carter to hold a meeting at Red Bank about the middle of March and take their signatures to the surrender.

As for satisfying Lemmie Paul, all Carter could do was tell him money would not be apportioned to Eel Ground without Red Bank's claims being considered. Carter warned the department that there was bound to be great dissatisfaction among the Red Bank Band if they did not get its annual rent that year as usual, as they thought they were being defrauded of their rights. Carter recommended that for 1895 the money be divided equally between the two bands.

The Big Hole lease money and the need for a chief at Red Bank were the core of a letter Dominic now sent to Hayter Reed. In it Dominic claimed that band business could not be handled without a chief, and that on February 17 he had been elected chief, though it was "not constitutional But they compell [sic] me to act on those Papers."[50] If the department appointed him, he would "work by the Order of the Governor in Council in Ottawa." He also requested an answer on the Big Hole money. Red Bank had also sent Carter a petition requesting the Big Hole money, and attached to it was a request that Dominic be made chief. When Carter visited Red Bank, however, he found band members were surprised that their petition had also included such a request. As perhaps the only literate band member, Dominic had presumably attached the request to the petition, probably drafted by him. Carter reported there was a desire for a chief, though some thought they could get along without one. As there were only a dozen families, Carter did not see the need, though if they really desired a chief there was no reason why Red Bank should not have a chief, and Carter would not stand in the way.

On the question of Red Bank being a separate band, Carter held the opinion that they should be separate from the Eel Ground band with regard to both

*Mi'kmaq Woman and Camp, New Brunswick*, ca. 1875.
Gift of the Mary Caroline Ellis Estate 4418, New Brunswick Museum, Saint John, NB.

property and government. If he was correctly informed, Red Bank had always been regarded as a separate band, and in the past they had their own chief. According to Carter, when Sock Francis Julian had died some years ago (Carter did not know his name or date of death), his brother Peter Francis Julian had succeeded without the formality of an election (Carter was unaware there had never been an election at Red Bank), but he had died a year ago.

Moreover, Charles Sargeant had always regarded Red Bank as a separate band and dealt solely with it when obtaining the surrender for the Big Hole fishing lease, with which Eel Ground had not been involved. For these reasons Carter recommended a division of the two bands. Red Bank was bound to be dissatisfied if they lost any of the lands of Big Hole or Indian Point reserves. They looked upon these lands as their own and declared to Carter that Eel Ground never before made any claim to them. In conclusion, Carter recommended it would be well to settle the matter definitively to prevent any further dispute.[51]

Hayter Reed remained determined to secure a surrender for Red Bank lands occupied by squatters. But to do so the department needed a description of lots occupied by squatters. He kept pressuring Carter to do so, but as Carter told him this could only be done by engaging a surveyor to do a complete survey. Because neither the department nor the squatters would pay for a surveyor, matters remained at an impasse.

Carter illustrated the position of the squatters, pointing out that on the south side of the reserve many of the them occupied lots without regard to division lines. They were thickly settled and there was no unoccupied land between them. Squatters on other lots had paid a little more attention to lot division lines, but none whatever to the division lines between their portions of the lots. All Carter's efforts to have the squatters employ a surveyor had met with refusal; they had lived for years on the lots and some of them were in miserably poor circumstances—too poor in many cases to buy the land. All Carter could recommend was to describe the lots by number.[52]

Hayter Reed gave Samuel Bray, the assistant surveyor in the technical branch, the task of recommending a course of action to deal with Carter's analysis of the squatters' position. Bray learned the lots had been surveyed in 1847, though he seems not to have seen the actual survey. Although, nearly all traces of this survey would have been obliterated, undoubtedly because of the lapse of time, he agreed with Carter no new survey should be undertaken. A subdivision survey would be necessary to determine each squatter's holdings, but the low value of land did not warrant such an expense.

Neither did Bray believe that the lands' value warranted the expenses attending ejection of the squatters. Instead, he recommended a surrender be taken either of the whole of the Red Bank Reserve, excepting such portion or portions as may be required for the actual use of the Red Bank Band, or a surrender of only the occupied and vacant lots, except those actually sold and patented, described simply by number as recommended by the agent. Hayter Reed accepted Bray's recommendations on using the lot numbers provided by Carter in December 1893. He was to insert these lot numbers in the surrender so the different lots could be identified on the official plan. When a sale was made to a squatter, the department would then require the necessary survey. Indian Affairs directed Carter to obtain from band members owning Big Hole, Indian Point, and Red Bank a joint surrender. Afterwards, the department would make a proper apportionment of the remainder of the reserves between Red Bank and Eel Ground.

Hayter Reed also wrote to both Carter and Dominic to say the department would not be disposed to settle the matter of separate bands or a Red Bank chief until the band agreed to a joint surrender of the lands occupied by whites in the Red Bank Reserve and when a proper apportionment of the other lands between the two bands was completed. Dominic replied that at present he would not consent to "Dispose of any of these lands," the separation of Red Bank and Eel Ground bands was well known, and he wanted to know about the Big Hole money.[53]

In his answer to Dominic, Hayter Reed, though "he wished to accede to Dominic in any way conducive to the well being of your Indians, [said he] could

*Mi'kmaq Fishing Scene, Miramichi, New Brunswick,* ca. 1900–1910.
X14915 New Brunswick Museum, Saint John, NB.

not comply with Dominic's request until the land matters in which the Indians of Eel Ground and those of Red Bank were jointly interested [were] settled."[54] Were the department to take any steps to dispossess the white men of their holdings, when they had been living for many years on the lands referred to, the band members would be put to very heavy expense, and in the end the proceedings might result in failure.

Reed concluded by saying the department had ruled, "after a careful consideration, that it would be wise to allow the white men to remain unmolested, provided they pay for the lands they occupy; but before we can compel them to pay, we must have a surrender from the majority of the Indians interested in the lands."[55] Reed trusted that Dominic would assist the department in bringing about a settlement as soon as possible. Dominic could then rely upon the department doing all it could to meet his wishes in other respects. Reed said the Big Hole licence money would be sent immediately to Carter for distribution among those entitled to it.

In December 1894, Carter had received from Eel Ground a communication with the signatures of forty-three Eel Ground Band members, who had come to an agreement to make the surrender required by the government in regard to the Big Hole Tract and Indian Point. In sending this document to Indian Affairs,

Carter suggested it would be well, before the division of reserves took place, to submit to a joint meeting of the Red Bank and Eel Ground bands the question of surrendering these tracts as well as the portions of Red Bank squatted upon. If all those on the list from Eel Ground voted to surrender, then, Carter said, they would constitute a majority of both bands.

Because there was no chief at Red Bank, such individuals as John Dominic and Lemmie Pierre Paul continued to write the department as they saw fit, with it remaining unclear to what extent they spoke for the band. This likely explains the letter Peter Paul Julian sent in mid-March of 1895 to the minister of Indian Affairs. He wanted the minister to send money for those "poor Indians" at Red Bank who were in "Very poor circumstances."[56] Peter Paul told the minister that the four-mile block at Big Hole was no use to them the way it was. The lands settled by whites should be sold for whatever price could be got. The minister could sell lands on the North West Miramichi and also the Little South West Miramichi. Red Bank had not received the money from the Big Hole lease, and the band was badly in need of it. Peter Paul asked the minister for an answer about selling the lands and when they would receive the lease money. Peter Paul also told Reed that the only Julians left at Red Bank besides himself were Peter Francis Julian and Bernard Julian, and concluded with a rhetorical flourish, "I will look after every thing the Same as my Grandfather."

John Dominic also sent off a letter to the department in which he said the Red Bank Band would hold a meeting with Carter on April 11, about land matters and the dispute with Eel Ground. Carter would also be attending a meeting on the previous night at Eel Ground. Dominic said he would write after this Eel Ground meeting. However, when Dominic wrote two days later, he reported that his band had refused to attend the Eel Ground meeting and Carter had not come to Red Bank for a meeting on April 11.[57]

In fact, Carter had called for a meeting of Red Bank and Eel Ground band members at Eel Ground for April 10. At the meeting he submitted the proposed surrender. Of the approximately seventy band members above age twenty-one in the two bands, thirty-five were in attendance. Dominic was right about Red Bank Band members refusing to go; only two attended. These two protested "against the Eel Ground Band having anything to do or say concerning the Big Hole, Red Bank and Indian Point Reserves and then withdrew from the meeting."[58] Twenty-three, or about two-thirds of those present, then signed the surrender.

Although previously Indian Affairs had sent Carter blank Forms 65 and 66 for him to fill in, it now sent a completed Form 65. It began, "The Indians owning the Big Hole, Indian Point and Red Bank Reserves," and continued to describe the lands being surrendered as follows: "Indians owning the Big Hole, Indian Point and Red Bank Reserves…for and acting on behalf of the whole people of our said Band in Council assembled, Do hereby release, surrender… that certain parcel or tract of land and premises situate, lying and being in the Parish of North Esk…containing by admeasurement [no acreage inserted] be the same more or less and being composed of Lots number…on the South Side of the Little South West Miramichi River and Lots number…on the North Side…all of the above Lots being in the Red Bank Indian Reserve (so called)."[59]

The Form 65 description continued with enumerating the lots for Big Hole and Indian Point reserves. The surrendered lands were entrusted to the department to sell and credit with interest "to us and our descendants as to the department of Indian Affairs may deem right." This was followed by the usual witnessing clause to be signed by Carter and the list of twenty-three Eel Ground Band member signatures, dated April 10, 1895. Form 66 required Carter and Chief Peter Julian to sign that the surrender document had been assented to "by a majority of male members of the said Band of Indians of the [no band name inserted in blank space] of the full age of twenty-one years then present."[60] Their signatures had to be witnessed by a magistrate, which John Niven did on the following day, April 11.

Although Dominic apparently believed Carter would come to Red Bank on the next night, Carter made no mention of any such meeting in his correspondence with the department. At the department, Dominic's letters had been interpreted as agreement by Red Bank to sign a surrender if a meeting were held there. Such an interpretation is open to doubt. In his April 10 letter, Dominic stated, "we will hold a meeting with Mr. Carter on april 11th the 7 oclock evening about land maters and the Desputes Between Elinground and red Bank to be settled." Then in his April 12 letter, he said he had promised "to Sende you a Notifyation about this mator When closed But i am sorow to Say Mr. Carter Did Not com to atend it on april 11th and one at 10th of Elinground my Band Would not go to Elinground for a meeting than But if thar Be one hear Held according to Law Every Man Will attend it."[61] Certainly, Dominic made no explicit reference to surrendering the lands and never used the word "surrender." As well, Indian Affairs seems not to have been concerned with what authority Dominic possessed within the Red Bank Band to write the letters in the first place.

Besides Dominic's letters, J. D. MacLean, the Departmental Secretary, questioned whether the surrender should be sent to the Governor-in-Council for approval in view of the circumstances described in Carter's letter, though otherwise it followed the regular form. MacLean did not detail his concerns. Not one Red Bank Band member signed the surrender and only twenty-three from Eel Ground had signed, a majority of those present, but less than one-third of the seventy eligible males in the two bands.

Also, Carter must have decided not to insert any band name, as required, because he could not very well put in Red Bank, when none had signed. Nor could he insert Eel Ground because Chief Peter Julian had relinquished any claim he and Eel Ground had to Red Bank lands. Indian Affairs was not prepared to disallow the surrender and give up its policy of a joint surrender to cover all three reserves. Instead, Hayter Reed now directed Carter to submit a similar surrender document to the Red Bank Band and provide, as before, a completed Form 65 describing the lots to be surrendered. Reed also wrote Dominic informing him that Carter was to call a meeting at Red Bank to obtain a surrender of the lands occupied by squatters on the Big Hole, Indian Point, and Red Bank reserves. Carter could not call a meeting because the majority of Red Bank members were engaged in stream driving; they had requested to let the matter stand until their return.

On June 6, Carter returned to Red Bank to have the surrender executed. He reported there were nineteen men above the age of twenty-one. Of these, fourteen were present. Carter had "great difficulty in inducing these Indians to sign" the document. At length he succeeded in having all fourteen sign, but they did so only "on condition that the Big Hole Reserve was declared to belong to them and not to the Eel Ground band."[62] They also requested a copy of the surrender be sent to them. Form 65, the surrender document proper, with its fourteen signatures, read exactly as that signed at Eel Ground on April 10, but importantly differed in that Carter inserted below the line "C, D, E of the Big Hole Reserve (so called)" the words "reserving of Big Hole and all other fishing privileges."[63] Form 66, the annex, however, sworn by Carter and John Dominic, named "Red Bank Indian Reserve" in the clause assented to by a majority of the male members of the band. This clause was almost certainly included because of the importance to Red Bank members of retaining sole ownership of the fishing privileges. In the same document, where Dominic as the chief of the band is mentioned, Carter inserted "Acting" chief. On June 7, John Niven witnessed the signing by Carter and Dominic.[64]

In Ottawa Hayter Reed was displeased. He curtly informed Carter he was returning the surrender document and "the emendation [Carter's alteration of the document by inserting "reserving of Big Hole and all other fishing privileges"] made therein be struck out and the Surrender re-acknowledged."[65] Carter would observe, "by the change made the very reverse of what the department desired has been effected." On July 2, Carter forwarded a surrender "duly re-acknowledged."[66] Just what Hayter Reed meant by "re-acknowledged" and how Carter interpreted the instruction is open to question. On the extant "original" copy of Form 65 is stamped "Department of Indian Affairs, June 10, 1895," and Carter's emendation is crossed out. The date June 10 can only mean this document was the one Carter used for the June 6 signing at Red Bank and then forwarded to Indian Affairs, which received it on June 10. It also must be the same document Reed sent back to Carter to be "re-acknowledged" and have the emendation struck out, because it is inked out. Carter returned the document on July 2, and the cover sheet is stamped, "received July 5."

Almost certainly the issue between Reed and Carter was over re-acknowledgement. Before returning it on July 2, Carter had apparently done no more than ink out the emendation and considered that sufficient re-acknowledgement. Indian Affairs went ahead and prepared a letter, dated July 9, for the minister's signature to obtain Governor-in-Council approval to the surrenders. The minister's letter submitted in duplicate the "surrenders...made by the Indians owning the Big Hole, Indian Point and Red Bank Indian Reserves...of certain lots... more particularly described in the said surrenders, which lots are occupied by squatters, the object of the surrenders being to enable the department to sell the lots to the parties of occupation."[67] The surrenders had been "assented to, executed and attested in accordance with the provisions of the Indian Act." The originals were to be returned to Indian Affairs and the duplicates kept as a record in the Privy Council.

On the gazetted order-in-council for the Eel Ground Surrender (No. 366A), recorded August 6, 1895, is the notation "Accepted by the Governor-in-Council on 25th July 1895." No such statement appears on the Red Bank Surrender (No. 366B), which was also recorded on August 6, 1895. But what does appear is the deposition sworn by Carter and Dominic at Richibucto on July 25. Apparently, to obtain the necessary signatures Carter had to insert a clause, which from the wording would seem to have secured to Red Bank ownership of the Big Hole Fishing Station and the $150 annual lease money. Carter does not state he read out the inserted clause at the Red Bank meeting. In his letter describing his difficulty in obtaining signatures, he clearly indicated he had to agree to the condition that Red Bank owned Big Hole, so he most likely read out his inserted clause.

The clause, of course, referred to "fishing privileges" and not to full ownership of Big Hole as implied in Carter's letter, but it seems for both Red Bank and Eel

Ground the real issue was the lease and annual payments. There is no evidence Carter ever told the Red Bank signees that the document they had signed had been amended to delete the reference to reserving Big Hole and the fishing privileges or that they received a copy. It is unknown what explanation he gave Dominic, whom he must have called to come to Richibucto for the deposition.

Carter had never been happy about Indian Affairs' insistence on dividing Big Hole between Red Bank and Eel Ground. He would now actively find evidence supporting Red Bank in the dispute and express his opposition to a division. In September 1894, when Chief Peter Julian wrote the minister of Indian Affairs, laying claim to all reserves on the North West Miramichi, he said he had "all the grants and papers showing his direct claim from my people [the Julian family] down to this day." Just what documentation Julian and others at Eel Ground and Red Bank held in this period became an important factor in Indian Affairs' dealings with reserve lands. In his letter to the minister, Julian claimed the lands had been "granted to my forefathers the tribe Jullian" for their loyalty to the British Crown. During Chief Peter Julian's Ottawa visit later in November 1894, he produced as evidence of Eel Ground's claim to Big Hole and Indian Point a licence of occupation granted by the New Brunswick government, dated March 5, 1805.[68]

The document Chief Peter Julian gave Indian Affairs was an interim licence and not the final licence of occupation, which came in 1808. Although the New Brunswick Council minutes do not state it, W. D. Hamilton considers that "the Indian name lists compiled at the time show that the Little South West tract was specifically given in 1808 to Francis Julian and his band at Red Bank, and the Indian Point (Indiantown) and Big Hole tracts to Andrew Julian and the Indians of the North West."[69] Whatever the likelihood of this being the case, in 1894 Indian Affairs was sufficiently impressed with the 1805 licence that it was "disposed to approve" of Eel Ground obtaining Indian Point and Big Hole.[70]

John Dominic at Red Bank likely heard of Chief Peter Julian's visit to Ottawa, for later in November he wrote again to Hayter Reed about the claim of Red Bank Indians to Big Hole and Indian Point Reserves.[71] In reply, Reed directed Dominic to forward this document, which, after copying, would be returned to Red Bank.[72] Dominic did not send any document to Ottawa, but in April 1895, Carter sent a "copy of an old grant from King George of the Big Hole tract to the old Red Bank Chief as King as he is styled."[73] Red Bank had refused to forward the original because the band was afraid to let it go. Carter thought it appeared to be a petition, but "the Red Bank Indians claimed it was a grant and that in

1794 King John Julien hand[ed] it to [his son] Francis Julian [1729–1830] and afterwards [Francis's son] Barnaby Julian [d. 1854]."

When Carter visited Red Bank on June 6, 1895, to have the surrender executed for Red Bank lands occupied by squatters, band members showed him "a very old document over 100 years old and almost illegible which they claimed was a grant or confirmation of a previous grant or license to John Julian, King of Micmacs (as he was therein styled) and his followers of the reserves on the Miramichi River."[74] The great-granddaughter of John Julian possessed the document, but refused to part with it.

At the time of the grant, Red Bank Band members told Carter the two bands of Red Bank and Eel Ground were united, with the great body of band members living at Red Bank. On "King" John Julian's death (ca. 1805), the lands were divided with Red Bank taking Red Bank Reserve, Indian Point, and Big Hole; Eel Ground, which then had no more than half a dozen families, got Eel Ground and Renous Reserves. It had been only in the previous forty years that Eel Ground's population had increased because of its location near Chatham and Newcastle. Band members went on to list the chiefs for both bands to the present time.[75] All this information the great-granddaughter of John Julian and an old man substantiated. When they wished Carter to take their statements on oath, Carter explained he had no authority to administer an oath in such cases.

Other than the 1805 interim licence, Indian Affairs still had no other documentation to substantiate any new division of the reserves between the two bands. On the receipt of Carter's letter outlining what Red Bank members had told him, Indian Affairs requested Carter to provide evidence "as to the alleged division of the Reserves" and how the division was carried out.[76] As noted earlier, Carter knew his predecessor, Charles Sargeant, had regarded the two bands as separate and believed that Red Bank owned Big Hole because he dealt only with Red Bank when making the 1892 Big Hole Fishing Station lease with its explicit wording of Red Bank ownership. Indian Affairs, of course, held the original of the surrender document, but none of its staff ever mentioned it as evidence of Red Bank's possession.

In his search for more evidence, Carter first sought out Michael Flinne, the Eel Ground schoolteacher, to have him question Tom Barnaby. Carter considered Barnaby, an ex-chief, "one of the most intelligent Indians in Eel Ground." Flinne had never heard of any division, but Tom Barnaby believed the bands did come to a mutual agreement to make a division, probably more than one hundred years earlier. Flinne asked when the plans of the reserves were given to the bands, and Barnaby replied that "a government officer named Perley came among the Indians and surveyed some if not all the Indian lands."[77] Barnaby obviously confused Moses Perley's 1841 visit and the resulting surveys by David Sadler, of which it seems no one had an explicit remembrance.

Carter next contacted Thomas Harvey Ramsay. A lumberman, mill owner, and merchant at Red Bank, Ramsay, for purely personal interest it seems, had been gathering all available information he could on "Miramichi Micmac history."[78] Carter considered Ramsay "better informed on matters concerning the Miramichi bands and their lands than any other man."[79] Ramsay wrote to Carter:

> from my own knowledge and from Inquiries, which I have made the Indian Reserves at Red Bank, and Eel Ground are separate, and have always been so. As far back as the oldest inhabitants can remember, these two reserves have had separate Chiefs. Eel Ground has never had any control of Red Bank Band or their lands. In 1836 the Government gave Barnaby Julian [Second Red Bank Chief] Control of Red Bank[,] Big Hole & Indian Point Reserves and they have kept them up to date. There was a division Between Red Bank & Eel Ground About One Hundred Years ago. Red Bank reserve had a much larger population than any Other reserve on the Miramichi Branches at that time.[80]

Ramsay went on to list the successive chiefs for each band. His statement that in 1836 the New Brunswick government gave Barnaby Julian control of Red Bank, Big Hole, and Indian Point reserves was likely a reference to its 1836 commission appointing him "Chief of the Micmac Indians of Miramichi and its Dependencies," but which said nothing about control over reserves.[81] Carter also questioned some of the Eel Ground Band members. They admitted Big Hole belonged to Red Bank. They suggested, however, that since the death of the last Red Bank chief, Peter Francis Julian, in 1893/94, leaving that band without a chief, the bands should again be united, presumably under Eel Ground's chief Peter Julian. As a consequence of the two bands' union, they believed Eel Ground should have a share of all the lands.[82]

Although the information Carter had obtained was not as clear and positive as he would wish, he was "forced to the conclusion that there must have been in the past a division of allotment of the Indian lands of the Upper Miramichi between the two bands."[83] He was certain up to the death of Peter Francis Julian, as Red Bank's last chief, that both bands "acted upon such a division, either express [*sic*] or implied." In view of these facts, Carter recommended the old arrangement be left to stand.

Such a conclusion based on oral tradition did not satisfy Hayter Reed. He wanted supporting documentary evidence before making a decision on Eel Ground's claim based on the 1805 interim licence of occupation. Having been unable to obtain from John Dominic the document supposedly from George III giving Red Bank both Big Hole and Indian Point reserves, Reed directed Carter in July to obtain the document.[84] It seems Carter tried to obtain it from Dominic, though without success, for Dominic wrote Reed that the document was "misLade [*sic*]."[85] He thought it was at Eel Ground at Tom Barnaby's house. He would get it and send it to the department. In October Reed again directed Carter to obtain the document.[86] Carter reported that he had endeavoured to get it from "an Indian of Eel Ground, but he was away, though Carter intended to visit the reserve in the following week and would try and induce the Indian who has, or who is claimed to have possession of it to give me a Copy."[87]

Meanwhile, Red Bank Band members were making inquiries twice a week on when they could expect the Big Hole fishing lease money. Indian Affairs would not release the money until the Big Hole issue was resolved. Carter called on Indian Affairs to make a final decision on the ownership of Big Hole.[88] He had also continued to search for the document Dominic said was in Thomas Barnaby's possession, without success. His failure, however, spurred Indian Affairs to write New Brunswick's surveyor general office for any record of a grant made to "King" John Julian and on the division of reserves. All that could be found was Governor John Parr's 1783 licence of occupation.[89] A search of Indian Affairs' records found nothing, other than at Confederation each band had their own chief and the censuses since 1882 had always been given separately for the two bands.[90]

After receiving Carter's letter of October 30 calling for a decision, J. D. MacLean recommended a division be made as soon as possible. The problem for the department, having put themselves in such difficulty, was an acceptable rationalization for keeping whatever they promised Peter Julian about Big Hole when he had visited in November 1894. It has been suggested earlier in this text that Indian Affairs made an implicit or informal agreement with Julian over Big Hole and Indian Point for obtaining Eel Ground's agreement to surrender lands occupied by squatters. How serious the department considered the matter was revealed by Hayter Reed's decision to go to Red Bank and Eel Ground to endeavour to reach an amicable settlement of the question.[91] In the end, Reed sent in his stead George Chitty, a timber inspector from the technical branch, who arrived in the midst of heavy snowstorms on March 5. Chitty sent notice via messenger to Red Bank that he intended to hold a meeting in the Eel Ground schoolhouse on March 11 "with a view to effecting a settlement between the Bands of the disputed claims to ownership of Big Hole and Indian Point Reserves," and asking for a full attendance.[92]

On the evening of the meeting, fifty members of both bands attended, with Carter acting as the chair. Carter reported to the deputy superintendent general on Chitty's address to the assembled band members: "on the desirability of having their differences amicably arranged, urged them to a settlement, as being in their best interests, and said that no chief could be elected at Red Bank until after the existing dispute was adjusted, and that no distribution of the money arising from the lease of Big Hole fishing ground would be made until it was determined to whom payment should be made."[93] After a short discussion among the gathered band members, Chief Peter Julian handed Chitty a "paper," which stated that he claimed Big Hole Reserve for Eel Ground as a descendant of "King" John Julian.

Some members of the Red Bank Band handed Chitty a similar document. Chitty then proposed as a settlement that the Big Hole Reserve should be divided between them, with the northerly part to belong to the Red Bank Band and the southerly part to the Eel Ground Band. Furthermore, Chitty proposed that Indian Point should belong to Red Bank and that money accruing from the fishing lease should be divided equally between the two bands. From the ensuing discussion came an agreement, which Carter committed to writing for the division of Big Hole and the division of rent from the fishing licence.[94]

Chitty returned to Ottawa with a copy of the agreement, but Reed considered it "such an important matter" that he directed Carter "to procure the marks of the Principal if not all the Indians whose names are shown on the Resolution."[95] Carter had the resolution duly attested by thirteen Red Bank members and thirty-eight from Eel Ground.[96] Although the surrender of Red Bank lands occupied by squatters had been executed on October 24, 1895, the department did not send it to Cabinet for approval until July 1896 and after the Eel Ground Schoolhouse Agreement had been approved by Cabinet.

The protracted problems Indian Affairs had with obtaining a surrender of Red Bank lands were entirely of its own making. As deputy superintendent general, Hayter Reed was especially responsible for the resulting confusion. His first error was his refusal to accept what William Carter told him of the necessity of a complete survey before a surrender could be obtained. To compound matters, Reed dealt directly with Peter Julian when he came to Ottawa. By the time he arrived, officials had come to believe the 1783 licence of occupation for lands on the North West Miramichi, of which Julian had written, related to Red Bank Reserve and that Red Bank belonged to Eel Ground. Although never explicitly stated, Hayter Reed and his officials, in their naïveté, almost certainly reached an informal agreement with Julian. In exchange for Indian Affairs giving Big Hole and Indian Point reserves to Eel Ground, Julian agreed on behalf of Eel Ground to surrender the lands on the three reserves occupied by squatters.

Red Bank did not have a chief, but as mentioned, John B. Dominic stepped up to assume the mantle, hoping to be so appointed. As a result, Indian Affairs' officials found themselves desperately attempting to deal with Red Bank and Eel Ground feuding over ownership of Big Hole and the fishing lease worth $150 annually. As Carter tirelessly pointed out to the department, Big Hole and the fishing lease unquestionably belonged to Red Bank. To extricate themselves from the entanglement department officials had created, Indian Affairs used their control over the lease payment to force Red Bank to agree to a shared arrangement.

A far more serious matter was Hayter Reed's insistence that Carter have Red Bank agree to a surrender, though he knew the band members were opposed. Carter secured acquiescence, but only by including the emendation "reserving of Big Hole and all fishing privileges." By insisting that Carter remove the emendation, and without informing the Red Bank signatories, Hayter Reed had ordered an employee of his department to commit an illegal act. Furthermore, he sent the Red Bank surrender to the Governor–in–Council, stating the Red Bank signatories had attested to the surrender in accordance with the Indian Act, knowing the signatories had signed only with the explicit understanding that it contained a clause relating to Big Hole. Such an act can only be described as intentionally deceitful.

With the surrender now obtained, Indian Affairs could proceed to sell lots to the squatters, but the squatters proved to be utterly intractable, refusing to purchase. They believed, and with good reason, that because they had remained in possession for so long, they would not be removed. Frustrated with failed attempts to have the squatters pay, Indian Affairs turned to the Department of Justice. In 1901 Warren Copley Winslow, agent for justice resident in Chatham on the Miramichi, was given the task of securing either the sale or the squatters' removal. As already noted, Indian Affairs had been determined not pay for a survey but to make the squatters pay; however, it was finally accepted that a survey had to be completed before Winslow could proceed. Although sixteen lots were listed in the surrender, there were many more squatters because some lots had three or four more families squatting on them. Surveys were done and at Indian Affairs were compiled into a single colour-coded plan (see Plan of

Red Bank Indian Reserve on final page of insert). Winslow persevered with obtaining sales and in the end there were twenty-nine, which came to $1,482.

William Carter's failure to collect payments from squatters ultimately led to his dismissal in 1908. In 1912 he gave up his law practice in Richibucto and moved to Vancouver. He became known as a capable lawyer and was appointed deputy provincial attorney general. In 1928 he became official administrator of the City of Vancouver.[97] His nemesis, Hayter Reed, retired from government service in 1897 and was manager of the Canadian Pacific Railway hotel chain from 1905 until 1915. He died in Montreal in 1936.

Through the 1895 surrender and previous grants under the 1844 act, Red Bank lost all productive frontal lands on both sides of the Little South West Miramichi within its reserve boundaries. Red Bank had been reduced from its original 10,000 acres to 6,150 acres. Red Bank First Nation (now Metepenagiag First Nation) submitted a specific claim, which was validated by the Department of Justice in 2010. In the following year, an appraisal for loss of use was contracted to Altus Group. Negotiations for compensation resulted in an award of $28 million.

NOTES

1. Record of Commission Book, October 2, 1866, RS538, B.1, 1857–1876, PANB.

2. His appointment caused Richard Hutchinson, the Liberal member for Northumberland, to ask for the tabling of all correspondence and documents relating to the position, including salary and duties. Joseph Howe, as secretary of state, tabled the documents on April 29, 1872, but they were not printed in the *Sessional Papers* and were destroyed when the Centre Block burned in 1916.

3. For a biographical sketch of Sargeant, see W. D. Hamilton, *Dictionary of Miramichi Biography: Biographical Sketches of Men and Women who Played a Part in Public Life on the Miramichi Northumberland County, New Brunswick, Canada* (Privately Published, 1957), p. 3.

4. Sargeant to Deputy Superintendent General, June 11, 1877, RG10, vol. 2,003, file 7,535, DAANDC.

5. Ibid.

6. Reverend William Morrisey to F. F. Spragge, Deputy Superintendent General, August 4, 1872, RG10, vol. 1,870, file 650, DAANDC.

7. See J. D. MacLean to Carter, August 13, 1901, and Carter to MacLean, August 20, 1901, RG10, vol. 2,522, file 107,222-2, DAANDC.

8. *Union Advocate*, Newcastle, May 31, 1893.

9. Superintendent General of Indian Affairs to His Excellency, the Governor-in-Council, September 20, 1898, Letter Book, April 8–October 7, 1893, RG10, vol. 1,113, DAANDC. No other correspondence has been located relating to Carter's appointment. In Prime Minister Sir John Thompson's papers, no correspondence was found from Edward Leger, the Kent County MP. In his correspondence with Thompson, Northumberland's MP, Michael Adams, made no mention of the appointment.

10. "William Doherty Carter," W. D. Hamilton, *Dictionary of Miramichi Biography*, p. 62.

11. Carter to Deputy Superintendent General, December 6, 1893, RG10, vol. 2,522, file 107,222-2, DAANDC.

12. W. P. Flemming, Deputy Surveyor General, to J. D. MacLean, Secretary Indian Affairs, August 24, 1898, and MacLean to Carter, September 16, 1898, RG10, vol. 2,522, file 107,222-2, DAANDC.

13. Indian Affairs to Carter, December 15, 1893, RG10, vol. 2,522, file 107,222.

14. Deputy Superintendent General to Carter, July 5, 1894, RG10, vol. 2,522, file 107,222-2, DAANDC.

15. Carter to Deputy Superintendent General, July 12, 1894, RG10, vol. 2,522, file 107,222-2, DAANDC.

16. Deputy Superintendent General to Carter, July 16, 1894, RG10, vol. 2,522, file 107,222-2, DAANDC.

17. Carter to Deputy Superintendent General, August 25, 1894, RG10, vol. 2,522, file 107,222-2, DAANDC.

18. His commission can be found in RG1, vol. 169, p. 45, August 30, 1783, PANS. For Peter Julian's descent from John Julian, see biographical sketches of "John Julian" (1720s–ca.1805), "Nicholas Julian" (ca. 1783–1868), "John Nicholas Julian" (ca. 1810–1888), and "Peter Nicholas Julian" (1854–1938) in W. D. Hamilton, *Dictionary of Miramichi Biography*, pp. 196–8.

19. *Sessional Papers*, Fourth Session of Sixth Parliament, 1890, vol. 10, no. 12, p. 174.

20. *Sessional Papers*, First Session of the Fourth Parliament, 1891, Annual Report, vol. 15, no. 18, p. 142.

21. For Mi'kmaw resistance to elections of chiefs and having chiefs, see Martha Elizabeth Walls, *No Need of a Chief for this Band: The Maritime Mi'kmaq and Federal Electoral Legislation, 1899–1951* (Vancouver: UBC Press, 2010).

22. See "John Nicholas Julian," Hamilton, *Dictionary of Miramichi Biography*, p. 196.

23. For Chief Thomas Barnaby and the following troubles at Eel Ground, see W. D. Hamilton, *The Julian Tribe*, pp. 36–38.

24. Ibid.

25. Order-in-council, 3309/89, November 13, 1895

26. Peter Julian to Minister of Indian Affairs, September 1, 1894, RG10, vol. 2,522, file 107,222-2, DAANDC. Where it is stated that John Niven wrote letters on behalf of Julian it is based on handwriting analysis and his witnessing of letters.

27. Deputy Superintendent General to Carter, September 15, 1894, RG10, vol. 2,522, file 107,222-2, DAANDC.

28. Ibid.

29. Carter to Deputy Superintendent General, September 20, 1894, RG 10, vol. 2522, file 107,222-2, DAANDC.

30. Deputy Superintendent General to Carter, September 15, 1894, RG10, vol. 2,522, file 107,222-2, DAANDC.

31. Carter to Deputy Superintendent General, September 20, 1894, RG10, vol. 2,522, file 107,222-2, DAANDC.

32. Ibid.

33. Ibid.

34. Ibid. In using "elective," Carter likely meant the chiefships were not simply inherited but involved a band decision. Red Bank was not to have an Indian Affairs supervised election for chief until 1896.

35. Carter to Deputy Superintendent General, September 12, 1894, RG10, vol. 2,522, file, 107,222-2, DAANDC.

36. Indian Affairs to Carter, October 5, 1894, RG10, vol. 2,522, file 107,222-2, DAANDC.

37. Petition of Barnaby and others , January 31, RS7, vol. 40, 169, PANB.

38. Carter to Deputy Superintendent General, October 10, 1894, RG10, vol. 2,522, file 107,222-2, DAANDC.

39. Ibid.

40. Ibid.

41. W. D. Hamilton, *The Julian Tribe*, p. 73

42. For schools, see W. D. Hamilton, *Old North Esk Revised* (Fredericton, NB: The Mi'kmaq-Maliseet Institute, University of New Brunswick, 1984): 41.

43. Carter to Deputy Superintendent General, February 14, 1895, RG10, vol. 2,522, file 107,222-2, DAANDC.

44. Dominic to Hayter Reed, March 1, 1895, RG10, vol. 2,703, file 128,698-2, DAANDC.

45. Carter to Deputy Superintendent General, October 30, 1894, RG10, vol. 2,522, file 107,222-2, DAANDC.

46. Carter to Deputy Superintendent General, November 21, 1894, RG10, vol. 2,522, file 107,222-2, DAANDC.

47. John B. Dominic to Hayter Reed, November 28, 1894, RG10, vol. 2,522, file 107,222-20, DAANDC.

48. Surrender, No. 322, Recorded September 19, 1892, Instrument No. 5626-175, Land Registry, Indian Affairs, DAANDC.

49. Carter to Deputy Superintendent General, February 14, 1895, RG10, vol. 2,522, file 107,222-2, DAANDC.

50. Dominic to Hayter Reed, March 1, 1895, RG10, vol. 2,703, file 128,698-2, DAANDC.

51. Carter to Deputy Superintendent General, March 13, 1895, RG10, vol. 2,703, file 128,698-2, DAANDC.

52. Carter to Deputy Superintendent General, March 2, 1895, RG10, vol. 2,522, file 107,222-2, DAANDC.

53. John Dominic to Hayter Reed, Red Bank, March 25, 1895, RG10, vol. 2,603, file 121,698-2, DAANDC.

54. Hayter Reed to John Dominic, April 3, 1895, RG10, vol. 2,603, file 121,698-2, DAANDC.

55. Ibid.

56. Peter Paul Julien (sic) to Minister of Indian Affairs, March 18, 1895, RG10, vol. 2,522, file 107,222-2, DAANDC. Quincy [?] M. [?] witnessed the letter and presumably wrote it for Peter Paul. The letter is barely legible. A search of 1901 census for North and South Esk parishes had not revealed anyone with remotely that name.

57. John B. Dominic to Your Honor of the Department of Canada, April 10, 1895 and John B. Dominic to Your Honor the Supt. General of Ottawa, April 12, 1895, RG10, vol. 2,522, file 126,432, DAANDC.

58. Carter to the Deputy Superintendent General, April 12, 1895, RG10, vol. 2,522, file 107,222-2, DAANDC.

59. Surrender No. 366A, Form No. 65, Instrument No. 5627-175, Land Registry, Indian Affairs, DAANDC. Accepted by Governor-in-Council, July 25, 1895.

60. Ibid.

61. John B. Dominic to Your Honor of the Department of Canada, April 10, 1895 and John B. Dominic to Your Honor the Supt. General of Ottawa, April 12, 1895, RG10, vol. 2,522, file 126,432, DAANDC.

62. Carter to Deputy Superintendent General, June 8, 1895, RG10, vol. 2,522, file 107,222-2, DAANDC.

63. Surrender No. 366B, Form 65, Instrumental No. 5626-175, Land Registry, Indian Affairs, DAANDC.

64. Surrender No. 366B, Form 66, Instrumental No. 5626-175, Land Registry, Indian Affairs, DAANDC.

65. Deputy Superintendent General to Carter, June 13, 1895, RG10, vol. 2,522, file 107,222-2, DAANDC.

66. Carter to Deputy Superintendent General, July 2, 1895, RG10, vol. 2,522, file 107,222-2, DAANDC.

67. Draft, Superintendent General of Indian Affairs to His Excellency the Governor-in-General in Council July 1895, RG10, vol. 2,522, file 107,222-2, DAANDC.

68. See Peter Julian to Minister of Indian Affairs, September 1, 1894, RG10, vol. 2,522, file 107,222-2, DAANDC; and Deputy Superintendent General to Carter, November 16, 1894, RG10, vol. 2,522, file 107,222-2, DAANDC. Enclosed was a typed copy of the licence.

69. W. D. Hamilton, *The Julian Tribe*, p. 15.

70. Deputy Superintendent General to Carter, November 16, 1894, RG10, vol. 2,522, file 107,222-2, DAANDC.

71. John B. Dominic to Hayter Reed, November 28, 1894, RG10, vol. 2,522, file 107,222-2, DAANDC.

72. Hayter Reed to John B. Dominic, December 6, 1894, RG10, vol. 2,522, file 107,222-2, DAANC.

73. Carter to Deputy Superintendent General, June 8, 1895, RG10, vol. 2,522, file 107,222-2, DAANDC.

74. Ibid.

75. Ibid.

76. Deputy Superintendent General to Carter, July 4, 1895, RG10, vol. 2,522, file 107,222-2, DAANDC.

77. Michael Flinne to Carter, July 16, 1895, RG10, vol. 2,522, file, 107,222-2, DAANDC.

78. W. D. Hamilton did not include Ramsay in his *Dictionary of Miramichi Biography* but kindly provided to the author the following information: "Lumberman, mill owner, and merchant at Red Bank in the early 1890s. For whatever reason, he gathered the available facts concerning the history of the local bands and was the best informed person on that subject whom Carter encountered." He died in 1896 in his fifty-ninth year. Nothing of his research seems to have survived.

79. Carter to Deputy Superintendent General, July 17, 1895, RG10, vol. 2,522, file, 107,222-2, DAANDC.

80. T. H. Ramsay to Carter, July 17, 1895, RG10, vol. 2,522, file, 107,222-2, DAANDC; and enclosed in Carter to Deputy Superintendent General, October 15, 1895, RG10, vol. 2,522, file 107,222-2, DAANDC.

81. Commission, September 20, 1836, Item 94, MGH54, HIAL.

82. Carter to Deputy Superintendent General, July 17, 1895, RG10, vol. 2,522, file, 107,222-2, DAANDC.

83. Deputy Superintendent General to Carter, February 26, 1896, RG10, vol. 2,522, file 107,222-2, DAANDC.

84. Deputy Superintendent General to Carter, July 23, 1895, RG10, vol. 2,522, file, 107,222-2, DAANDC.

85. John Baptiste Dominic to Deputy Superintendent General, Red Bank, July 30, 1895, RG10, vol. 2,522, file, 107,222-2.

86. Deputy Superintendent General to Carter, October 9, 1895, RG10, vol. 2,522, file 107,222-2, DAANDC.

87. Carter to Deputy Superintendent General, October 15, 1895, RG10, vol. 2,522, file 107,222-2, DAANDC.

88. Carter to Deputy Superintendent General, October 30, 1895, RG10, vol. 2,522, file, 107,222-2, DAANDC.

89. Deputy Superintendent General to Andrew Inches, Deputy Surveyor General, November 18, 1895, T. G. Loggie to Deputy Superintendent General, November 25, 1895, Deputy Superintendent General to Loggie, November 27, 1895, Deputy Superintendent General to Loggie, January 20, 1896, and Loggie to Deputy Superintendent General, January 23, 1896, RG10, vol. 2,522, file, 107,222-2, DAANDC.

90. J. D. MacLean to John McGinn, November 9, 1895, John McGinn to Deputy Minister, memorandum, November 14, 1895, and S. Stewart to Deputy Minister, memorandum, November 15, 1895, RG10, vol. 2,522, file, 107,222-2, DAANDC. Stewart noted that the department had no papers for the period prior to Confederation.

91. Deputy Superintendent General to Carter, February 26, 1896, RG10. vol. 2,522, file 107,222-2, DAANDC. Carter to Hayter Reed, March 4, 1896, RG10, vol. 2,522, file 107,222-2/138,307, DAANDC. Carter wrote Reed of how pleased he was that Reed intended to visit Eel Ground and Red Bank.

92. Chitty to Hayter Reed, Ottawa, March 28, 1896, RG10, vol. 2,522, file 107,222-2, DAANDC.

93. Carter to Deputy Superintendent General, May 14, 1896, enclosure, RG10, vol. 2,522, file 107,222-2, DAANDC.

94. Carter to Deputy Superintendent General, May 14, 1896, RG10, vol. 2,522, file 107,222-2, DAANDC.

95. Carter to Deputy Superintendent General, May 14, 1896, RG10, vol. 2,522, file 107,222-2, DAANDC.

96. Ibid.

97. See "William Doherty Carter," W. D. Hamilton, *Dictionary of Miramichi Biography*, p. 62.

# CHAPTER 9

# THE 1919 SURRENDER OF TABUSINTAC LANDS AND THE 1974 REMOVAL OF SQUATTERS FROM RED BANK VILLAGE

In the summer of 1894, William Carter had visited Tabusintac Reserve.[1] As a result of his report on the visit, Indian Affairs instructed him it had no desire to dispossess the squatters of their holdings, provided the Tabusintac Band was willing to surrender the lands squatted upon and the persons in occupation were willing to purchase.[2] Carter was further instructed to determine whether the band was willing to surrender the occupied lands and forward to the department a description of these lots. He should also state the price per acre for which he considered lots should be sold.[3] Presumably, Carter acted on his instructions, but Indian Affairs did not take up the question of Tabusintac lands until 1912, when it received a report from R. A. Irving, superintendent of northeastern New Brunswick, concerning white peoples' occupation of lands on Tabusintac Reserve.[4] At the time, staff recommended a surrender be undertaken; however, they did not act on it until two years later, when they again recommended instructions be sent to Irving to obtain a surrender from the Burnt Church Band, who, in fact, were the owners of this reserve, to enable the department to carry out sales to the occupants of the lands, as named in Irving's 1912 report.[5] Deputy Superintendent General Duncan Campbell Scott accepted the recommendation. He wrote Irving about the decision to submit a surrender of the lands occupied by squatters to the Burnt Church Band in accordance with the Indian Act.[6]

Irving proceeded to post a notice, dated November 2, 1914, that "a meeting would be held on Wednesday, the eleventh day of November, 1914 at one o'clock for consideration of the surrender of certain parcels of land containing 1,315 acres for thirteen lots in the Tabusintac Reserve."[7] All these lots had been unsold on the transfer of reserve lands at Confederation. Seven of the lots on the north side and six of the lots on the south side were also unsold at the time. Presumably, Irving put up for surrender only those lots occupied by squatters. No meeting was likely held, though, because Irving died sometime in November 1914. His eventual successor, John Sheridan, apparently took no action, as no surrender was made.

The question of a surrender of lots arose again in November 1918 in combination with Indian Affairs' desire to have Burnt Church surrender timber rights on the Tabusintac Reserve. Earlier, in the latter part of 1917, the department had decided to proceed at law against the lumber firm of Harding & Taylor for timber trespass on the Tabusintac Reserve. Instructions were sent to Sheridan on October 23, 1917, to employ a lawyer to proceed against the firm.[8] Dealing with timber trespass on Tabusintac Reserve had become a major concern for Indian Affairs. It certainly was an important factor in the department's determination to obtain a surrender of unpatented lands occupied by squatters and of timber lands: it was prepared to withhold timber permits from petitioning band members to obtain consent for a surrender.

At a meeting held at Burnt Church on October 24, 1918, a motion was passed unanimously to allow acting chief William Francis to make application for any person to obtain permits to cut three hundred pieces of logs each on Tabusintac Reserve, which Sheridan sent to the department.[9] Indian Affairs then wrote John Sheridan in relation to the request, directing him to inquire "whether or not the Indians are desirous of surrendering the whole of the timber on the Tabusintac Reserve for sale, and to participate in a distribution of ten per cent of the proceeds, the balance of the money derived from the sale to be placed to their credit."[10] Sheridan reported he took up the matter of a surrender with Chief Francis, who said the band was not willing to surrender the lands. Sheridan told the department:

> The matter of surrendering the land is drilled into the Indian by White men who live near this land and along with the Indians are cutting all the lumber upon the land. It has been reported to me by men who know, that in less than ten years the lumber will be cleaned off. The permits the Indians receive from year to year does [sic] not seem to be of any benefit to them, as soon as any of them become incapacitated in any way, the department has come to their aid. The

lumber land[s] at present are quite valuable, and I fully believe a fair sum of money could be realized from them.[11]

Indian Affairs decided to send H. J. Bury, a departmental timber inspector, to look into timber matters in northeast New Brunswick.[12] During February, Bury reported on timber trespass on Red Bank, Eel Ground, Big Hole, and Tabusintac reserves.[13] Apparently, Sheridan was in poor health, because in early December 1918, Indian Affairs had written him if his health conditions improved, he should proceed with the election for a Burnt Church Band chief.[14] After Sheridan advised the Burnt Church Band would be holding a band election for a chief on April 1, the department determined that as Bury would be at Burnt Church Reserve on April 1, he would preside at that meeting for the election of a chief and councillors in order to avoid the expense—and also presumably because of his ill health—of Sheridan having to be present. Sheridan was asked to send the requisite notice to the "Acting Chief" advising the band to hold their nomination meeting before April 1.[15]

On that date, three events took place. Paul Taylor was elected chief and William Dedam and Sandy Mitchell were elected councillors at the band election, which would be confirmed by the department on April 23.[16] At a special meeting of the Burnt Church Council, it passed a resolution petitioning the department "to grant permits for 500 logs each" to eighteen named band members. At some point on the day, the band surrendered 2,900 acres, consisting of all the unpatented land on the north and south sides of the Tabusintac River.[17]

The surrender document specified that half the money received from sales of the lands was to be paid to the individual band members.[18] Indian Affairs authorized Sheridan to issue the permits for the cutting of five hundred logs to each of those mentioned in the April 1 band resolution. The extant correspondence does not reveal what, if any, relationships there were among the three events of April 1, or their sequence. Chief Paul Taylor, who held the office of "guardian" for preventing trespass at Tabusintac, lost this position because the department considered that "In view of the fact of the Indians having given a surrender of the occupied lands on this Reserve recently it is not anticipated that any trespass of a serious character will occur in the future and it is therefore not necessary to incur any more expense in the matter."[19] Sherdian reluctantly issued the permits because he believed those receiving them intended to sell them to lumbermen.[20]

The 1919 Tabusintac surrender would prove to be the last occasion that Indian Affairs could secure a surrender in New Brunswick as a means of dealing with squatters. However, it would take the Red Bank Band nearly a century to have squatters removed from its lands, while stubbornly refusing to surrender the lands so the squatters could receive legal title, as had been the practice of Indian Affairs.

At the turn of the twentieth century, Red Bank Village was a continuous line of houses and other buildings on both sides of a new highway. There were seventy or so white families making up the village outside of the reserve. Within Red Bank Reserve, a dozen band families were occupying about fifty acres. Their dwellings were small but comfortable. St. Thomas Church was the main building on the reserve. The band would not have a school building of its own until 1917. Most families seemed to have lived to the northwest of the church and along a road that followed generally the south bank of the Little South West Miramichi up to the great Oxbow meadow. Land near the river was fertile, and families engaged in farming to a greater extent than other bands in the Northeastern Agency; a number had horses and cattle. William Carter considered Red Bank Band the most progressive in the agency.[21]

Chief John Tenass, of whom Carter thought highly, had first been elected in 1896 and would remain chief, with apparently a single interlude, until succeeded by his son Mitchell (called Michael) in 1920.

It appears no whites were living within the village area of the reserve, though one individual from Red Bank Village had obtained a ninety-nine-year lease in 1895 from band member Lemuel Peter Paul to a hay field that ran up the eastern boundary of the reserve towards the river. Paul and members of his family continued to lease lands within the reserve. The first house erected by a white squatter appeared around 1909/11. No other buildings appeared until the 1920s, when five more whites obtained lands in the village. By 1935 there were such commercial establishments as a general store, a pharmacy, a barbershop, and a blacksmith shop, as well as more houses.

Over a period of thirty years, this movement of whites onto reserve lands in the village and the construction of new buildings took place in the full knowledge of successive Indian Agents (all were political appointees until the late 1940s). Moreover, because of the proceedings resulting from the 1895 surrender, both those band members who made the leases and those receiving the leases knew that such leases were illegal, and in nearly all cases they clearly stated the land in question was on the reserve. The prevailing attitude seems to have been that once leaseholders/squatters had made such improvements as building a house or commercial establishment, they would never be evicted and would eventually obtain legal title. Unlike the squatters of 1895, those in the village were well off and included among them a doctor and two merchants.

In early July 1935, Indian Affairs sent H. J. Bury, who had secured the 1919 Tabusintac surrender, to visit Red Bank Reserve to ascertain those portions of the reserve occupied by whites without the sanction of the department. He reported that band members were now "fostering an agitation to eject these white locatees [sic] as being on their reserve without proper authority."[22] He further reported the occupants of these lots were concerned about their position. It is likely they had made their concerns known through their Member of Parliament. Successive MPs would become involved in the issue at their behest. The local agent was Charles Hudson, and he had done nothing to stop the illegal squatting; in fact, he may have encouraged it.

Bury seems to have accepted what the squatters told him, much of which was incorrect in details of each lot's history. He reported that he had discussed the situation fully with the band at a meeting with Hudson present. Band members, he wrote, appeared "disposed to surrender" to lease for twenty years renewable those lands occupied by squatters with houses and other buildings. For other lots, such as those leased for pasture and which the band wished to reclaim, occupants would have to be paid compensation. In Bury's opinion, the plan, as he laid it out, would "dispose of any further trouble, and the only alternative will be for the department to definitely rule (preferably by Order in Council) that the Indians must not molest the present white occupants, and recognize the position of the latter as squatters."[23]

If Bury believed that the Red Bank Band members had been silenced and the concerns of the squatters dealt with satisfactorily, he was gravely mistaken. Immediately after Bury departed, Chief John Augustine, Councillor Michael Tenass, and twelve band members wrote to Superintendent General T. G. Murphy, requesting him to "take part of our affairs promptly we bluffed [sic]."[24] They reported Bury and Charles Hudson had been at Red Bank "to settle some of our lands were unlawfully held and occupied by white people and we all agree that we want all our lands to be restored to us."[25] Indian Affairs decided instead to follow Bury's advice by drafting a resolution for Charles Hudson to have Red Bank band members sign. The resolution required the signatories to agree to whites obtaining proper leases, while those in possession of lands outside the village proper would be compensated as a charge against band funds. Hudson had to report that after spending two hours of explaining the resolution, the band would not sign.

Moreover, the band did not trust Hudson to present their case, so they wrote directly to Indian Affairs' secretary, A. F. McKenzie. They said the document

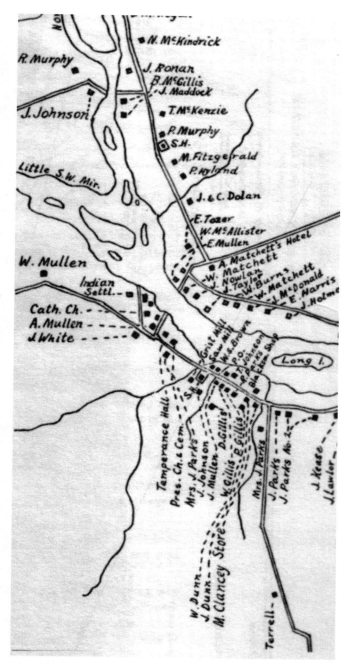

Sketch made from Roe & Colby map of 1876, showing Red Bank Village.
Courtesy Natural Resources Canada

that Hudson wished them to sign omitted a number of important points. They were starving and freezing in winter and their cattle were going hungry because the whites had taken their best farmlands. They had surrendered all the lands on both sides of the Little South West Miramichi. And on the front part of the reserve much of the land was dry sandhills unfit for farming. Any good land was held unlawfully by whites, while some Red Bank families had not enough land for gardens. As well, there were forty-three children, most of whom were attending school and who would need land. They claimed that when Bury came he had not taken time to see what they were "actually crying for" but had stopped with them for only over half an hour.[26] He had spent most of his time with Father Ryan, the local Roman Catholic priest, and the white people.

The band believed that Ryan had "convinced the whole department to do everything his own way, which is contrary to the Indian Act."[27] They had been "having trouble" with him ever since he had come to Red Bank in 1921. Indeed, he had been trying to remove the band from this reserve. Frederick Claude Ryan was a controversial priest, who was continuously embroiled in disputes with religious teaching orders, and others, but the government retained him as a part-time inspector of schools for more than twenty years.[28]

Officials were unmoved by the band's letter and continued with their policy as laid out by Bury. Indian Affairs engaged a surveyor to carry out a survey of the village lots whose boundaries should be made to conform as much as possible to the parcels as fenced. The surveyor placed iron posts at all angles marking corners, but within a short time all the posts disappeared.

Neither the band nor Indian Affairs pursued the squatter issue until May 1944, when Michael Tenass wrote an angry letter to the department about a Myrtle Somers who had been living on his property at Oxbow for over ten years.[29] Other than investigating her occupancy, nothing happened immediately. But the creation in May 1946 of a Joint Senate and House of Commons Committee to examine the Indian Act provided Red Bank an unusual opportunity to protest against continuing squatting. Among the committee's terms of reference was "The encroachment of white persons on Indian Reserves."[30] On behalf of the committee, Norman Lickers, a distinguished Six Nations lawyer engaged to act as committee counsel and liaison officer, wrote all bands announcing the establishment of the special joint committee, detailing its terms of reference and soliciting their views on changing the Indian Act legislation and administrative practices. After a Red Bank Band meeting attended by seventeen members, the band council wrote Norman Lickers with a list of their concerns. On the subject of Treaty Rights and Obligations they wrote:

We, the members of Red Bank at the Council, do not want any change in regards Our rights, according to Treaty…There are a number of trespassers on our reserves [Red Bank IR 4 &7 and Big Hole], We want this stopped. We want the full authority of our reserve. All trespassers should respect the Indian Act. We want more support from the department concerning these matters…The Indian Council has considered this [encroachment of white persons] an offence. We want that stopped, and any land now occupied by white persons to be returned to the Band.[31]

After hearing witnesses in Ottawa, the special joint committee recommended the establishment of a royal commission comprising members of the joint committee.[32] As part of its mandate, it was to visit reserves in Eastern Quebec and the Maritimes. On October 22, 1946, the commissioners came to Red Bank. John Augustine acted as spokesman for the band. He told the committee: "As far as our land on the Reserve we have lost 75 per cent of our original Indian Reserve of Red Bank. Our white neighbours take up our Reserve…They think it is heaven to get in the Indian Reserve. We understood that the Department of Indian Affairs was to protect Indian rights, Indian ground, Indian timber, land. With all our efforts we have tried our best to get the government to take action but without avail."

The commissioners noted in their report disfavour that persons other than reserve members were within the limits of the reserves. They noted Indian Affairs was taking steps to terminate such encroachments. These steps included action to remove squatters from Red Bank. Ministerial approval was given to send notices to the squatters to remove. The recently appointed agent, A. Lee Fraser, was to deliver or send notices to move by May 31, 1948. Two of the squatters left the reserve, but the others remained. No further efforts were made to remove them because departmental policy changed—no longer would forcible removals be a policy. Roy McWilliam, the local MP, detailed the legal concern the department had to consider in a 1951 letter to one of the squatters, Stanford McKibbon, who had sent McWilliam leases he had from Red Bank Reserve members for his property.

McWilliam had held extensive discussions with officials at Indian Affairs. He explained that under the Indian Act, "there was no authority for any individual Indian or band to sell reserve land." The only way to perfect title at the present time was for the band to surrender lands to the Crown for sale to McKibbon. Unfortunately, because of the decision of the Judicial Committee of the Privy

Council (*St. Catherine's Milling & Lumber Co v. the Queen*), the department was not in a position to ask the band for a surrender for sale or lease because the result of such a surrender would have been to vest title "in the Crown in the right of the Province of New Brunswick."[33] Until there was agreement with New Brunswick, it would be impossible for Indian Affairs to assist McKibbon. No further attempts were made during the 1950s to deal with the village squatters.

However, on March 5, 1958, the governments of Canada and New Brunswick signed a Memorandum of Agreement "in order to settle all outstanding problems relating to Indian reserves in the Province of New Brunswick and to enable Canada to deal effectively in future with lands forming part of the said reserves."[34] Each government ratified this Memorandum of Agreement by passing similar acts to confirm it.[35] As a result of the agreement, it was now possible for Indian Affairs to accept surrenders of Indian land in New Brunswick. It did not apply to previous surrenders.

The squatter issue arose again when preparing the instructions for undertaking the 1960 boundary and subdivisions surveys at Red Bank Reserves Nos. 4 and 7. V. J. Caisse of the Atlantic Regional Office was sent to Red Bank in mid-October 1959 "to report on the claims of non-Indians" occupying reserve land. It took him to February 1960 to produce a report he entitled, "Report on Various Claims by Non-Indians Occupying a Portion of Red Bank Indian Reserve No. 4, New Brunswick." He had to rely greatly on oral history because for many transactions spanning half a century, there was no written documentation available. Further deed searches by him provided some of the missing documentation, but the oral content of Caisse's report remains the main source for the lot occupation histories.[36] When sending off the report to Ottawa, F. B. McKinnon, regional supervisor, mentioned he had spoken to Chief John Peter Augustine who had "volunteered that it would be most unfair to request the people occupying [lots in the village] to vacate this land."[37] Augustine suggested they be given a grant on payment of a survey.

Word that a survey was to be undertaken caused some of the white families to contact Roy McWilliam, who wrote Indian Affairs of their concern over "titles to lands they have occupied, or held possession of, over the years."[38] The rationale for a survey was that most of the families were successors in title to persons "who [had] obtained some form of lease or agreement with the Indians many years ago." The purpose of the survey was to create a composite plan showing the location of the various lots. Once the survey was completed, Indian Affairs intended to ask the band to consent to a surrender for sale so the occupants could obtain clear title. The survey was completed by 1962 for twenty-five lots. The band council, however, took the position that the lots should be rented or leased on a yearly basis.

Matters dragged on until there developed a major confrontation between the band and the province's Department of Highways over the construction of a replacement bridge across the Little South West Miramichi. In 1970 the bridge linking Red Bank and Sunny Corner was destroyed. A year later Department of Highways began construction of a new bridge on the same alignment as the old with the southern end and approach within reserve land. Red Bank Band presented a demand for $100,000 compensation.[39] This demand for compensation became entwined with the squatter problem because at the same council meeting that passed the motion for compensation also passed the motion: "Further negotiations with non-Indians on claimed Indian lands will be acceptable on a rental basis only."[40]

Tension increased to the point that G. A. Percy Smith, the local MP, wrote to Jean Chrétien, as minister of Indian Affairs and Northern Development, in June and July 1971 on the urgency of dealing with a worsening situation. Percy Smith called on Chrétien to come to the Miramichi and obtain a first-hand report on what was a very dangerous situation.[41] Chrétien was away, but it seems no consideration was given to his coming to the Miramichi. In mid-July a public meeting was held to discuss the bridge issue, attended by 150 persons, mainly "Indians and Indian Affairs officials." Roderick Brown, regional director of Indian Affairs, addressed the meeting, stating "the Red Bank Indians had the support of other bands across the province in their demand for compensation for taking Indian land: History [he said] is in the making here." He continued, "There has been a land question in Red Bank for a long time," and, "For a long time the chief and his council have claimed that non-Indians are living on their land. When you have to tolerate this for a long period of time and some one [sic] says 'let's relocate the Indian people' then I believe you have a right to feel you are in trouble."[42]

As far as the Department was concerned, there were two main issues: the building of the bridge and the claims to land. Brown then noted that for a long time the "Indians and non-Indians at Red Bank have lived together and regardless of what happens you will have to live together when this is over."[43] If the "land is proven to be Indian land then, the department and the council will have to decide on what course of action to take." Following this meeting, officials from Indian Affairs met with Chief Donald Ward (elected in 1972) in early December and told him the "Department were [sic] prepared to initiate action to recover Lots 1 to 25 in the village for the Band."[44] Later in the month the band council passed a resolution that a referendum be held "to decide if the non-Indians living on reserve land are to be removed."[45] Such a referendum was held in February 1973 and proved "unanimous" in requesting the department "to remove the 24 non-Indian families from the reserve and if necessary initiate legal action under Section 31 of the Indian Act."[46]

In April 1973, P. B. Lesaux sent out a registered letter to all illegal occupants of lots, stating Indian Affairs would negotiate with each a settlement, and where circumstances warranted, it would pay compensation. Indian Affairs now had an appraisal completed on each of the lots, which totalled $174,608. Indian Affairs received permission to make *ex gratia* payments to individual occupants. Most squatters were gone and the keys handed to the band by the end of 1973. A few held out for more compensation, though they all eventually settled for the appraised value and had left the village by early in the new year. Indian Affairs had planned to turn over all the houses to the band and use the funding allocated to Red Bank for housing to give to another band. However, before departing, the occupants of houses for which they had received payment made sure they were left uninhabitable. Chief Donald Ward went to Ottawa and had the original housing funds restored to Red Bank.

The 1974 Removal of Squatters from Red Bank Village marked the finale of Indian Affairs being able to obtain surrenders of reserve lands to deal certainly with squatting in New Brunswick. It also represented a change of attitude by staff who had to accept that a new relationship was necessary: no longer could staff assume the department would always get its way when dealing with reserve lands.

# NOTES

1.  W. D. Carter to Department, September 12, 1894, RG10, vol. 2,522, file 107,222-2, DAANDC.

2.  Ibid.

3.  Ibid.

4.  Note on sources for the 1919 surrender: No file has been located for the 1919 surrender. For what follows I have relied on scattered documents and two particular sources. First are the Departmental Letter Books for 1918 and 1919. These contain departmental outgoing correspondence, which often has references to incoming letters and reports. Most references to Tabusintac were found in the indexes under "Sheridan: New Brunswick East." The second source was the Departmental Indexes of Incoming Correspondence by date with a brief note on the content of each incoming item. The missing file for the 1919 surrender is likely file number 107,222-7, but my efforts and those of the Library and Archives Canada staff to locate the volume in which this file could be found proved unrewarding. Although the matter of timber trespass seems to have played a formative role in the 1919 surrender, the file dealing with Tabusintac Timber, RG10, vol. 7,834, file 30,055-6, DAANDC, has no references to any correspondence that relates to the 1919 surrender.

5.  W. A. Orr to Deputy Minister, October 21, 1914, RG10, vol. n/k, file 107,222/7, DAANDC.

6.  Deputy Superintendent General to R. A. Irving, October 26, 1914, RG10, vol. n/k, file 107,222/7, DAANDC.

7.  Quoted from R. M. J. J. Superintendent, Miramichi Indian Agency to H. W. Hennigar, Lands Division, November 5, 1969, vol. n/k, file 271/30-1-11, Atlantic Region.

8.  The references that follow come from the Departmental Letter Books for 1918.

9.  Chief William Francis to Councillor Paul Taylor, October 24, 1918, RG10, vol. 7,834, file 30,055-6, DAANDC.

10. Department to John Sheridan, November 22, 1918, RG10, vol. 7,834, file 30,055-6, DAANDC.

11. John Sheridan to Department, December 10, 1918, RG10, vol. 7,834, file 30,055-6, DAANDC.

12. Department to John Sheridan, January 10, 1919, RG10, vol. 5,744, p. 341, DAANDC.

13. Departmental Index of Incoming Letters, February 18, 1919, RG10, vol. 3,546, p. 245, DAANDC.

14. Department to John Sheridan, December 3, 1918, Departmental Letter Books, RG10, vol. 5,740, p. 322, DAANDC.

15. Department to John Sheridan, March 13, 1919, RG10, vol. 5,753, p. 492, DAANDC.

16. Department to John Sheridan, April 23, 1919, RG10, vol. 5,759, p. 694, DAANDC.

17. Certified Copy of a Report of a Committee of the Honourable the Privy Council, approved by His Excellency the Governor General, on April 22, 1922, Order in Council, P.C. 867, DAANDC Land Registry No. 1354.

18. Ibid.

19. Department to John Sheridan, April 16, 1919, RG10, vol. 5,759, p. 34, DAANDC.

20. John Sheridan to Department, April 28, 1919, RG10, vol. 7,834, file 30,055-6, DAANDC.

21. Department of Indian Affairs, Sessional Papers, no. 27, vol. 11, Session 1,903, p. 60.

22. H. J. Bury to Mr. Williams, Illegal Occupancy by Whites of Certain Portions of the Red Bank Reserve, July 18, 1935, RG10, vol. 8,384, file 55/18-12-10, DAANDC.

23. Ibid.

24. Chief John Augustine, Councillor Michael Tenass, and twelve band members to the Hon. T. G. G. Murphy, Superintendent General, July 18, 1935, RG10, vol. 7,998, file 271/32-10-4-2, DAANDC.

25. Ibid.

26. Chief John Augustine and Councillor Michael Tenass to A. F. McKenzie, Secretary, August 13, 1935, RG10, vol. 7,998, file 271/32-10-4-2, DAANDC.

27. Ibid.

28. For Ryan see W. D. Hamilton, "Frederick Claude Ryan," *Dictionary of Miramichi Biography* (privately published, 1997), p. 337. Ryan was not favourably disposed towards Indians.

29. Michael Tenass to Indian Affairs, May 17, 1944, Michael Tenass to Department of Indian Affairs, Ottawa, August 20, 1945, and Indian Agent, unsigned, to Indian Affairs, September 4, 1945, RG10, vol. 8,384, file 55/18-12-10, DAANDC.

30. Debates, House of Commons, 22nd Session, 20th Parliament, vol. 11, May 13, 1946, Motions for Papers, Indian Affairs, Joint Committee to Consider Amendments to the Act and Indian Administration Generally, p. 1446.

31. Seventeen Red Band Members to Norman E. Lickers, Liaison Officer, Joint Committee on Indian Affairs, July 8, 1946, found in Appendix AZ, Special Joint Committee, p. 882, Claims and Historical Research Centre, DAANDC.

32. For a history of the Joint Committee, see John F. Leslie, "Assimilation, Integration or Termination?: The Development of Canadian Indian Policy, 1943–1963," PhD diss., Carleton University, March 1999, pp. 112–178.

33. G. Roy McWilliam to Stanford McKibbon, July 13, 1951, E-5673-06021, Surveys & Reserves, Red Bank, IR 4, General File, vol. 1, Atlantic Region.

34. An Act to Confirm an Agreement between the Government of Canada and the Government of New Brunswick respecting Indian Reserves, *Statutes of Canada*, 1959, 7-8 Elizabeth II, p. 329.

35. New Brunswick's confirming legislation received royal assent April 18, 1958.

36. Copies of Caisse's report turn up in a number of places. One is in file 271-30-10, Red Bank, Miramichi Agency, Indian Affairs. Although undated, for other sources it was dated February 16, 1960 the report was entered into the Indian Land Registry, Department of Indian Affairs and Northern Development, No. 566-176 D, April 20, 1971. For the author's research, see Brian Cuthbertson, "Narrative History: 1974 Removal Red Bank Village Lots 1–25, prepared for the Joint Working Group of Red Bank First Nation and Specific Land Claims (2001)," DAANDC and copy in PANB.

37. F. B. McKinnon to Indian Affairs Branch, February 16, 1960, file 55/30-10, DAANDC.

38. G. Roy McWilliam to H. M. Jones, Director of Indian Affairs, October 7, 1960, file 55/3-10, Indian Affairs.

39. Relevant documents concerning compensation are R. D. Brown to C. W. Miner, July 6, 1971, D. Gourlay to Regional Director, Maritmes, July 28, 1971, John B. M. Baxter, New Brunswick Minister of Justice, to Jean Chrétien, July 26, 1971, and H. B. Robinson, Deputy Minister, to John B. M. Baxter, August 16, 1971. In the end compensation amounting to $20,000 was paid.

40. Band Council Resolution No. 22, July 21, 1971, file 271-30-10, Red Bank, Miramichi Agency, Indian Affairs.

41. G. A. Percy to Jean Chrétien, July 6, 1971, file 271-30-10, Red Bank, Miramichi Agency, Indian Affairs.

42. *Saint John Telegraph Journal*, July 14, 1971.

43. Ibid.

44. Band Council Resolution No. 15, December 12, 1972, file 271-30-10, Red Bank, Miramichi Agency, Indian Affairs.

45. P. B. Lesaux, Director Indian-Eskimo Economic Development Branch, to J. Ciaccia, Assistant Deputy Minister Indian and Eskimo Affairs, February 23, 1973, file 271-30-10, Red Bank, Miramichi Agency, Indian Affairs.

46. Privy Council Order 1973-10/3192, October 16, 1973, authorizing *ex gratia* payments.

# CHAPTER 10

# JUSTICE AT LAST

After the establishment of New Brunswick in 1784, the Crown Lands office faced the immense task of allocating lands for the thousands of Loyalists. Although George Sproule had been appointed surveyor general in 1784, he did not take up the post until the spring of 1785. No consideration was given to the Maliseet and Mi'kmaq until, during the escheat proceedings of the Davidson-Cort grant, the government obtained knowledge of the 1783 licence of occupation for the twenty thousand acres given to John Julian. The first attempt at dealing with the issue of setting aside lands for the Mi'kmaq and Maliseet was Surveyor General George Sproule's instructions in 1798 to Stephen Millidge to go to Northumberland County, which then encompassed all the eastern shore of the province, to ascertain the limits of the Mi'kmaw villages.

There is also no evidence that New Brunswick officials even had any knowledge of the existence of the Royal Proclamation of 1763, let alone considered that the government was in any way bound by its provisions relating to Aboriginal lands. During the debates over the 1844 act, there was no doubt that title to lands set aside as reserves for the Maliseet and the Mi'kmaq was vested in the Crown. Although in 1789 Provincial Secretary Jonathan Odell stated as government policy that the Mi'kmaq and Maliseet would not receive large tracts of land but only enough for them to engage in farming, the government went ahead and allocated substantial tracts, especially at Buctouche and Richibucto. Sproule reported in 1803 that 116,160 acres had been allocated for the two tribes. However, the only licence of occupation issued, for which the documentation is certain, was for Eel Ground Reserve in 1789. Not included in the total was sixteen thousand acres, reputedly set aside in 1801 for a reserve at Tobique, which meant a possible 130,000 acres had been allocated. When next the surveyor general provided a "Schedule of Indian Reserves" in 1838, the total had fallen to 61,258 acres occupied by around 1,300 Mi'kmaq and Maliseet, and there were believed to be at least 150 squatters. Most of the reduction had come from an executive council decision in 1824, as the result of settler petitions, to reduce Buctouche Reserve from 40,960 to 4,665 acres and Richibucto from 51,320 to 5,720 acres. Other than surveys of the Miramichi Reserves, at Pockemouche River and the sixteen thousand acres of Tobique Reserve, Crown Lands office had no more than vague descriptions for the others.

Squatting occurred on all the reserves, though their distance from white settlement largely determined when it began. On the Miramichi, it began first in the 1790s, if not before, but squatters did not appear on Tobique Reserve until 1815. An unforeseen consequence was that the Julian family began selling and leasing lands to the squatters. At Buctouche and Richibucto, chiefs and others sold or leased reserve lands. This further complicated any attempts the government might make to deal with the blatant squatting on reserve lands. Its first attempt consisted of a proclamation in 1815 threatening prosecution of persons committing trespass. There is no record of any prosecutions and there would never be any because of the fear of violent reactions from squatters and that courts might require the Crown to reimburse squatters for improvements. Other than appointing unpaid Indian Commissioners, and the assembly grudgingly continuing to vote funds for relief, the government had no inclination to do anything more.

Two events were to bring significant and unexpected change. The first resulted in August 1838 from Lord Glenelg, the colonial secretary, specifically directing Lieutenant-Governor Sir John Harvey to furnish him with a report on the state of the Aboriginal inhabitants in the province. For his reply, Harvey sought the views of the Indian Commissioners, who were of one mind that the extensive tracts of lands reserved for Mi'kmaq and Maliseet were of no use to them and that some of the lands should be sold to provide a fund for the aged and infirm. Harvey had no interest in matters connected with the Mi'kmaq and Maliseet and simply sent off the commissioners' replies. He probably believed that would be the end of the matter. However, Lord Normanby, who had succeeded Glenelg as colonial secretary in 1839, in replying to Harvey, broached the idea of selling part of the reserves. Moreover, he was prepared to leave the sale of reserve lands to the discretion of the government and assembly. Those wanting to dispose of reserve lands immediately recognized that Normanby's dispatch of July 27, 1839, meant the government could proceed to sell the lands without further reference to the colonial authorities.

The second event was the arrival in 1841 of the reform-minded Sir William Colebrooke to succeed Harvey as lieutenant-governor. He took an immediate and unprecedented interest in the welfare of New Brunswick's Mi'kmaq and Maliseet. In Moses Perley he found a kindred spirit. Between them, they worked out a policy that would involve the gathering of the Mi'kmaq and Maliseet population into a number of villages. Within these villages, families would receive allotments of land in anticipation that they would become farmers. There would be schools and similar institutions, though Colebrooke firmly believed in mixing Native and white children in the classroom. Those in the villages would continue to have a general interest in the remaining reserve lands with funds arising from leasing or other arrangements used for their benefit.

Colebrooke was never able to adjust to the political realities of New Brunswick's pre-responsible government. This was especially true of his inability to deal with an assembly that had gained control of virtually all government expenditures. In his desire to improve conditions for New Brunswick's Maliseet and Mi'kmaq population, he faced two interrelated issues. The first was that, notwithstanding Lord Normanby's 1839 dispatch, his own legal advisers held the New Brunswick government could not dispose of reserve lands without explicit instructions from the British government. The second was that in order to implement his policy, the central feature of which was the establishment of villages, he needed legislation. If the legislation came from the government, it would meet strong opposition from the likes of John Ambrose Street and John Wesley Weldon, who wanted to obtain reserve lands to advance settlement in their respective counties. However, Street's bill ran into opposition because of his strongly held position that all proceeds from sales should remain within the county of their origin. After much debate, which was widely reported by the newspapers of the day, there was a compromise that a majority could support, though it took John Weldon, speaker at the time, to break a tie vote by voting in favour.

The 1844 act, as finally passed, reflected an uneasy compromise between what Colebrooke desired and the determination of those whose primary interest was summed up in the act's preamble, which emphasized that reserve lands obstructed settlement. The legislative council insisted on attaching a suspending clause, necessitating approval by the Colonial Office before it became law, though it was probably unnecessary.

Opposition to implement the 1844 act by selling reserve lands first arose in Northumberland County. After William Salter was named commissioner under the act, he immediately set to work to have the reserves surveyed. Both the Julians and John Gonishe, on behalf of the Burnt Church Mi'kmaq, petitioned against the sale of reserve lands. A delegation came to Fredericton to complain about William Salter's doings. Thus began a conflict between Salter and Colebrooke over whether sales of reserve lands should benefit the Mi'kmaq, in furtherance of the government's policy, or whether the sales should open the lands to settlement, with little or no consideration of their wishes. A complicating factor was the demand of squatters to purchase by installments, which Colebrooke refused to allow. When Salter finally arranged for a sale, he found to his chagrin there was little inclination to purchase. Moses Perley's direct involvement further complicated matters. His antipathy to the Julians, who claimed the whole ten thousand acres of the Red Bank Reserve as their sole property, caused him to advocate the annulment of the relevant licences of occupation. By 1848 Colebrooke's ability to influence proceedings was virtually nil, as his days as governor were numbered.

His successor, Sir Edmund Walker Head, accepted that it was impossible to reconcile the interests of the Aboriginals and the squatters. He abandoned Colebrooke's plans for Indian villages and an Indian Fund. In their place he admitted that Aboriginals would remain "wards of Her Majesty's Government." He also ordered Perley not to interfere again in matters relating to reserves. Although their position was considerably weakened, the Miramichi Mi'kmaq continued to protest against any loss of their lands. They implored Head to withhold his assent to any sale as an act of justice. With Perley now removed from any involvement, Salter adopted a policy of divide and rule so he could ensure there would be no further opposition to his wishes. Still, in 1862 the Burnt Church Mi'kmaq petitioned against Salter remaining as commissioner, without success. Salter's real problem was with the squatters whose interests he had so favoured. When the major sale of Red Bank's lots took place in September 1849, few were sold. Another attempt a year later resulted in the same outcome. Sales of Tabusintac lots between 1853 and 1867, though often unsuccessful, did result finally in squatters obtaining 1,301 acres.

Although the Red Bank sales of lots proved to be an abysmal and embarrassing failure for the government, and especially for Salter, they were as well disastrous for the Miramichi Mi'kmaq. With thirty lots still occupied by squatters in 1868, sales under the 1844 act had not dealt with the squatter problem on the reserve. Although the government had notified all squatters who did not purchase that they would be ejected, none ever were. The squatter problem was left to fester. If the sales had created an Indian Fund to provide a steady yearly income of £167, as projected by both Salter and the surveyor general, it would have been of immense benefit to the Red Bank Band. Instead, the actual sales generated a potential annual income of around £41, all of which disappeared into the provincial Treasury. As result of sales, the band lost with the river frontage lands what income the Julians had gained from leases. Although the Northumberland County Mi'kmaq—as with those in other counties—were intended to be beneficiaries of the sales, they obtained absolutely nothing.

After the Department of Indian Affairs assumed responsibility for New Brunswick reserves and appointed Charles Sargeant as Indian Agent, there was no attempt to deal with the squatters until William Doherty Carter succeeded as agent in 1893. Immediately on his appointment, the department ordered him to report on squatting at Red Bank. Problems between Carter and Indian Affairs began right away. They were directly the result of the department ignoring Carter's reports on the extent of squatting and how the squatters had occupied lands without regard for any dividing lines. The department obstinately refused to have a full survey done so that accurate descriptions by metes and bounds could be obtained. This was essential for a surrender to be made in accordance with the Indian Act. The department's insistence, nonetheless, of having a surrender done, resulted in a document of highly questionable legality according to the Indian Act of the day.

Indian Affairs' dealings with and promises to Chief Peter Julian displayed such ignorance of the history of the Miramichi reserves that it meant certain failure in its attempt to deal with the squatters. That Hayter Reed was prepared, at one point, to come to Red Bank and Eel Ground to personally bring about an amicable settlement over ownership of Big Hole, and with it the salmon pool licence, was most extraordinary behaviour by a deputy superintendent general. However, far more serious was his insistence that Carter remove the emendation "reserving of Big Hole and all fishing privileges" from the surrender document. Doing so, without informing the signatories, was a dereliction of his responsibilities as deputy superintendent general, both to the Red Bank Band and to the government he served.

As the Julians had leased reserve lands, so did the Buctouche Band. However, John Weldon and William Chandler, appointed Indian Commissioners under the 1844 act, authorized grants for lands which had been leased or reputedly sold, and did so knowing it was illegal. A similar pattern developed on the Richibucto Reserve. After Lieutenant-Governor Head authorized sales under the 1844 act, John Weldon and Peter Merzerall were appointed commissioners. They made no attempt to sell lots in accordance with the act. Almost certainly their reason was the need for complete surveys. In 1851 Merzerall completed surveys for both reserves, on which were designated areas described as Indian Encampments or Indian Clearances. He and Weldon submitted a report to government on the results of the survey, which has not survived.

Up to that point, there seems to have been no reaction by either the Buctouche or Richibucto bands. But it was this report that caused Chief Thomas Nicholas of Buctouche to challenge its contents and to level such charges as the blinding of his oxen. The government was sufficiently concerned about the conduct of Weldon and Merzerall in their capacity as commissioners that it ordered a full inquiry. In what became known as the "Livingston Report," though it did not state so specifically, the evidence was clear that past sales approved by Weldon and Merzerall had been illegal and that provisions of 1844 act had been ignored. Most of the lands illegally purchased by squatters from 1850 onwards had had the sanction of Weldon and Merzerall.

A major consequence of these sales sanctioned by Weldon and Merzerall was that those who had purchased had no clear title. In attempts to deal with this issue there would be three so-called surrenders. The first surrender was undertaken by Indian Agent Francis Pouliot, which was done on September 3, 1870. For the required oath, John Weldon, now a Justice of the New Brunswick Supreme Court, came to Buctouche. Although both Pouliot and Weldon should have been aware that a surrender had to be assented to by a majority of the band, only five members of the Buctouche Band were present—hardly a majority. Nevertheless, he and Weldon proceeded. Moreover, Pouliot prepared a description of the lands to be surrendered that seemed to have included nearly the whole reserve and was not confined to the lots ostensibly being surrendered.

A second surrender of April 27, 1871, involved a lot that had not been included in the first surrender. Both surrenders were accepted by the Privy Council. What Pouliot had done, with the apparent consent of Indian Affairs and with the collusion of Justice John Weldon, was to reduce the Buctouche Reserve from 4,655 acres (its extent in 1867) to about 350 acres. It was all for naught, because Pouliot had made no attempt to identify lots as a means of describing land for which patents were desired.

The third surrender was a direct consequence of Gilbert Girouard's election to Parliament in 1878. He, like his predecessors, was determined to resolve the titles issue. He had Indian Affairs order Charles Sargeant to visit Buctouche to submit to the band the advisability of surrendering the lands occupied by white people. However, the Buctouche Band had no interest in a surrender of lands and were divided into two factions over who should be chief. There was also a major falling out between Sargeant and Girouard because the latter so favoured the white settlers and had no concern whatever for the Buctouche Band.

After Sargeant failed to secure a surrender under the Indian Act, Girouard took matters into his own hands, with the result that the settlers agreed to pay $300 into Buctouche's Indian account at the department and to pay another $70 immediately to the band members. This agreement bore no resemblance to a surrender under the Indian Act of 1876. The department termed the agreement "an informal surrender," for which it never proceeded to obtain an order-in-council; nevertheless, beginning in August 1882, it issued seventy-seven patents for a total of 3,215.9 acres on the conveniently specious grounds that all the lots claimed by their white occupants had been previously surrendered, under the 1870 and 1871 surrenders. What the three surrenders achieved—though none conformed to the provisions of the Indian Act—was to reduce Buctouche Reserve from 4,665 acres to 350 acres, for which the Buctouche Band members received $370.

What had transpired at Buctouche could not have been more different than at by far the largest reserve of eighteen thousand acres at Tobique, which was also the one with the clearest separation between its Maliseet occupants and squatters. There were thirty or so families on the north side of the Tobique River and thirteen, or possibly sixteen, squatters occupying lands on the river's south side. From the first intimation that the government wished to sell the south part of the reserve, the Tobique Band opposed any such sale unless all the proceeds went directly to the band. The need for a proper survey meant no sales could take place. Finally, in 1853, the government paid for a survey that determined the reserve's boundaries, in the process confirming it consisted of 18,394 acres. The surveyors also surveyed the bounds of nineteen lots where the squatters resided and determined they occupied 2,539 acres. Unlike sales on other reserves, a sale held at Tobique in January 1854 resulted in all the squatters except one purchasing lots. Only one paid outright, while the remainder paid only the first installment.

There was no further attempt to deal with the continuing squatter problem until 1867, when there was a proposal made to the government for the sale of lands in the rear portion of the reserve in one block and also lands on the north side of the Tobique River. A survey was undertaken to divide the rear lands into lots of one hundred acres each. This was probably made in anticipation of the Dominion government assuming responsibility for reserve lands in the hopes of gaining immediate possession of these rear lots. Tobique Band members were certainly aware of such plans because they sent off a petition to Governor-General

Lord Monck in March 1868. Although the band had agreed the south portion could be sold, it was with the understanding the proceeds were to be applied to the band's benefit. The land situation at Confederation was that 93 acres had been sold and grants issued. Another 1,244 acres had been sold, but not fully paid for. The income from sales had been $1,751, of which the Tobique Band had received none. Another $1,186 was still owed. Moreover, much of the high-quality timber had been cut, for which the band received no recompense.

Until visiting superintendent William Fisher reported the sum still owed by squatters, the department had no knowledge of the situation at Tobique. It initially assumed it would be a simple matter to collect the outstanding amounts from the squatters. It would be some time before officials in the department were disabused of that notion. Nor did officials expect the degree of political pressure that would be exerted on behalf of the squatters by the Hon. John Costigan. But it was unexpected intervention of lawyer George Gregory, on behalf of one of the squatters, who challenged the assumed right of Indian Affairs to issue letters patent: in short, title to reserve lands in New Brunswick rested with the province and not the Dominion government. Gregory's highly disturbing intervention was followed by the New Brunswick government's minute of December 19, 1890, which also assumed title of reserve lands was with the province, while wishing to obtain Tobique Reserve for the purpose of settling immigrants.

What became apparent was that none of the officials—including particularly long-serving Deputy Superintendent Lawrence Vankoughnet—knew there had never been any formal surrenders of land taken by the governments of New Brunswick and Nova Scotia. Nor was there any knowledge of New Brunswick's 1844 act, though agents had been reporting about lands sold before Confederation. Vankoughnet chose to prepare a reply to New Brunswick's minute for presentation to the Privy Council, which deliberately misrepresented circumstances surrounding the selling of Tobique lands before and after Confederation. It used incredibly obtuse language to disguise the fact that there had never been a surrender of Tobique lands.

Equally unexpected for Indian Affairs was Agent James Farrell's unilateral decision to secure a surrender, using documents created by a Fredericton solicitor, in apparent ignorance of the proper forms required under the Indian Act. The department had the option of requiring Farrell to take a surrender in accordance with the Indian Act, but it chose instead to ignore Farrell's surrender—in fact, to deny its very existence. It only came to light around 1971, when Tobique First Nation raised the matter of the reputed surrender. As reprehensible as was Vankoughnet's and other officials' conduct in the matter of a reputed Tobique surrender, it amply portrayed the deceitful lengths he and his officials would go to defend their bureaucratic turf.

William C. Wicken in *The Colonization of Mi'kmaw Memory and History, 1794–1928* (2012) explores how five Nova Scotia Mi'kmaw men at a trial in 1928 of the Grand Chief of the Mi'kmaw people, Gabriel Sylliboy, remembered a treaty their ancestors had signed with the British Crown in 1752 at Halifax. Wicken analyzes petitions of Mi'kmaw leaders submitted in 1794, 1825, 1849, and 1853 in which they referred to the 1752 treaty, but in different, changing contexts. In what follows, I have adapted Wicken's approach in describing the remembrances by Mi'kmaw and Maliseet leaders who, in opposing the selling of their lands under the 1844 act, asserted their lands had been permanently granted by the Crown. These selections are also ample evidence of Maliseet and Mi'kmaw opposition to New Brunswick's and then Indian Affairs' determination to sell reserve lands for the purpose of dealing with squatters.

No petitions that mentioned King George III and loyalty have been found until petitions from Mi'kmaw and Maliseet leaders began stating opposition to the selling of reserve lands to squatters under the 1844 act. The first such opposition came at Moses Perley's meeting with the Burnt Church Mi'kmaq in October 1841, when he asked what lands they wanted reserved for the exclusive use of the tribe. The Burnt Church Council replied they wished "all the land at Burnt Church Point and also the reserve on the north side of the creek as given them by King George when the French were driven away." This suggests a remembrance of the 1783 licence of occupation given to John Julian, though Burnt Church lands were not set aside until 1802. Also, there were probably tribal memories of the signing of treaties in Halifax in 1761, which involved acceptance of King George III as their king.

In 1845, in reaction to William Salter submitting to the government a survey of the Little South West lands, Barnaby Julian sent a petition, which began by stating how he and his tribe had made extensive clearances on the Little South West Reserve land that had been "given to Barnaby Julian's grandfather, John Julian, for his loyalty and services to the British Crown and all the Julian family had unequivocally remained faithful and loyal." The petition concluded with John Gonishe, Chief of Burnt Church, and others, who all were agreed that the "Honourable Council [should] take into consideration and leave [reserve lands] as it was given them at first by His Majesty King George the third as they Aborigines of this land and born here on this ground."

In August 1848, the Miramichi Mi'kmaq heard that Lieutenant-Governor Sir Edmund Head planned a visit, seventeen chiefs assembled in council at Burnt

Church. They prepared a petition in which they said the tribe was fast fading away and "the reserves of land in different sections of the County reserved for the use of the tribe by his Late Majesty King George III...is the only source left to them for a scanty subsistence in their helplessness. And which lands they cling to with the utmost tenacity as hallowed to them by the graves of their ancestors and from which they never wish to be parted in life from a resting place for their bones in death."

John Dibblee, as the result of his 1845 visit to Tobique, reported that when the Tobique Band learned of the government's intention to sell off "Lands known as the Indian reserve," they determined to petition against any such sale. The petitioners stated they were "very much adverse [sic] to having their lands sold. They had always considered the lands known as the Indian reserve to have been granted by the British Government for the benefit of the Melicite tribe of Indians."

When, in 1868, the Tobique Band became aware of plans to sell reserve lands north of the Tobique River, they sent a petition directly to Governor General Lord Monck, i.e., to the Crown. They described the creation of the reserve in 1800 and how they had derived little benefit on the lower side of the Tobique River because of squatting. The petition concluded in describing how repeated representations had been made to the executive of New Brunswick regarding the injustice done to the tribe, all to no purpose. The tribe now appealed to his Excellency for "that justice which has been denied them in New Brunswick and to which they feel have strong claims having been noted for their loyalty when occasion required." This reference to having been noted for their loyalty probably related to the War of 1812, and perhaps also especially to what is called the "Aroostook War" of 1839 in the border dispute with Maine.

Officials at Indian Affairs had no knowledge whatever of the history of Miramichi reserves. It was, therefore, a sudden revelation when Peter Julian claimed Red Bank lands in his letter of 1894 to the minister of Indian Affairs, asserting that William Carter had no authority to sell any lands and "to deprive me of the last piece of Indian territory on the Noble Branch of the North West Miramichi which was granted to my forefathers the tribe 'Julian' for their loyalty to the British Crown."

In September, 1894, when Chief Peter Julian wrote again to the minister of Indian Affairs, laying claim to all Indian reserves on the North West Miramichi, he repeated that he had "all the grants and papers showing for his direct claim from my people [the Julian family] down to this day." In a further letter to the minister, he claimed the lands had been "granted to my forefathers the tribe

Julian for their loyalty to the British Crown." After John Dominic heard of Julian's visit to Ottawa, he wrote Hayter Reed that "the Indians of Red Bank Have written Claim from King George III of the Big Hole and Indian Point Reserves, which they can produce at any time." Although Carter carried out a search, he could never locate any such documents. It is possible that John Julian's licence of occupation of 1783 was the missing document that had been preserved over generations: "all the grants and papers showing his direct claim from my people [the Julian family] down to this day."

Whatever the probability, both the Maliseet and Mi'kmaq shared a common understanding that their lands had been reserved for them by the Crown and in perpetuity. Going back to the 1760–61 treaties of Peace and Friendship, in which they had pledged their loyalty to King George III, they expected, in the words of John Gonishe, chief of Burnt Church, the government to "leave [reserve lands] as it was given them at first by His Majesty King George the third as they Aborigines of this land and born here on this ground."

As noted in Chapter 1, New Brunswick officials seemed to have been completely unaware of the existence of the Royal Proclamation of 1763. During the debates on the 1844 act it was assumed by all parties involved that full title to reserve lands was vested in the Crown. If there was any knowledge of the Royal Proclamation, Moses Perley would surely have cited it. Moreover, officials at the Colonial Office, including law officers of the Crown, seemed to have been equally unaware of its existence; otherwise, colonial secretaries would have drawn attention to it in their correspondence relating to the sale of reserve lands. That it could have any relevance to New Brunswick's reserve lands seems to have arisen as the result of *St. Catherine's Milling & Lumber Co. v. The Queen*, which became the vehicle for settling a constitutional dispute in 1889 between the governments of Ontario and Canada. Lawyers for the former argued that the Royal Proclamation was of no force in the legal elaboration of "Indian rights." This case was cited in *Burk v. Cormier* (see chapters 6 and 7). During this trial Chief Justice Sir John Allen of the New Brunswick Supreme Court cited opinions given from the bench in the St. Catherine's milling case that all un-granted lands belonged absolutely to Ontario. He gave his opinion on this view in forceful language: "There has never been any doubt in this Province, that title to the land in the Province [was] reserved for the use of the Aboriginals—like all other un-granted lands—in the Crown, the Aboriginals having, at most, a right of occupancy." The Act 7 Vic. cap. 47, XLVII, passed with a suspending clause and confirmed by the Queen in 1844, fully recognized this.

Recent scholarship, however, has challenged this opinion that the Royal Proclamation of 1763 has no validity relating to New Brunswick's reserve lands. Nancy Ayers in "Aboriginal Rights in the Maritimes," as noted previously, considers there is "little doubt that the Royal Proclamation issued by the Imperial Crown in 1763 applied to the area now comprising the three Maritime provinces."[1] She argues that the 1763 Royal Proclamation provides authoritative confirmation of a recognized Indian interest in all lands in their possession at that time. Moreover, "Once issued, the 1763 Proclamation became part of the law of the colony. It has the force of a statute and has never been repealed."[2] Jack Stagg, in his analysis of Nova Scotia and the Proclamation, concludes that Aboriginals undoubtedly possessed and occupied lands in Nova Scotia, which had never been ceded to or purchased by Great Britain. Thus, "Indian lands in Nova Scotia should have been accorded the same protection against encroachment and non-Indian occupation as any other parts of the British dominions at time of the proclamation."[3]

## RESEARCHING FIRST NATIONS

When I was approached in 1996 to undertake historical research to support a specific claim by Red Bank First Nation, little did I realize that I would complete eighteen similar reports for Red Bank, Tobique, and Buctouche First Nations in succeeding years. Red Bank's lawyer Ronald Gaffney explained Indian Affairs was encouraging New Brunswick First Nations to submit specific claims seeking compensation for reserve lands lost because of New Brunswick's passage of the 1844 act. This was an important change of policy for the department because most of the lands had been lost before Confederation and therefore when New Brunswick was responsible for the Mi'kmaq and Maliseet nations. Another departure in policy was the agreement to form a Joint Historical Research Working Group involving Red Bank First Nation and staff of the Specific Claims Directorate of then Indian and Northern Affairs. The aim of the Working Group was to direct historical research and the preparation of a report leading to the Red Bank First Nations' claim for reserve lands sold under the 1844 act. I believe that was to be a first attempt at such a collaboration by the department.

It was agreed that I would research the enactment and implementation of the 1844 act as it concerned Red Bank lands. Although Leslie Upton in his *Micmacs and Colonists* had described the provisions of the act, he had not dealt with the history of its drafting or particulars of its passage. It was agreed that I would research the creation of the Little South West Reserve and the sale of reserve lands from 1844 to 1868 when the Dominion Government assumed responsibility for Indian affairs. I was able to proceed fairly rapidly because the staff of the Provincial Archives of New Brunswick sent many reels of microfilm to me in Halifax. This allowed me to conduct the research from my residence. As I was required also to provide with my report bound copies of all primary and secondary documents used, which had to be indexed by date and reference, I could with ease make copies from the microfilm. The terms of reference were broadened to include the Royal Proclamation of October 7, 1763.

When it became apparent that by Confederation many lots remained either unsold or the occupants had not completed payments owed, Indian Affairs agreed to another contract. It was prepared to fund a narrative history of the Red Bank 1895 Surrender. The research showed the department's bureaucracy in a most unseemly light. This was particularly so for Deputy Superintenant Hayter Reed's actions that would lead to the surrender being declared void and result in a compensation payment to Red Bank of $28 million.

The Department did insist on obtaining full payment owed by squatters. The last payment was made in 1946. The Joint Historical Research Working Group agreed that a number of small research projects be funded. With these completed, all claims by Red Bank were dealt with. After decades of losing lands to squatters and enduring the vile actions of the likes of William Salter and Hayter Reed, justice had been finally done.

A Joint Historical Research Working Group was similarly established for Tobique First Nation. As in the case of Red Bank, the working group required a historical report on 1844 sales. It was followed by the 1892 alleged surrender of Tobique Reserve and the attempts by officials to deny any such surrender ever took place. Tobique was by far the largest reserve in Atlantic Canada. The working group required a report on the sales of Tobique lots for the period 1844 to 1977. Because appraisers needed to be able to determine for each lot the period of time that squatters had occupied it, the report had to provide 115 separate lot histories that in the end involved 1,463 documents. Although the 1892 surrender has been validated, the amount of compensation agreed upon has not been made public. However, there is sufficient information to place the compensation figure at as much as $50 million.

The last report I was to complete under the joint arrangements was for a narrative history of Tobique and Beechwood dams on the Tobique and Saint John rivers. In the 1950s and into the next decade, New Brunswick Power constructed the two dams. It gave ample assurances that there would be no interference with the salmon fishery. This assurance was of special concern to Tobique Reserve because of the fishery's importance to its economy. By the time the dam at the mouth of Tobique River was finished, the salmon fishery had been destroyed. Power lines and roads had been run over reserve lands with little concern for the damages caused.

Although Indian Affairs was responsible for ensuring that Tobique's unquestioned interests would be protected, the officials failed miserably to do so. In dealing with NB Power they were spineless. It was painful to write of their conduct and deal responsibly with NB Power officials. In January 2006, I submitted my report, the last I would do under the auspicious of a Joint Working Group. Since then it has been submitted for validation at Indian Affairs. I am unaware of any decision, though I would consider that compensation could run into many millions.

Since the last Tobique report, Indian Affairs has ended its policy of assistance for researching possible specific claims. I would argue that this does not end the possibility of obtaining justice for loss of lands. What was even unthinkable a decade or two ago, historical research and the courts have given cause to reconsider as possible. For New Brunswick First Nations, it is whether the validity of the 1844 act could withstand a legal challenge. An examination of all issues of the New Brunswick *Royal Gazette* from 1849, when the first notice appeared of an auction of lots, as provided for in the 1844 act until the last such notice appeared on July 3 in 1867, revealed that a total of twenty thousand acres were put up for auction. Although Red Bank and Tobique would not be eligible, other reserves could presumably claim compensation.

# NOTES

1. Nancy Ayers, "Aboriginal Rights in the Maritimes," *Canadian Native Law Reporter* 2, no. 1 (1984): p. 64. She notes that Chief Justice MacKeigan of the Nova Scotia Supreme Court in *R v. Isaac* "held that the Proclamation in its broad declaration of Indian rights applied to Nova Scotia, including to Cape Breton" (by inference to New Brunswick also). Ayers also draws attention in her article at page 6 to the fact that Lord Justice May in *The Queen v. The Secretary of State for Foreign and Commonwealth Affairs* "agreed with the Nova Scotia Supreme Court in *Isaac*, and other Canadian courts, which have held that the 'the provisions of the Royal Proclamation did and do extend to the Provinces of Nova Scotia and New Brunswick.'"

2. Ayers, "Aboriginal Rights in the Maritimes," p. 6.

3. Jack Stagg, *Anglo-Indian Relations in North America to 1763 and an Analysis of the Royal Proclamation of 7 October 1763* (Department of Indian Affairs and Northern Development, 1981), p. 386.

# INDEX